MONETARY AND FINANCIAL POLICIES IN DEVELOPING COUNTRIES

The role of monetary stability and financial condition in economic growth has produced one of the most passionate debates in economics. Much of the evidence in this debate is inconclusive and influenced by extreme cases. *Monetary and Financial Policies in Developing Countries* brings together diverse views on the subject within a coherent framework. The work includes:

- a balanced assessment of empirical findings and their theoretical foundations on the role of money and finance in economic growth;
- a balanced assessment of financial liberalisation experience in developing countries;
- an examination of the money supply process and its controllability, and the practice of monetary policy in developing countries;
- an assessment of findings on the stability of demand for money and the reliability of the relationship between money and economic activity in developing countries;
- an analysis of monetary policy as an instrument of economic stabilisation;
- a study of the relationship between money, credit, the balance of payments, inflation and the exchange rate system;
- a reflection on market and government failures and institutional framework to minimise these failures.

The book is composed of two complementary parts, the first dealing with the role of money and finance in economic growth and the second with the role of monetary and financial policies in stabilisation. This volume will be a valuable guide for all those interested in how developing countries can best create a stable macroeconomic environment for maintaining economic growth.

Akhtar Hossain is Lecturer in Economics at the University of Newcastle, Australia. He has published widely on development and macroeconomic issues and his research interests include development economics, monetary policy, balance of payments and financial liberalisation. **Anis Chowdhury** is Senior Lecturer in Economics, University of Western Sydney, Macarthur. He has published extensively on macroeconomic and development issues. His research interests include macroeconomics, growth and structural change and political economy.

ROUTLEDGE STUDIES IN DEVELOPMENT ECONOMICS

MONETARY AND FINANCIAL POLICIES IN DEVELOPING COUNTRIES

Growth and Stabilisation

Akhtar Hossain and Anis Chowdhury

London and New York

We dedicate this work to Professor Malik Khosru Chowdhury and Professor Mirza Mozammel Huq of Jahangirnagar University, Bangladesh, who gave us our first lessons in economics and cultivated our interest in the discipline, but did not live long enough to see published the work of two of their students.

First published 1996
by Routledge
11 New Fetter Lane, London EC4P 4EE

Simultaneously published in the USA and Canada
by Routledge
29 West 35th Street, New York, NY 10001

© 1996 Akhtar Hossain and Anis Chowdhury

Typeset in Garamond by
Florencetype Ltd, Stoodleigh, Devon

Printed and bound in Great Britain by
Mackays of Chatham PLC, Chatham, Kent

British Library Cataloguing in Publication Data
A catalogue record for this book is available from the British Library

Library of Congress Cataloguing in Publication Data
A catalogue record for this book has been requested.

ISBN 0–415–10870–5

CONTENTS

CONTENTS

ILLUSTRATIONS

FIGURES

TABLES

PREFACE

Should monetary policy be used to minimise short-run deviations of actual output from the potential? Should monetary policy be used to stabilise the price level and other monetary variables such as exchange rates and interest rates rather than output? More importantly, what role does money and finance play in promoting the long-run growth of an economy? These are questions that have fascinated both academics and policy-makers ever since money became an essential feature of an economy. While money's short-run stabilisation role has received much attention in the developed world since the great depression of the 1930s, it is money's long-run growth-promoting role that has been the predominant focus in developing countries. The question that policy makers confront in developing countries is whether a country can achieve a high rate of growth without monetary stability – through a repressed financial sector and forced savings via inflation. The past two and half decades, especially since the early 1970s, have witnessed significant advances in both theoretical understanding of and empirical findings on the issue.

Although there is conflicting evidence on the relationship between monetary stability, financial repression and economic growth, there is a general consensus that large repressions and high inflation rates are detrimental to economic growth. Furthermore, it is now increasingly realised that the short-run stabilisation role of monetary and financial policies cannot be separated from their long-run role of promoting economic growth. In other words, the monetary and financial policies must provide a stable macroeconomic environment in the sense of maintaining realistic exchange rates, interest rates and a stable price level which keep the balance between aggregate demand and aggregate supply and at the same time enhance savings and investment rates necessary for raising economic growth.

This book surveys the recent developments in monetary and financial policies in developing countries with a view to making them accessible to advanced undergraduate and higher-degree students in economics and finance. It will also be useful to a wider body of policy makers and researchers. It brings together diverse views on monetary and financial policies in a coherent framework and offers a balanced assessment of empirical findings and their theoretical foundations. It also reflects on broader issues such as openness, assignment problems, central bank independence, constitutional safeguards and prudential regulation of the financial sector.

In writing this book we have benefited from discussions with our friends and colleagues. We owe our gratitude to all of them. In particular to Professor P.J. Drake, Vice-Chancellor, Australian Catholic University, Professor M.L. Treadgold of the University of New England, Professor S. Rashid of the University of Illinois-Urbana Champaign, and Professor C. Kearney of the University of Western Sydney, Macarthur, who have kindly read the manuscript and offered many valuable comments. Ms Janice Carroll of the University of Newcastle has patiently drawn and redrawn our diagrams. Of course, we must mention our families, especially since our wives both had to cope with newborn babies while we were engulfed in this work.

1

INTRODUCTION

A successful economy is one which has at least two main features. First, its actual real output does not fluctuate much from natural real output.[1] Second, its natural real output grows at a rapid, but steady pace. While the determination of the level and the rate of growth of natural real output is the focus of growth theory, the determination of actual real output relative to natural real output is the concern of stabilisation theory, and together they form the subject matter of macroeconomics. Implicit in macroeconomic theories are questions about the role of economic policies in growth and stabilisation (Branson, 1989). The two main macroeconomic instruments are fiscal policy and monetary policy. This book provides a survey of issues pertaining to the role of monetary and financial policies in growth and stabilisation in developing countries. As pointed out by Drake (1980), the earlier literature defined finance narrowly to mean only government revenue and expenditure (public finance). However, for the purpose of this survey, finance is defined broadly to include all aspects of borrowing and lending which affect the money supply.

In the literature for developed countries the role of monetary and financial policies is associated with the taming of business cycles.[2] In contrast, the role of monetary and financial policies in developing countries is linked with the promotion of economic growth and development. Such a dichotomy in the role of monetary and financial policies reflects the differences in economic issues and priorities of policy-makers in developed and developing countries. Although the principal preoccupation of policy-makers in developing countries is to attain rapid growth and change in the composition of output, the concern for growth of output and structural change is not independent of the concern for price stability and external balance (Coats and Khatkhate, 1984). For example, as the experience of Latin American countries shows, if the inflationary pressure that emerges during the process of development is ignored and the inflation rate is allowed to rise rapidly, resources will be allocated inefficiently, and this will ultimately impede development. The Latin American experience also demonstrates that higher inflation rates in these countries *vis-à-vis* their trading partners are a major cause of the loss of their competitiveness and, hence, the worsening of their balance of payments position. The exchange rate crisis that emanates from worsening balance of payments leads to capital flight which adversely affects the growth of output. On the other hand, the overwhelming lesson from the experience of East Asian newly industrialising economies (Hong Kong, Korea, Singapore and Taiwan) and South East Asian countries (Indonesia, Malaysia and Thailand) is that in the long run the growth of real income and overall monetary equilibrium, defined to include both the domestic price level and the external sector, are mutually interdependent.

Thus it can be argued that the objectives of a stable price level, the balance of payments equilibrium and economic growth are intertwined. Any demarcation in the roles of monetary and financial policies in growth (long-run) and stabilisation (short-run) in developing countries is artificial and somewhat misleading. Monetary and financial policies have both short-run and long-run roles. In the short run, monetary and financial policies should maintain such key macroeconomic variables as real interest rates, inflation rates and exchange rates at levels which will ensure the balance between aggregate demand and aggregate supply (or gross investment and gross savings). In the long run, these key macro variables must also enhance both savings and investment rates so that the economy grows at a faster rate. If monetary and financial policies fail in their short-run roles, the resulting inflation and balance of payments problems will affect the long-run objective of raising savings and investment rates adversely. Similarly, if the savings rate continues to be low, the economy will have perpetual and unsustainable external imbalance. Therefore, the essential role that monetary and financial policies can play in developing countries is to provide a stable macroeconomic environment conducive to economic growth.

TAMING BUSINESS CYCLES: THE ROLE OF MONETARY POLICY IN THE SHORT RUN

Figure 1.1 shows the hypothetical case of an economy which passes through recurrent business cycles. The smooth upward-sloping line represents the growth path of trend or natural real output. The actual real output fluctuates around the growth path of natural real output. The deviation of the actual real output from natural real output is called the real output gap. Obviously, a positive real output gap occurs during a boom, and a negative real output gap occurs during a recession. A positive (negative) real output gap also represents a condition where the rate of actual unemployment is below (above) the rate of natural unemployment.

There are many factors which may cause business cycles. In general, business cycles may originate from either the demand side or the supply side of the economy in the form of random shocks, implying that they do not have any significant effect on the trend path of the economy.[3] In fact, the factors

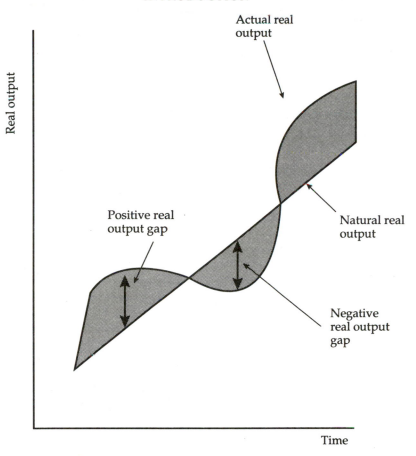

Figure 1.1 Hypothetical business cycles and the output gaps

that cause business cycles can be examined with an aggregate demand (AD) and aggregate supply (AS) model.[4]

Figure 1.2 shows that at time period t_0 the economy is in equilibrium at point A where aggregate demand equals aggregate supply. y_0^n is the level of natural real output at the given levels of capital stock, population, and the state of technology. Any deviation of the actual real output from natural real output will arise when there is a shift in either the short-run aggregate demand curve (SAD) and/or the short-run aggregate supply curve (SAS) by economic disturbances. Business cycles represent such output fluctuations around the growth path of trend output during a time period within which long-term factors of production are assumed to remain roughly constant.

In a market economy demand disturbances may originate from a number of sources, including private demand shocks, such as shifts in private

3

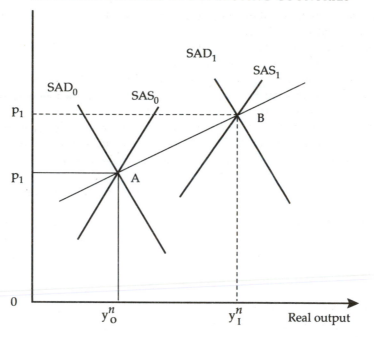

Figure 1.2 Movement of the real economy over time

consumption or investment spending, and changes in both government spending and net exports. A positive (negative) demand shock will create a positive (negative) real output gap. Like demand shocks, there can be supply shocks, such as crop failures, changes in the terms of trade, and technological innovations. A positive (negative) supply shock will create a positive (negative) real output gap. As there can be a large number of independent demand and supply shocks to an economy within a particular period of time, actual real output can be considered a normally distributed random variable with a mean equal to natural real output and a constant variance. Given that actual real output (y) equals natural real output (y^n) plus transitory real output $(y - y^n)$, the mean level of real output at period t_0 equals the level of natural real output y^n_0. (That is, $E(y) = E(y^n) + E(y - y^n) - \mathrm{Cov}(y^n, y - y^n) = y^n$, provided that y^n and $(y - y^n)$ are independent and $E(y - y^n) = 0$.) Similarly, the mean level of real output at period t_1 will equal the level of natural real output y^n_1. The movement of the economy from A to B during the period t_0 to t_1 represents the rise in natural real output as a result of the increase in each of the factors that determine the long-term growth of the economy – labour force growth, capital accumulation and technical change.

4

What should be done about business cycles is a subject of intense debate. When the lengths and the amplitudes of business cycles are large, they can create macroeconomic problems such as unemployment and inflation.[5] As both unemployment and inflation impose economic and social costs, many economists believe that economic policies should be used to stabilise business cycles. However, what form of economic policies would achieve short-run economic stability remains a debatable issue. Because monetary policy is an important macroeconomic instrument, the debate is about whether it should be used in the same way that fiscal policy is used to stabilise business cycles. Keynesian policy activists hold the view that as monetary policy is capable of damping business cycles, it should be used along with fiscal policy for stabilisation. On the other hand, monetarist policy non-activists are not so enthusiastic about the role of monetary policy in stabilisation because they are concerned that any discretionary monetary policy may destabilise, rather than stabilise, the economy. Issues relating to stabilisation in developing countries, and in particular the role of monetary policy, are examined in Chapters 5–8.

PROMOTING ECONOMIC GROWTH: THE ROLE OF MONETARY POLICY IN THE LONG RUN

Figure 1.3 shows that an economy without business cycles does not necessarily represent a success because such an economy may be stagnant. It indicates that, given similar mild business cycles, an economy would be considered successful when it grows faster compared with an economy which grows slowly. Economic growth being a prerequisite for an improvement in the economic condition of the poor in developing countries, the natural real output must grow at a rapid and steady pace.

Therefore, the predominant concern of policy-makers in developing countries is to promote economic growth, both in aggregate and per capita terms. One area of policy debate is whether monetary and financial policies can accelerate economic growth so that per capita income rises on a sustained basis. In terms of Figure 1.3, the question is whether monetary and financial policies can make the growth path of natural real output steeper and also minimise the deviations of actual output from the potential. In terms of Figure 1.2, this means maintaining a balance between aggregate demand and supply while moving from one period to another and at the same time making the time path AB flatter.

Sources of growth and monetary policy

Money's role in enhancing the growth rate can be elaborated by Solow's (1956, 1957) much-celebrated production function approach to growth accounting. Consider the following linearly homogeneous production function:

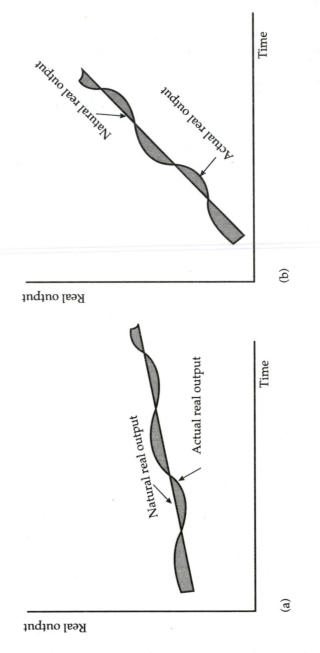

Figure 1.3 Rate of economic growth as a measure of success (a) A slowly growing economy (b) A rapidly growing economy

$$y = f(k; T)$$ (1.1)

where y is per capita output, k is the capital–labour ratio, and T is the state of technology. Assume that the above per capita production function satisfies the standard property that the marginal product of capital is positive ($\delta y/\delta k > 0$), which diminishes as the capital–labour ratio increases ($\delta^2 y/\delta k^2 < 0$).

From equation (1.1) the growth rate of per capita output (g_y) can be written as

$$g_y = \tau + \epsilon_k g_k$$ (1.2)

where τ is technical progress, ϵ_k is the elasticity of output with respect to capital input, and g_k is the growth rate of the capital–labour ratio (or capital deepening). It shows that per capita real output growth originates from two sources: technical progress and capital deepening. When there is no technical progress, the growth of per capita real output depends on the growth of the capital–labour ratio alone. Implicit in the question of whether monetary and financial policies can affect economic growth is the question of whether they can induce technical progress and/or raise capital deepening.

The earlier literature on this area examined the role of monetary and financial policies in raising savings and capital accumulation. Although there is general agreement regarding the impact of monetary and financial policies on savings and capital deepening, the specific policy measures and the way they work remain unsettled. The works that followed Tobin's (1965) model, and generally are Keynesian in nature, show that inflationary monetary and repressive financial policies promote growth by inducing portfolio shifts from financial assets to real capital, and/or by forced savings brought about through either transferring resources from the private to the public sector or income distribution in favour of the capitalist class. On the other hand, McKinnon (1973) and Shaw (1973) hold the view that inflationary monetary policy and financial repression retard growth as they discourage savings and financial intermediation between savers and investors, and reduce efficiency of investment. The theoretical and empirical literature pertaining to the role of monetary and financial policies in economic growth is reviewed in Chapters 2–4.

It is important to note that Solow (1957) and Nelson (1964) show that growth results predominantly from technical progress and not from the growth of either labour or capital. For example, according to Solow (ibid.), about 88 per cent of economic growth in the United States during 1909–49 could be accounted for by what he called 'technical progress', while the remaining 12 per cent could be explained by the increase in capital per worker. However, in Solow's growth model, technical progress is exogenous, and there is no economic explanation of why in a free-market economy technical progress occurs. If technical progress is exogenous and plays such a dominant role in economic growth, can monetary and financial policies make any substantial contribution to economic growth? Solow's findings imply that the contribution of monetary and fiscal policies is limited since they are aimed at raising savings and thereby the growth of capital whose contribution to output growth is small, and these policies cannot affect technical progress which is the dominant contributor to growth. Thus, Solow's results are pessimistic about the ability of policy to change the growth path (Branson, 1989: 644). If technical progress is disembodied (freely available to all), a further implication of exogenous technical progress is that the growth rates of all economies will converge over time. But it was not the case in reality (Gordon, 1993; Lucas, 1988).

Therefore, the Solow growth model has been found to be inadequate, particularly due to the restrictive assumption that technical progress is exogenous. As a result, substantial research activities have been directed towards explaining technical progress within the model itself. A new class of growth models under the name of endogenous growth theory paradigm has been recently developed in which technical progress is the outcome of market activity in response to economic incentives (Gordon, 1993; Lucas, 1988; Romer, 1986, 1990). The new endogenous growth theory considers human capital along with physical capital as a major source of growth because any lack of human capital may lower the productivity of physical capital. Human capital however does not originate in a vacuum; it is linked to education, training, and research for product innovations and ideas.

While in the Solow growth model the effect of a rise in savings on economic growth is temporary, saving plays a crucial part in the new endogenous growth theory. For example, saving is necessary for investment in areas which contribute to human capital formation and thereby to growth. Thus, there is potential for a substantial monetary and financial policy effect on growth, provided that it influences capital accumulation (physical and human) and induces technical progress by education, training and research. To begin with, monetary and financial policy can affect growth through the 'Solow channel' of savings and capital accumulation (physical and human). Second, since technical progress is often assumed to depend on investment in both physical and human capital (Arrow, 1962; Gordon, 1993), the role of capital in growth may be larger than is suggested by the Solow growth model. Thus, monetary and financial policies within the endogenous growth model affect the long-term growth path not just through capital deepening (more capital), but also through better and newer capital.

One policy implication of the new endogenous growth theory is that unless large capital investment (physical and human) is made in developing countries, it is unlikely that there will ever be an economic convergence between poor and rich countries. Even in an open economy there is no guarantee that foreign savings will supplement low domestic savings in developing countries and thereby promote higher economic growth. The inflows of foreign capital and technology in developing countries are dependent on their political, social and economic conditions. Macroeconomic policies in general, and monetary and financial policies in particular, by maintaining economic stability play a critical role in attracting foreign capital and embodied technical progress from abroad.

PLAN OF THE BOOK

The book has two main parts. The first part examines the role of monetary and financial polices in the economic growth of developing countries. The second part examines the role of monetary and financial policies in stabilisation. Since stabilisation and growth are intertwined, the two parts of the book overlap and complement each other. The following provides an overview of various chapters in the book.

Money, inflation and economic growth: theory and evidence

Chapter 2 reviews the theoretical literature on money and growth in developing economies. In particular, it examines the role of inflationary finance in growth and evaluates the theoretical literature on financial liberalisation. The channel through which money growth and inflation may affect economic growth is through its impact on the real interest rate that affects capital accumulation. The presence of such an effect was postulated by Metzler (1951). By applying the Metzler model, Mundell (1971) showed that anticipated inflation raises the nominal rate of interest by less than the rate of inflation and thus lowers the real rate of interest and gives an impetus 'to an investment and an acceleration of growth'. The modern literature on money and growth, however, began with Tobin (1965), who argues that, as the nominal interest rate or return on money is zero, an acceleration of inflation following an acceleration of money growth would lower the real return on money and make it less attractive to hold, as asset-holders compare the return on money with the return on capital. A higher rate of inflation would then encourage a portfolio shift away from money and into capital and thereby raise output through capital deepening. This is known as 'the Tobin effect' and the presence of it suggests that money is not super-neutral.

Besides the insight of the Tobin model of growth, the rationale for inflationary finance in developing countries is that they cannot mobilise sufficient resources for development finance through the conventional tax system. Inflationary finance thus became attractive to many developing countries as a route to economic progress. However, Mundell (1965) formally established the relation between inflationary finance and economic growth and showed that the maximum rate of growth that could be achieved by deficit financing was rather small. Furthermore, as pointed out by Dornbusch and Reynoso

(1989), there was indeed a danger of causing high inflation for a marginal rise in economic growth.

The underlying assumption of inflationary financing is that investment is the limiting factor in growth. It thus implies that if the financial sector is repressed by interest rate ceilings then inflation will result in a low real interest rate which may encourage investment. However, the financial liberalisation hypothesis of McKinnon (1973) and Shaw (1973) is based on the classical notion that saving is the constraining factor in economic growth. It thus advocates a high real interest rate policy to enhance the savings rate, induce financial deepening and improve investment efficiency. These salutary effects in turn contribute to economic growth. However, the empirical foundation of the financial liberalisation paradigm has not been so robust. The lack of robustness of empirical findings has been compounded by burgeoning arguments that directly challenge the doctrine of financial liberalisation. A stronger critique of the financial liberalisation hypothesis maintains that a repressed financial system facilitates economic growth.

Following the review of theoretical literature, the empirical literature on money, inflation and growth relationships in developing countries is reviewed in Chapter 3. It reveals that there is a positive relationship between money supply growth and inflation. Such a relationship becomes prominent when money supply growth exceeds about 10 per cent per annum. The relationship between inflation and economic growth is however complex. Low or moderate inflation is found to be positively correlated with economic growth, but very high or hyperinflation has a negative relationship with economic growth. There is no significant relation between inflation and economic growth in a large number of developing countries. In the case of financial repression, only persistently large negative real deposit rates were found to misdirect savings. Similarly, random and non-price allocation of investment negatively affect the productivity of resources. On the whole, the nature of the relationship between financial liberalisation and economic growth is found to be episodic.

Issues in and lessons from financial liberalisation reform

Chapter 4 provides the background on financial reform liberalisation in developing countries since the early 1970s and then examines the issues in, and draws lessons from, financial reform. The 1950s and 1960s were the heyday of financial repression in developing countries. Many leading economists prescribed financial repression for the promotion of economic growth. The governments of developing countries actively promoted financial repression because they found it economically attractive and politically convenient. Beginning in the mid-1970s a large number of developing countries in Africa, Asia and Latin America have undertaken financial liberalisation reform of one form or another. Financial liberalisation reform has not been an outright success or failure in developing countries. There are cases where financial liberalisation reform experiments went badly. There are also cases where financial liberalisation reform experiments have had considerable success.

Financial reform experiences of developing countries, and those of Latin America in particular, have led to a reassessment of the general case for financial liberalisation reform. There are two broad explanations of the failures of these reforms in Latin American countries. Neo-structuralist economists consider that these failures vindicate their view that financial liberalisation reform is essentially a theoretical aberration unrelated to the objective conditions of financial markets in developing countries. By contrast, the protagonists of financial liberalisation reform blame macroeconomic instability, the lack of prudential regulation and supervision, and the incorrect order of liberalisation for the failures of Latin American financial liberalisation reform.

By now some lessons have been learnt from the reform experiences in developing countries. First, financial liberalisation needs to be preceded by macroeconomic stabilisation. Second, financial reform should be accompanied by a prudential regulatory and supervisory body, particularly to counter any pervasive moral hazard problem from deposit insurance. Third, to avoid destabilising capital flows, care must be taken in opening the capital market. Fourth, a gradual and phased reform is appropriate for developing countries, where there are difficulties in imposing monetary and financial discipline and in creating appropriate institutions and human skills for prudential regulation and supervision of financial institutions. Fifth, the government must persuade the public of the credibility of financial reform. Sixth, financial liberalisation does not guarantee competition in the financial sector because of the uncompetitive and oligopolistic nature of the financial system in developing countries. Finally, the lesson from financial reform is that a market-based financial system is not the panacea for all success.

Monetary policy as a tool of economic stabilisation

Having examined the roles of monetary and financial policies in economic growth, the book takes up the issues relating to the stabilising role of monetary and financial polices in developing countries. Chapter 5 examines the question of whether monetary policy can be used to stabilise a developing economy following either demand or supply shocks. There are at least two pertinent questions relating to economic stabilisation. First, how prevalent is demand shocks in a developing economy? Second, how sensitive is a developing economy to a demand shock? The Keynesians and monetarists are divided on these issues. While the Keynesians consider that demand shocks are rampant and tend to persist, monetarists argue that demand shocks are infrequent and not persistent. It is revealed that developing countries are not prone to demand disturbances. Moreover, given that the real wage rates, interest rates and exchange rates in developing countries are flexible, it is possible that any demand shock to the economy would be neutralised without active stabilisation measures by the government. However, unlike the demand shocks, the developing countries are more prone to supply shocks. The question is whether a monetary authority should adopt a hands-off policy following a supply shock. An examination of the issue by applying an analytical model shows that the conduct of active monetary policy is problematic following a supply shock. For example, an expansionary monetary policy following a negative supply shock may cause sustained inflation. Indeed, in contrast to the popular view, the monetary authority may require to adopt a contractionary monetary policy to avoid the danger of inflation.

Design and conduct of monetary policy

The empirical evidence reviewed in Chapter 3 showed that there is a close association between money growth and inflation, but the long-run relationship between money and economic growth is at best weak. This implies that monetary policy can be used for price stabilisation. The effectiveness of monetary policy depends on the controllability of money supply and the reliability of the link between money supply and the ultimate targets of inflation, output and balance of payments. Chapter 6 examines the money supply process in developing countries. It finds that money supply in developing countries is largely endogenous. The endogeneity arises from the link between the monetary base and government budget deficits, and balance of payments developments. While the link between money supply and balance of payments developments is the outcome of a fixed or pegged exchange rate policy followed by many developing countries, the absence of a well-developed capital market is the main cause of the link between the monetary base and a budget deficit. Due to the absence of a developed capital market, budget deficits are often financed by borrowing from the central bank. There are, however, three broad hypotheses regarding the linkage between budget deficits and nominal money supply. The first, found in the literature on hyper-inflation, is that the monetary authority uses money creation to finance the public-sector deficits. The second view, more prominent in the writings of the structuralist school, is that the authorities have imperfect control of the fiscal apparatus and that, under these conditions, money creation is the only source of finance. The third and emerging view is the political economy explanations for the direct link between budget deficits and monetary expansion.

It is also revealed that monetary policy in developing countries has been passive and accommodating to developments in the real sector. Among the instruments of monetary control, credit ceilings and reserve requirements loom large, although one of them is effective at any point in time. These instruments are used predominantly to achieve developmental goals rather than price stability, except in a few cases. The lack of a well-developed capital market makes it difficult for any effective open market operations. The prospect for using discretionary monetary policy to fine-tune the economy in developing countries is poor due to institutional constraints on the flexibility of specific monetary instruments, an absence of well-developed information systems giving rise to relatively long problem-recognition lags, and a lack of full internal economic integration. The recent liberalisation of the financial sector in developing countries has not improved the situation because the money multiplier has become unstable in response to interest rate changes, and financial innovations have caused traditional measures of monetary aggregates inappropriate.

The debate on the reliability of monetary policy centres around the way the disequilibrium in the money market works its way through to the real sector of the economy. Central to the issue is the stability of the demand for money. Chapter 7 examines money demand behaviour in developing countries. It is found that money demand is rather stable and that, contrary to the theoretical possibility, financial deregulation did not make it unstable.

Money, credit and balance of payments

After the generalised floating of major currencies in the early 1970s, most developing countries chose not to float their currencies freely and instead opted for pegged exchange rate arrangements of one kind or another by fixing their currencies to a single hard currency or a basket of hard currencies. Such an arrangement created a number of issues relating to the conduct of monetary policy. First, the goal of monetary policy changed from inflation control to stability of the balance of payments, and therefore the intermediate target of monetary policy changed from the growth of the money supply to the growth rate of central bank credit. Second, domestic inflation remained pegged to world inflation.

The monetarist view that monetary policy should be conducted by monetary targeting with the objective of price stabilisation is based on two fundamental assumptions. First, there exists a stable money-demand function. Second, the monetary authority conducts monetary policy under a floating exchange rate system so that the monetary authority can have control over the money supply. When the above conditions are satisfied inflation becomes a monetary policy variable, in the sense that by setting the growth rate of the money supply to a predetermined level the monetary authority can determine the rate of inflation. Thus a monetary policy independence associated with a floating exchange rate system can provide a choice of inflation.

However, monetary policy independence is both good and bad for a country. It is good because, if a country wishes, it can in principle choose a tailor-made inflation rate. It is bad because when a country lacks fiscal–monetary discipline, it may create an excessive and non-optimal rate of inflation. Hence a floating exchange rate system (and monetary policy independence) may be a curse in disguise. Chapter 8 develops the relationships among money, credit, balance of payments and inflation under fixed and flexible exchange rate systems.

Fiscal and monetary constitution

Chapter 9 reflects on issues pertaining to market failures and the role of the government. It is suggested that private-sector-based, incentive-compatible policies can improve market performance while at the same time minimising the possibility of government failures. It is argued that in the absence of constraints on inefficient governments in many developing countries, characterised by large budget deficits, high inflation and unsustainable balance of payments deficits, institutional arrangements such as fiscal and monetary constitutions may be necessary to achieve macroeconomic stability. While the fiscal constitution should be designed to restrict government's ability to embark on unfunded expenditure, the monetary constitution should make the central bank independent from other parts of the government. By constraining governments' debt and money-creation capacity, together they will constitute the necessary and sufficient conditions for inducing responsible macroeconomic management. In extreme cases a currency board may also be required to act as an additional anchor for the macroeconomic and financial stability necessary for economic growth.

NOTES

1 Natural real output represents a level of real output at which the inflation rate is constant, with no tendency to accelerate or decelerate (Gordon, 1993).
2 The business cycle is a recurring change in the level of economic activity around the path of trend growth. The sequence of events that constitute a business cycle – expansion, downturn, contraction and upturn – are not periodic (Dornbusch and Fisher, 1990; Wachtel, 1989).
3 This view is not accepted by all economists. For example, Campbell and Mankiw (1987) argue that the effect of random shocks to real output may be persistent over time. There is a growing body of econometric literature which tests for unit roots in the time series (Engle and Granger, 1991). The presence of a unit root, say, in real output implies that the effect of any random shock on real output is not transitory, but would persist over time.
4 Besides the demand and supply shocks, there can be policy shocks to the real economy. In general, they follow from decisions made by the government, and include changes in the money supply, the exchange rate and fiscal policy (Sachs and Larrain, 1993).
5 Hysteresis in unemployment is a macroeconomic problem linked with business cycles. Some economists argue that the natural rate of unemployment may be affected by movements in the actual rate of unemployment. For example, a high

actual rate of unemployment during a prolonged recession may raise the natural rate of unemployment. It means that, if the actual rate of unemployment can be kept low by stimulative policies, the natural rate may decline automatically (Blanchard and Summers, 1986; Gordon, 1988).

2

MONEY AND FINANCE IN ECONOMIC GROWTH
A theoretical review

One common economic goal of developing countries is raising per capita real income on a sustained basis.[1] There is however no consensus on any mechanism through which per capita real income can be raised rapidly and steadily over time, except that all the major approaches to development give emphasis on both capital formation and the effective use of capital.[2]

Although investment has been identified as a major determinant of growth, there remains controversy about the relative efficacy of different approaches to investment finance. In the literature two broad analytical approaches to investment finance can be identified.[3] They are the prior savings approach and the forced savings approach. According to the classical economists, prior savings are the determinant of investment and all savings find their investment outlets. The proponents of the prior savings view are averse to inflation and do not see the need for inflation for growth. Because investment is an alternative to consumption, they believe that any investment which is not financed by prior savings will generate inflation but no real income.[4]

On the other hand, economists who mainly follow the Keynesian school of thought do not consider prior savings as a requirement for investment for growth. According to this view, investment can be increased autonomously by the government without prior savings through monetary expansion. Such an investment will generate its own savings in at least four ways. First, if resources are underemployed, monetary expansion will increase aggregate demand and hence output and savings. Second, if resources are fully employed or if there are supply rigidities (as can be expected in developing countries), monetary expansion will generate inflation. Inflation in turn lowers the real rate of return on financial investment and thereby induces wealthholders to change their portfolio by investing in physical capital. The resultant rise in capital intensity increases output and hence savings. Third, inflation can also increase savings by changing income distribution in favour of profit earners with a higher propensity to save compared with that of wage earners. Fourth, inflation imposes tax on real money balances and thereby transfers resources to the government for financing investment.

Therefore, the precise role of monetary policy in growth is dependent on whether the prior savings or forced saving or a combination of prior and forced saving approaches to development finance is appropriate for developing countries. According to the forced savings school, since investment, not saving, is the constraint on growth, a low or negative real interest rate is necessary for the encouragement of private investment. To the extent that a high rate of inflation keeps the real interest rate low, inflation can be seen as a necessary price of economic development. Thus the policy implication that follows from the forced saving approach is financial repression characterised primarily by interest rate ceilings.[5] In contrast, the prior savings school believe that the role of monetary policy in developing countries should be to mobilise savings and channel them into productive investment by keeping the rate of inflation low so that the real interest rate remains positive over time. This forms the basis of financial liberalisation reform.

This chapter reviews the theoretical debate on the role of money and finance in economic growth and development. The review is selective and eclectic in nature, in the sense that the pure monetary growth theories are analysed along with the theories of finance and capital in economic growth and development. The view taken here is that ideas from these complementary branches of monetary economics have common threads and are equally useful for dealing with monetary policy and development issues in developing countries.

MONEY AND ECONOMIC GROWTH

As the term suggests, economic growth is a dynamic phenomenon. It deals with changes in real economic variables over time. The core issue in monetary growth theory, common to both forced and prior savings schools, is whether money has any effect on real variables in a growing economy in the steady state or in the transition towards the steady state. Answers, albeit inconclusive, to such questions can be found in the literature on neutrality and superneutrality of money.

Neutrality of money

One fundamental proposition in monetary economics is that money is neutral to the real economy – that is, to the determination of relative prices, employment and output. It is indeed a building block of the classical quantity theory, which states that a change in the quantity of nominal money causes a proportionate change in the price level, while real variables, such as employment, output and the real interest rate, remain unaffected.[6]

Fisher (1930) invoked the concept of money illusion[7] to account for short-run non-neutrality of money arising from fluctuations in real interest rates.

He wrote that 'The erratic behaviour of real interest is evidently a trick played on the money market by the "money illusion" when contracts are made in unstable money' (Fisher, ibid.: 415). However, the existence of money illusion is synonymous with the violation of the 'homogeneity postulate' (Haberler, 1941; Leontief, 1936; Modigliani, 1944), which in its refined form states that the demand and supply functions of goods and services are homogeneous of degree zero in money prices and in the initial quantity of financial assets, including money.[8]

The short-run non-neutrality of money is a prominent feature of the Keynesian monetary theory (Meltzer, 1988). It follows from the contention that since under the conditions of underemployment the price level does not rise proportionately to the increase in the quantity of money,[9] the resulting increase in the real quantity of money lowers the interest rate and therefore increases investment and real output.[10] Keynes (1936) accepted the classical view that the demand for labour depends on real wages and therefore employment can be increased by lowering the real wage rate. According to him, as nominal wages are more rigid than prices, any monetary expansion that raises the price level may raise output because of the reduction in the real wage rate. However, Keynes's assumption of rigid nominal wages is often interpreted as being based on the existence of money illusion on the part of workers. It follows from his suggestion that the supply of labour depends on the nominal wage rate so that a rise in the price level at a given level of the nominal wage rate is not seen by workers as a fall in the real wage rate. They supply more labour as the nominal wage rises with the rise in labour demand, implying that workers suffer from money illusion (Leontief, 1936). However, Leijonhufvud (1968) provides an alternative interpretation to the Keynesian labour supply behaviour. He argues that workers may continue to supply the same amount of labour in the event of a rise in the price level not because they irrationally identify nominal with real wages but because in a world of less than perfect information they may take time to learn of the changed value of money (Howitt, 1989).

Monetarist economists accept that in the short run money has an effect on the real economy. As Friedman (1992: 260) writes, 'In the short run, which may be as long as three to ten years, monetary changes affect primarily output. Over decades, on the other hand, the rate of monetary growth affects primarily prices.' However, his acceptance of the short-run non-neutrality of money is not based on money illusion; rather, it arises from expectational errors or imperfect information. As he writes,

> Over short periods, an unanticipated increase in inflation reduces real wages as viewed by employers, inducing them to offer higher nominal wages, which workers erroneously view as higher real wages. This discrepancy simultaneously encourages employers to offer more

18

employment and workers to accept more employment, thereby reducing unemployment, which produces the inverse relation encapsulated in the Phillips curve.

(Friedman, 1992: 258)

Despite such a plausible explanation of the short-run effect of inflation on real output, there is no convincing justification of Friedman's view that workers hold incorrect expectations for a significant period of time. Also, it is doubtful that employers have an information advantage over workers to such an extent over a considerable period of time that can generate a business cycle in output or employment (Gordon, 1993).

Lucas (1972) developed a macroeconomic model with optimising agents, decentralised markets and imperfect information. The use of imperfect information leads to an effect of unanticipated money shock on real output, but anticipated money does not affect real output. Fischer (1979a) also developed a model in which nominal wages are preset on the basis of lagged information on money and demand disturbances. His model, like the Lucas model, shows that demand and money shocks affect real output to the extent that they are unanticipated. The Fischer model works as in Keynes; because prices are flexible but nominal wages are fixed within a period, money shocks increase prices, decrease real wages and increase real output.

Therefore, it is evident that the short-run non-neutrality of money is broadly explained by the argument of imperfect information (Blanchard, 1990). Such an interpretation is more convincing than any argument which invokes the assumption of money illusion because money illusion contradicts the rational behaviour of economic agents.

Superneutrality of money

Closely related to the neutrality of money is the concept of superneutrality of money. One core question regarding the superneutrality of money is whether a change in the growth rate of nominal money affects the growth paths of real economic variables in the steady state with the exception of real balances, the steady state value of which may decrease with the rise in inflation following the increase in the growth rate of nominal money (Danthine, 1992). Superneutrality of money requires that the real interest rate, capital-intensity and per capita real output (or consumption) are independent of inflation and the rate of money growth.

Money growth may affect economic growth through its impact on the real interest rate and thereby on capital accumulation (Orphanides and Solow, 1990). The presence of such an effect is postulated by Metzler (1951). He argues that the real interest rate is a monetary phenomenon and that an increase in the growth rate of nominal money can affect capital accumulation. According to him, the central bank can affect the real interest rate through money market operations:

> [B]y purchasing securities, the central bank can reduce the real value of private wealth, thereby increasing the propensity to save and causing the system to attain a new equilibrium at a permanently lower interest rate and a permanently higher rate of capital accumulation.
>
> (Metzler, 1951: 112)

One criticism of the Metzler model is that he did not examine the effect of inflation on the interest rate and distinguish between a real and a nominal interest rate. He also did not link capital accumulation with economic growth (Orphanides and Solow, 1990).

By applying the Metzler model, Mundell (1963, 1971) shows that anticipated inflation raises the nominal rate of interest by less than the rate of inflation and therefore lowers the real interest rate and gives an impetus 'to an investment and an acceleration of growth'. One shortcoming of the Mundell model is that it does not consider the effects of anticipated inflation on real variables in the steady state, although he claims that any change in the real interest rate is a permanent change.

The supposed link between monetary expansion, inflation and growth through 'capital-intensity effect' has been more formally developed by James Tobin. In fact, the modern literature on money and growth began with Tobin (1965), who made a case against monetary superneutrality.

The Tobin model

The Tobin model is based on the one-sector neoclassical growth model of Solow (1956) and Swan (1956), and it rationalises the forced savings approach to development finance.

Assume that per capita real output (y) depends on the capital–labour ratio (k):

$$y = y(k) \qquad (2.1)$$

where $\delta y / \delta k > 0$ and $\delta^2 y / \delta k^2 < 0$.

In the non-monetary model, individuals save by acquiring physical capital and therefore k is the only form of wealth. However, in the basic monetary growth model, per capita real balances are considered an alternative form of wealth, so that per capita real wealth (w) equals per capita capital (k) plus per capita real balances (m):

$$w = k + m \qquad (2.2)$$

Per capita real balances may be assumed to depend on per capita real output and the opportunity cost of holding money instead of capital. The opportunity cost of holding money equals the real rate of return on capital

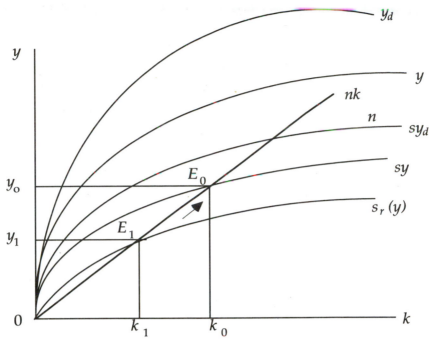

Figure 2.1 A neoclassical monetary growth model

(r_k) plus inflation (π), so that the demand for real balances can be expressed as

$$m = m(y, r_k + \pi) \qquad (2.3)$$

where $\delta m/\delta y > 0$ and $\delta m/\delta (r_k+\pi) < 0$.

Assume that the stock of nominal money is exogenously determined and that it grows at a rate of μ. When the demand for per capita real balances is constant, the equilibrium condition for the money market ensures that the rate of inflation equals the growth rate of nominal money less the growth rate of population (n), such that

$$\pi = \mu - n \qquad (2.4)$$

Assuming that the nominal interest rate (or return) on money is zero, Tobin (1965) suggests that a rise in inflation will lower the real return on money and make real balances less attractive to hold as assetholders compare the return on money with the return on capital. Therefore, a higher rate of inflation encourages a portfolio shift away from money and into capital and consequently raises real output because of the rise in capital intensity. This is known as 'the Tobin effect'. The presence of it suggests that money is not superneutral.

21

Figure 2.1 presents the standard one-sector neoclassical growth model. It explains how a rise in the growth rate of nominal money raises per capita real output. The initial equilibrium is at point E_0, where the savings curve (sy) crosses the capital requirement line (nk). At equilibrium the capital–labour ratio is k_0 and per capita real output is y_0.

To modify the real growth model into the neoclassical monetary growth model, per capita 'disposable income' (y_d) needs to be redefined as per capita output (y) plus changes in per capita real balances $(\mu - \pi) m$. That is, $y_d = y + (\mu - \pi) m$. Per capita disposable income is so defined because changes in real balances in the 'outside money' economy are regarded as a change in wealth and therefore a change in income. Using the quantity theory relationship in growth rate form, $\mu = \pi + g_y$ (velocity is assumed constant; g_y represents the growth rate of real output), the above definition of disposable income can be rewritten as $y_d = y (1 + xg_y)$, where x is the money–income ratio (m/y). Assuming that per capita saving (s) is a constant proportion of disposable income, the savings curve sy_d is drawn. It shows that when the economy grows, due to an increase in k, y_d, from which savings are made, so that the value of the ratio of savings to output rises. However, not all, but a portion of total savings is devoted to increasing real savings and then to increasing physical capital. Precisely, from savings sy_d, savings devoted to increasing real balances are given by $xg_y y$ leaving real savings $s_r(y)$ $(= sy_d - xg_y y)$. Real savings are plotted as $s_r(y)$. Given the capital requirement line nk, the equilibrium point is now at E_1 with the capital–labour ratio k_1 and per capita output y_1.

The effect of any monetary expansion that leads to inflation can be seen on the equilibrium capital–labour ratio and per capita output. From the definition of real savings $s_r(y)$ and its inverse relationship with the money–income ratio (x), it follows that any decline in the value of the money–income ratio (x) will shift the $s_r(y)$ curve upwards and therefore raise the capital–labour ratio and per capita output (Johnson, 1978: 165).

Since the rate of return on capital is fixed by either the capital–labour ratio or per capita output, the money–income ratio will vary inversely with inflation. Inflation is a policy variable which can be raised by raising the growth rate of the nominal money supply at a given rate of growth of population $(\pi = \mu - n)$. It suggests that the higher the rate of inflation, the lower the money–income ratio, and the intersection point E_1 is further to the right as the real savings curve $s_r(y)$ shifts upwards. The upper limit is the point E_0 where the rate of inflation is high enough to lower the money–income ratio to negligibility (Johnson, 1978: 165).

Critique of the Tobin effect

The conclusion drawn above is based on the implicit assumption that the stock of wealth remains constant with the rise in inflation. As Orphanides and Solow (1990) point out, the stock of wealth is endogenous dependent on the saving behaviour of individuals and is likely to change with inflation. When wealth is reduced because of the decline in real balances owing to inflation, inflation may not raise the capital–labour ratio and therefore the superneutrality condition of money may prevail. It indicates that the net effect of inflation on capital intensity depends on the interaction of the portfolio composition effect and the saving behaviour of individuals during inflation.

Levhari and Patinkin (1968) specified the savings rate as a function of the rates of return on capital and real balances and showed that the steady state impact of inflation on capital intensity could be positive or negative. They also pointed out that the role of money in the Tobin model is not adequately explained and showed that the Tobin effect cannot be obtained unambiguously when money is treated as a consumption or a production good. Dornbusch and Frenkel (1973) showed that when inflation has a positive effect on consumption, the Tobin effect simply disappears.

The classic defence of superneutrality of money came from Sidrauski (1967). He formulated a monetary growth model within a representative individual's utility-optimising framework where the individual's utility is a function of real consumption and of the flow of services of real balances. His important finding was that the sizes of the steady-state capital stock and real consumption are independent of inflation and the rate of money growth, implying that money is superneutral. However, as the opportunity cost of holding money rises with inflation, superneutrality does not extend to real balances and therefore any monetary expansion that generates inflation leads to welfare losses (Haliassos and Tobin, 1990).

Orphanides and Solow (1990) find that the difference in the Sidrauski and Tobin results lies in the specification of savings behaviour.[11] As in the case of Dornbusch and Frenkel (1973), when inflation has a positive effect on consumption the Tobin effect is neutralised in the Sidrauski model in which the portfolio decision and the savings behaviour are derived simultaneously. Orphanides and Solow also show that Sidrauski's neutrality results can be obtained in a model in which the transactions role of money is explicitly modelled.

In Sidrauski's model the marginal product of capital depends on the level of capital stock. As his model shows, in the steady state real balances are inversely related to the rate of money creation and the superneutrality results cannot be sustained if real balances enter in the production function. Therefore, an important variation of the Sidrauski model has been the inclusion of money as a factor of production. It is assumed that firms hold real balances to facilitate production, so that money acts as a complementary factor to capital:

$$y = y(k, m) \qquad (2.5)$$

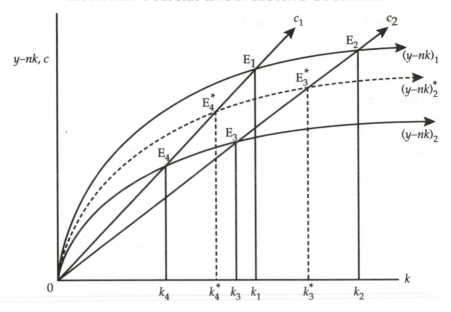

Figure 2.2 Effect of money supply growth (or inflation) on capital intensity (or per capita output)

Inflation lowers the productivity of and the return to the complementary input capital by lowering real balances in the steady state. The negative effect of inflation (or money growth) on productivity is opposite to the positive effect suggested by the portfolio view of Tobin (1965) in which money and capital are substitutable assets. Marty (1968) finds that, given the production function (2.5), the effect of a rise in inflation on capital accumulation is ambiguous and depends on the form of the production function. If the production function is concave, and the effect of real balances on the marginal product of capital is positive, inflation will lower capital holdings. Orphanides and Solow (1990) make the pertinent remark that whatever model is used for analysis, any complementarity between money balances and capital does create a negative effect of inflation on capital. Because inflation damages the efficiency of the transactions technology, the net productivity of capital, and hence the demand for capital, may be lower, particularly during high inflation.

Figure 2.2 shows that an increase in the growth rate of nominal money has an ambiguous effect on capital intensity and per capita output (or income). In the figure, an increase in the growth rate of nominal money from μ_1 to μ_2 is shown to have two effects. First, it will shift the consumption curve from c_1 to c_2 as the consequent higher rate of inflation reduces the real money balances and hence the disposable income, $y_d = y + (\mu - \pi)\,m$. Second, a rise

24

in inflation will lower the demand for real balances, and since real balances (m) are a complementary factor to per capita capital stock (k) in the production: $y = y(k, m)$, the decrease in the holding of real balances will lower per capita output. As a result, the net production curve will shift from $(y - nk)_1$ to either $(y - nk)_2$ or $(y - nk)^*_2$, two alternative positions. As both the consumption and production functions shift to the right, the net effect of an increase in the growth rate of the nominal money supply on capital intensity (or per capita output) will depend on the relative strength of two opposite effects of monetary expansion.[12] For example, in the figure, the capital–labour ratio is shown to increase from k_1 to k^*_3 when the production curve shifts from $(y - nk)_1$ to $(y - nk)^*_2$ and the consumption curve from c_1 to c_2. However, if the production curve shifts to $(y - nk)_2$ instead, the capital–labour ratio is k_3, which is lower than the initial equilibrium capital–labour ratio k_1.

In the literature on the superneutrality of money the question of whether changes in the growth rate of nominal money are superneutral when the economy is outside its steady state, but moving towards it, has received attention. Fischer (1979b) develops a model similar to Sidrauski's with perfect foresight and shows that although in such a model the steady-state capital stock is invariant to changes in the growth rate of nominal money, such a superneutrality does not prevail during the transition path to the steady state. Cohen (1985) provides an explanation of Fischer's results. He shows that the nominal rate of interest varies along the transition path because of two conflicting factors. On the one hand, a rise in inflation raises the nominal interest rate, and on the other, a decline in the real interest rate due to inflation pushes down the nominal interest rate. When these two effects cancel each other out, monetary policy cannot affect the nominal interest rate; otherwise, the nominal interest rate during the transition path may remain above or below its steady-state value. In such a situation, monetary policy may affect capital accumulation by influencing the nominal interest rate towards its steady state value (Haliassos and Tobin, 1990).

MONETARY EXPANSION, INFLATION AND ECONOMIC GROWTH

While the neutrality and superneutrality of money have been the focus of growth analysis in developed countries in the context of a fully employed economy, an important branch of the money-growth literature has been concerned with the role of inflationary finance – that is, financing of real budget deficits through money creation, in economic growth in developing countries. The original insight of inflationary finance came from the time of the Roman Empire (Gillis *et al.*, 1992). However, it caught the imagination of policy-makers in developing countries only in the 1950s and 1960s.

As indicated above, money creation generates forced savings through a rise in inflation which will either redistribute income from classes with low propensities to save to classes with high propensities to save (Thirlwall, 1989) or transfer income from the holders of money to the government through inflation tax.[13] The theoretical framework of the income distribution link between monetary expansion, inflation and economic growth has been provided by Kalecki (1976), Kaldor (1955–6), and Robinson (1962), while the inflationary tax link has been formally developed by Mundell (1965, 1971).

Inflation, income redistribution and economic growth

The Kalecki–Kaldor–Robinson model rejects the classical notion that savings determine investment. Rather, they argue that investment determines savings. Within their model the rise in the price level in response to excess demand in the commodity market, following any monetary expansion, raises savings through redistribution of income from wage earners to capitalists. Thus, investment is not constrained by saving, but by the tolerable rate of inflation on the part of wage earners. Thirlwall (1989) has explained the above argument in a precise way by using the following model.

Assume that the actual change in capital (dK) is a linear combination of planned savings (S_p) and planned investment (I_p), so that the actual growth rate of capital (dK/K) is given by

$$dK/K = a(I_p/K) + (1 - a)(S_p/K), \quad \text{where } a < 1$$

The rate of inflation (π) is assumed to be proportional to the degree of excess demand as measured by the difference between planned investment and planned saving, so that

$$\pi = b(I_p/K - S_p/K), \quad \text{where } b > 0$$

Substitution of this expression into the actual growth of capital equation yields,

$$dK/K = a\pi/b + S_p/K$$

Thus the actual rate of growth of capital is the sum of forced saving ($a\pi/b$) and planned saving per unit of capital (S_p/K). Forced saving occurs as the excess demand due to increased investment causes inflation which redistributes income in favour of profit earners and prevents the realisation of planned consumption. As Thirlwall (1989: 281) writes:

> Other things remaining the same, if prices rise faster than wages, real consumption will fall and real savings increase as long as the propensity to save out of profits is higher than the propensity to save out of wages ... [T]herefore, the effect of inflation on savings depends on two factors: first, the extent to which income is redistributed between wages and profits; and second, the extent of the difference in propensity to save out of wages and profits.

26

Inflation tax and economic growth

Following the standard inflationary finance model, the inflation revenue function $R(\pi)$ can be expressed as

$$R(\pi^e) = \pi^e x_1 = \pi^e x_0 e^{-\alpha \pi e} \tag{2.6}$$

where x_0 is the money–income ratio when expected inflation is zero, implying that the nominal interest rate equals the real interest rate $i_0 = r_0$, and x_1 is the money–income ratio when expected inflation is π^e, that is, $i_1 = r_0 + \pi^e$.

Figure 2.3 explains the collection of government real revenue from money creation that leads to inflation. The size of government real revenue generated from inflation tax is given by ABCD. As the model shows, the demand for real balances is inversely related to expected inflation or the nominal interest rate. It suggests that the size of real revenue from inflation tax is a function of expected inflation and that it follows a Laffer curve where it first increases and then decreases with inflation, implying that there is a revenue-maximising rate of inflation.

The classic work of Cagan (1956) shows that there is a steady-state rate of inflation at which the government can maximise its inflation tax revenue. In the steady state the revenue from inflation (R^π) (or the size of seigniorage) equals the stock of real balances (m) times the growth rate of nominal money (μ). However, when the economy grows at the rate of g_y, the yield from inflation tax equals the stock of real balances multiplied by sum of the growth rate of nominal money and the rate of growth of output times the income

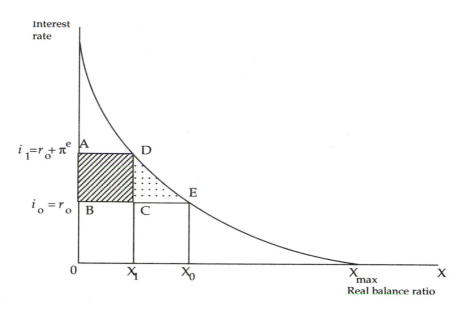

Figure 2.3 Real inflation revenue from money creation

elasticity of demand for money (η_m) – that is, $R^\pi = m(\mu + \eta_m g_y)$ (Friedman, 1971).

In the Cagan hyperinflation model in which money demand (m^d) depends on expected inflation, π^e, (for example, $m^d = e^{-\alpha \pi e}$), the revenue-maximising rate of inflation (π^*) is given by the inverse of the semielasticity (α) of demand for real money, so that

$$\pi^* = 1/\alpha \tag{2.7}$$

However, since in the general model real income is another determinant of money demand, the revenue-maximising rate of inflation (π^{**}) in a growing economy is given by the inverse of the semielasticity of demand for money minus the income elasticity of demand for money times the growth rate of real income, so that

$$\pi^{**} = 1/\alpha - \eta_m g_y \tag{2.8}$$

Equation (2.7) can be used to calculate the revenue-maximising rate of inflation in high-inflation developing countries. Khan (1980) estimated the semielasticities of demand for real money with respect to expected inflation for several developing countries and found that the estimates lie between 3 and 5. Substitution of these estimates yields the revenue-maximising rates of inflation ranging from 20 to 33 per cent per annum.

In equation (2.8) it is however obvious that the revenue-maximising rate of inflation is lower in a growing economy compared with that in a stagnant economy. For example, if it is assumed that the economy grows at the rate of, say, 4 per cent per annum and the income elasticity of demand for real money is, say, 2, as Khan (1980) found in several developing countries, the revenue-maximising rates of inflation will be somewhere between 12 and 25 per cent per annum.

However, Tanzi (1989) looks at the issue from the perspective of the net contribution of inflation to total government revenues. He suggests that the debate on inflationary finance should include the adverse effect of inflation on the conventional tax system, so that the net effect of inflation on total government revenue can be used as a criterion for deciding whether inflationary finance is economically justifiable.

Tanzi finds that one common feature of developing countries is that their tax systems are income inelastic and have a long collection lag, implying that the real value of tax revenue declines with inflation. Even in the case of a unitary elasticity of the tax system but a long tax-collection lag, the real value of tax revenue may decline with inflation. Assuming a unit elastic tax system, Tanzi uses the following formula to calculate the effect of inflation on the ratio of tax revenue to income (or tax burden):

$$T^\pi = To/(1 + \pi)^{\xi/12} \tag{2.9}$$

where T^π is the ratio of tax revenue to income when annual inflation is π,

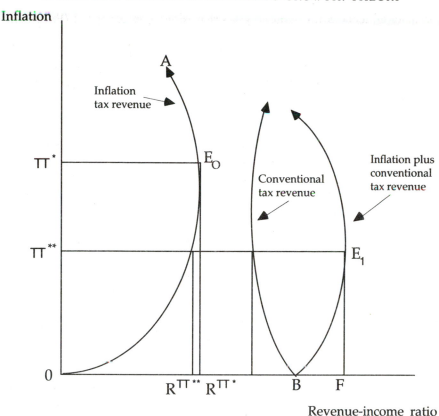

Figure 2.4 Inflation, tax revenue and inflationary finance

T_o is the ratio of tax revenue to income when inflation is zero, and ξ is the collection lag in months.

As indicated above, in a growing economy the revenue from deficit financing (or inflation tax revenue) is given by

$$R^\pi = (\pi + \eta_m g_y)\, m \tag{2.10}$$

Therefore, total government revenue (conventional tax revenue plus inflation tax revenue) is given by

$$TR^\pi = R^\pi + T^\pi \tag{2.11}$$

Taking the derivative of TR^π with respect to π, and setting it equal to zero, yields a value of π that maximises the total government revenue.

Figure 2.4 shows that inflation tax revenue (curve OA) is zero at zero inflation and reaches the maximum level when inflation is π^* (point E_0).

29

The conventional tax revenue is maximum when inflation is zero (point B), but it declines with inflation (curve BC). Total revenue (horizontal sum of inflation tax revenue and conventional tax revenue as shown in curve BD) is maximum at the point E_1 when inflation is π^{**}. Note that at the rate of inflation π^{**}, even though inflation tax revenue is $OR^{\pi^{**}}$, the net contribution of inflation tax revenue to total government revenue is just BF.

Therefore, it is found that since the ratio of tax revenue to income falls with inflation while inflation tax revenue rises with inflation up to a point, total government revenue reaches the maximum level at a rate of inflation which is lower than the rate of inflation at which inflation tax revenue is maximised alone.

It was found above that in a growing economy the revenue-maximising rate of inflation lies between 12 and 25 per cent per annum. However, when the adverse effect of inflation on the conventional tax system is taken into account, the revenue-maximising rate of inflation is likely to be at a much lower level. Therefore, Tanzi draws the following conclusion:

> [T]he existence of lags in tax collection implies that government gains from the pursuit of inflationary finance are likely to be lower than has commonly been assumed. If the lags are long and the initial tax burden is high, the loss in revenue may be substantial and may neutralize any gain coming from central bank financing of the deficit. This is an argument against inflationary finance that is quite different from the traditional one based exclusively on welfare-cost considerations of alternative sources of revenue.
>
> (Tanzi, 1989: 226–7)

The Mundell model

Mundell (1965) combined the growth analysis with the quantity theory of money and derived the following relationship between inflationary finance and economic growth:[14]

$$\pi = [(v/\phi\rho) - 1]g_y \qquad (2.12)$$

where π is inflation, g_y is economic growth, v is the velocity of circulation of money, ϕ is the fractional reserve ratio (in the relation between bank reserves and the nominal money) and ρ is the productivity of capital (or output–capital ratio).

Substitution of the plausible parameter values of v, ϕ and ρ ($v = 3$, $\phi = 0.3$, and $\rho = 0.5$) in equation (2.12) yields

$$\pi = 19g_y \qquad (2.13)$$

It shows that in order to raise the growth rate of output by 1 per cent, inflation needs to be raised by 19 per cent.

However, as the above relation is based on the assumption that the velocity of money is invariant to inflation, Mundell (1971) develops a case in which the velocity of money is an increasing function of inflation, so that

$$v = v_0 + \omega\pi \tag{2.14}$$

where v_0 is the rate of velocity at zero inflation and ω is the coefficient on inflation. Substitution of equation (2.14) into equation (2.12) gives the following relation

$$\pi = [(v_0/\phi\rho) - 1]g_y/[1 - (\omega/\phi\rho)g_y] \tag{2.15}$$

It shows that inflation is not a linear function of economic growth. The ratio of inflation to economic growth rises with economic growth, which means that the greater the growth rate financed by money creation, the larger will be the marginal increment of inflation. A limit will eventually be reached at which inflation will approach infinity, such that

$$g_y = \phi\rho/\omega \tag{2.16}$$

It is the value when the denominator in equation (2.15) is zero. For example, when $\omega = 10$ (the case discussed by Mundell), to raise the growth rate by 1 per cent will require an acceleration of inflation by 57 per cent per annum. And the maximum growth rate possible is 1.5 per cent per annum when inflation approaches infinity.

Inflationary finance and the danger of hyperinflation

The policy of inflationary finance has been criticised by Bailey (1956), Dornbusch and Reynoso (1989), Mundell (1965, 1971), Marty (1967, 1973), and Friedman (1971). The standard argument against inflationary finance is that it imposes welfare costs on money holders. However, the effective argument against inflationary finance in developing countries is that once a licence to print money is given to the government there is no guarantee that it will stop short of hyperinflation. Economists working on Latin American inflation history would testify that hyperinflation in Latin American countries was 'triggered by large budgetary deficits and sustained by subsequent ongoing deficits, virtual economic collapse, and steadily rising inflationary experiences' (Gillis et al., 1992: 340). Aghevli and Khan (1978) have developed a model for developing countries which shows that fiscal deficits perform a dual role as the original source of and the propagating mechanism for the inflationary process. They have used the idea of inflation-induced fiscal deficits which arise when government revenues rise slower than government outlays with inflation because of structural constraints in the fiscal system. Inflation-induced fiscal deficits may then become the dynamic force to sustain inflation. Therefore, although inflationary finance may start with an objective of achieving higher growth, it could end up with hyperinflation which may cause a retardation of growth.

Summing up

This review of the literature on inflationary finance and growth suggests that money creation to finance investment may have some influence on economic growth, but it is unlikely to be a major source of growth. Experience of Latin American countries shows that inflation is a hazardous means of economic growth. Rao (1952) delivered just such a message to planners in developing countries about forty years ago:

> I would prefer to say that the economic policy of deficit financing and disregard for thrift advocated by Keynes for securing full employment does not apply in the case of an underdeveloped economy ... [The] blind application of the Keynesian formulae to the problems of economic development has inflicted considerable injury on the economies of underdeveloped countries and added to the forces of inflation that are currently afflicting the whole world. The old-fashioned prescription of 'work harder and save more' still seems to hold good as the medicine for economic progress, at any rate as far as the underdeveloped countries are concerned.
>
> (Rao, 1952: 217–18)

FINANCE AND ECONOMIC GROWTH

Recent theoretical and empirical research suggests that financial markets can play an important role in economic growth. An efficient financial system transfers capital from savers to borrowers and directs resources to productive and profitable investment projects. The more productive is the investment, the higher is the growth rate of an economy (King and Levine, 1993; Zahler, 1993). An efficient financial market also enhances growth by pooling risks and facilitating transactions. As Stiglitz (1994: 23) has put it:

> Financial markets essentially involve the allocation of resources. They can be thought of as the 'brain' of the entire economic system, the central locus of decisionmaking: if they fail, not only will the sector's profits be lower than would otherwise have been, but the performance of the entire economic system may be impaired.

However, during the heyday of Keynesian revolution in the 1950s and 1960s, the importance of financial factors was largely ignored (Chandravarkar, 1992). Under the influence of the predominantly Keynesian forced-saving school most developing countries favoured low nominal interest rates and high inflation, which inevitably resulted in negative or very low real interest rates. The resultant financial repression is thought to be a major cause of low savings rates and the underdevelopment of their financial sectors.

Since the early 1970s the view that repressive financial policies raise investment and accelerate economic growth has come under criticism from the prior-saving school, particularly from the classic works of McKinnon (1973) and Shaw (1973). Although there are differences between the McKinnon and the Shaw models, they essentially suggest that financial repression (low or negative real interest rate) has a number of growth-inhibiting effects. First, low or negative real interest rates encourage current consumption and induce people to hold their savings in real, rather than financial, assets, because real assets are a better hedge against inflation. As a result, the financial sector remains shallow, which adversely affects the monetisation of the economy and the efficiency of transactions. Second, low or negative real interest rates generate excess demand for investible funds, which may create problems with credit rationing and rent-seeking activities. Third, low real interest rates create inefficiency in investment and induce investors to make capital-intensive investment which is incompatible with the country's factor endowments (Chowdhury and Islam, 1993; Fry, 1988). The McKinnon model in its basic form is taken up here.[15]

The McKinnon model of finance in economic development

The McKinnon model of finance in economic development is applicable to any fragmented economy with rudimentary capital markets. Entrepreneurs are constrained to self-finance as they do not have access to bank credits. Therefore, before making any investment in high-yielding physical capital, investors are required to accumulate funds in monetary forms. Money thus serves as a 'conduit' for capital accumulation.

The McKinnon model of finance takes the following simplified form:

$$m^d = m^d(y, iyr, d - \pi) \qquad (2.17)$$

$$iyr = iyr(r_k, d - \pi) \qquad (2.18)$$

$$iyr = syr = s \qquad (2.19)$$

$$s = s(g_y, d - \pi) \qquad (2.20)$$

$$\pi = \pi(\mu, g_y) \qquad (2.21)$$

$$g_y = \rho s \qquad (2.22)$$

where m^d is the demand for real money, y is real income (or output), iyr is the investment–income ratio, $d - \pi$ is the real deposit rate of interest, r_k is the real return on physical capital, syr is the savings–income ratio or the propensity to save (s), g_y is the growth rate of income (or output), μ is the growth rate of exogenously determined nominal money, and ρ is the fixed output–capital ratio.

Equation (2.17) shows that there is a complementary relationship between money and capital. All the partial derivatives of real money demand in equation (2.17) are positive. The complementarity between money and capital is

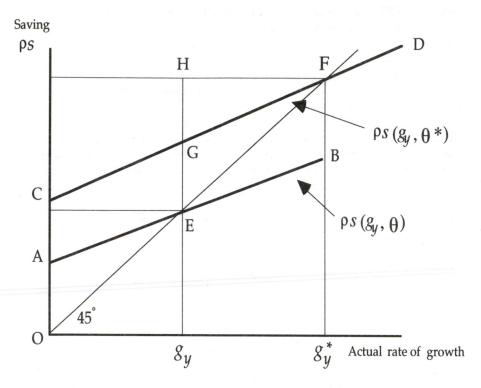

Figure 2.5 The propensity to save and the rate of economic growth

also shown in equation (2.18). All the partial derivatives of investment are positive. The investment function shows that any exogenous change that raises the return on capital, such as opening the economy to foreign trade or introducing the seed-fertilizer-irrigation technology in agriculture, would raise the desired level of investment and real money demand. Also, a rise in the real deposit rate of interest will raise savings and investment.

Equations (2.20) to (2.22) show the dynamic relationship between savings and growth.[16] At equilibrium the growth rate of income generates the desired savings that is sufficient to support the level of investment which is required to maintain that rate of growth.

Figure 2.5 shows the effect of financial reform on the propensity to save. E represents the initial equilibrium growth rate of output where the variable propensity to save line crosses the 45-degree line. The variable propensity to save line AB is drawn as a function of the growth rate of output. Assume that the initial financial structure of the economy is repressed with a low or negative real return on holding money and a small money–income ratio. Such an economy is denoted by the parameter θ. The variable propensity to

34

save line CD is drawn as a function of the growth rate of output after financial reform which raised sharply both the real return on holding money and the money–income ratio. Such a financial reform is denoted by the parameter θ^*. The consequence of such a financial reform is the shift in the savings line from AB to CD in which the slope of the line CD with respect to g_y is steeper than that of AB. The new equilibrium growth rate of output is g^*_y. It also represents a higher propensity to save.

The increment to the rate of saving has two parts. EG is the buoyant effect on savings of financial reform. McKinnon (1974) calls it 'the pure intermediation effect' – the increase in the propensity to save at a given growth rate of income. Since income is expected to grow faster when realised savings and investment rise, GH captures the growth dividend to savings – the portfolio effect when individuals maintain their portfolio balance in the face of economic progress. The steeper slope of the savings line CD indicates that the effect of growth on the rate of savings (reverse causation) is higher in a financially reformed economy compared with that in a financially repressed economy. Therefore, the essence of the McKinnon model is that financial reform promotes savings and economic growth.

A developed financial sector performs two growth-promoting functions. First, by sharing risks, it facilitates trade and specialisation. Second, it promotes capital accumulation. Although the role of a developed financial sector in facilitating trade and specialisation is well understood, the capital-accumulation-augmenting role of financial reform remains a controversial issue.

There are three aspects in the financial development–capital accumulation–growth link. They are the relation between the real deposit rate of interest and the rate of savings (or the volume effect of the real deposit interest rate); the relation between the real deposit interest rate and financial savings (or the composition/efficiency effect of the real deposit interest rate); and the relation between the real loan interest rate and the efficiency of investment. Although economic theory does not offer a clear-cut prediction as to the overall influence of interest rates on saving, the proponents of financial liberalisation hold the view that a rise in real interest rates will encourage households to save more.

A rise in the real deposit rate of interest is believed to promote financial deepening because savings may be held in financial, rather than non-financial, asset forms. It improves the efficiency of intermediation between savers and investors. Compare it with the condition when the nominal interest rate is set below the inflation rate, which creates a negative real interest rate that lowers the demand for financial assets as savers are encouraged to invest in real rather than in financial assets. As a consequence of the decline in financial savings, the supply of loanable funds declines and the financial sector becomes shallow.

Effective utilisation of capital is one important determinant of growth. In many developing countries it is not always the lack of capital but the lack

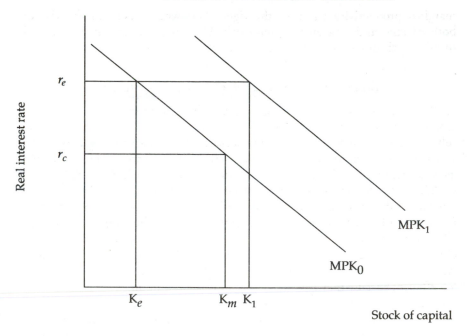

Figure 2.6 The relationship between real interest rate and capital stock

of effective utilisation of capital that might have kept their economic growth low. It is argued that when real interest rates are negative or very low, there is little incentive to use capital more efficiently since excess capacity is costless. Hence, a rise in the real interest rate is expected to raise the effective utilisation of capital. As Fry points out:

> Overtime, shift work and other measures that increase effective utilisation of plant and machinery are not worthwhile when keeping the capital stock idle is costless. Under such circumstances, the measured capital stock exceeds the effective capital stock.
>
> (Fry, 1991: 30)

The above contention can be explained with the help of a simple diagram (Figure 2.6). MPK_0 represents the returns to capital before the interest rate reforms. If the ceiling interest rate is r_c which is below the market (equilibrium) rate r_e then the measured capital stock (K_m) will be higher than the equilibrium stock (K_e). When the interest rate ceiling is removed and the rate moves towards the equilibrium rate, the marginal efficiency of capital rises along MPK_0 and the capital stock approaches to K_e so that the measured capital stock is equal to equilibrium stock. However, it is also argued that with interest rate reforms and improved utilisation of capital there will be an increase in total factor productivity, causing a shift in the

36

marginal productivity curve to the right. This would result in the rise of both effective and measured capital stock. Thus, financial reform is expected to raise both quantity and quality of investment.

Critique of the financial liberalisation hypothesis[17]

As the review of empirical findings in the following chapter will reveal, the empirical foundation of the financial liberalisation paradigm has not been so robust. The doctrine of financial liberalisation has been challenged both on theoretical and empirical grounds. One variant of the critique, known as the 'new structuralist' critique, uses empirical findings such as Wijnbergen's (1982, 1985) that the major effect of financial reforms in Korea was a huge portfolio shift of savings away from the unregulated (informal) to the regulated (formal) market without any concomitant increase in the volume of savings. Thus, whether financial reforms will enhance growth depends on the relative efficiency of the formal financial sector in allocating investable funds. According to Choo (1990) and Fischer (1989), informal credit markets are less efficient because they have a narrow information base and a limited capacity for risk-pooling. On the other hand, the informal credit market can economise on overhead costs, which may outweigh its limitations pertaining to risk-pooling. An implication is that one cannot make an *a priori* statement about the efficacy of the formal *vis-à-vis* informal credit market.

The new structuralist critique of the financial liberalisation hypothesis also draws on so-called Cavallo effect (Cavallo, 1977). The essence of the argument is that in developing countries firms depend on borrowing for their working capital. Thus the diversion of funds from the informal market as a result of financial liberalisation will reduce the supply of loanable funds because bank deposits require reserves. This will, therefore, create a credit squeeze and raise working capital costs with the predictable outcome of stagflation (Bruno, 1979; Taylor, 1979, 1983). Obviously, the validity of this argument hinges upon the substitutability between the formal and informal sector deposit instruments. Kapur (1992) argues that the informal and formal sector deposits are not close substitutes. While the informal sector primarily provides high-yielding but illiquid deposit instruments, arising from zero reserves, the bank deposits are more liquid; both have their own roles in the utility function of wealth holders. Even if there is some portfolio shift towards the formal sector, Kapur maintains that the total supply of productive credit may not necessarily decline. He derives his results by considering the motive of the government which receives a 'windfall' seigniorage gain as the monetary base increases with the rise in reserves due to higher deposit takings. The government can channel this newly created monetary base to development banks or to commercial banks themselves.

A stronger critique of the financial liberalisation hypothesis, often characterised as the new view of the role of finance, maintains that a repressed financial system would facilitate rapid economic growth (Amsden, 1989, 1991; Lee, 1992; Wade, 1988, Stiglitz, 1994). In developing this argument, it is useful to start with the distinction that Zysman (1983) makes between a capital-market-based and a credit-based financial system. In a capital-market-based financial system, securities are the main sources of long-term business finance. Lenders (and borrowers) can choose from (and use) a broad spectrum of capital and money market instruments.

On the other hand, in a credit-based system, the capital market is weak and firms rely heavily on credit to finance investment. To the extent that banks are the main suppliers of credit, it makes firms dependent on banks. If banks are themselves dependent on government, then firms essentially become dependent on government as well. In such an institutional environment, financial repression (in the form of government-directed credit) is alleged to have certain advantages (Wade, 1988: 134). First, 'a credit-based system permits faster investment in developing country conditions than would be possible if investment depended on the growth of firms' own profits or on the inevitably slow development of securities market'. More importantly, productive investment is less affected by speculative stock-market booms and busts. Second, a credit-based system tends to avoid the bias towards short-term profitability that often appears to be associated with a stock market system. It stems from the argument that lenders of long-term finance are interested in the ability of borrowers to repay the loans over the long term. Hence, long-term performance becomes the dominant consideration, entailing a focus on such issues as the ability of organisations to develop new products, cost competitiveness, and so on. These therefore become the criteria that managers are concerned with, rather than the short-run performance in the stock market. Finally, a state-dominated financial system provides the government with the necessary political clout to implement its industrial strategy. As Wade (1988: 134) puts it, 'firms are dissuaded from opposing the government by knowledge that opponents may find credit difficult to obtain'.

Stiglitz (1994) argues that many of the arguments against financial repression are based on a number of errors in previous empirical studies. To begin with, earlier studies failed to distinguish between small and large repression, and let large repression influence the results. Second, high negative rates of returns are primarily a symptom of a wider range of government failures, and it would be incorrect to infer that the low level of economic growth is caused by financial repression. Third, the claim that financial repression leads to inefficient allocation of resources is based on the failure to recognise the distinction between credit and other markets.

Stiglitz maintains that market failures related to informational asymmetry is endemic in financial markets,[18] and economies with imperfect information or incomplete markets are not constrained Pareto-efficient.[19] In such situations, feasible government interventions can make all individuals better off. Stiglitz has outlined a number of ways in which financial repression (low interest rate) policy can enhance growth.

First, according to him, the low interest rate policy can be viewed as a mechanism of resource transfer from the household to the corporate sector where such transfers are costly. If the marginal propensity to save of the corporate sector is higher than that of the household sector, then the aggregate savings will rise. This argument is similar to the Kalecki–Kaldor–Robinson model.

Second, lower interest rates could increase the expected quality of borrowers by minimising the adverse selection and incentive problems. This effect would be even greater if the government were assumed to have some positive selection capabilities. Furthermore, by reducing the cost of capital, financial repression (low interest rate policy) increases the firm's equity which, in turn, reduces the prospect of bankruptcy. In addition, when more of their own capital is at stake, firms are more likely to select good projects.

Finally, as lower interest rate creates excess demand, directed credit policy can be used as an incentive scheme. Government can set up a contest such that those who perform better in terms of some measurable target (for example, foreign exchange earnings) will get more excess to capital.

A very similar argument in favour of financial repression can also be found in C.H. Lee's internal capital market hypothesis. Using the East Asian example, Lee (1992) suggests that a state-dominated, credit-based system operates as a *de facto* internal capital market. The state cultivates a long-term and close relationship with borrowing firms. The atmosphere of trust and cooperation created as a result of this close relationship allows lender monitoring to be carried out effectively and efficiently; in the case of East Asia, export targets were used to monitor performance. The outcome is that transaction costs are minimised. Hence, what is apparently considered a phenomenon of financial repression is in effect a *de facto* internal capital market that is more efficient than private capital markets.[20]

While the above arguments are suggestive and interesting, we can, however, construct cogent counter arguments. For example, we must be careful not to confuse a credit-based system with a state-controlled credit-based system. Financial repression is a necessary feature of the latter, but not the former. More importantly, the major advantages of a credit-based system as identified by Wade do not require the existence of state controls (and hence financial repression). The only way in which financial repression can contribute to economic growth in this framework is to presuppose that a strong-willed government has the capacity to overcome the inadequacies of private capital markets without the corresponding risk of government failure. Stiglitz (1994: 32) himself pointed out that governments may resolve market failure imperfectly as some interventions could be motivated by special interest group pressures. Moreover, the government is markedly disadvantaged in assessing risks and premiums due to the large element of subjectivities involved (Stiglitz, 1994: 28).[21]

There are also inadequacies of the internal capital market hypothesis. It is sufficient to emphasise that the notion of transaction cost minimisation is not unique to a state-controlled financial system. It is also worth noting that the efficacy of the internal capital market has been exhaustively studied in the case of Japan, but in the Japanese internal capital market the state does not play a major role (Frenkel, 1991).

The hypothesis of the superiority of lender monitoring in a state-controlled financial system is also questionable when we take account of the interactions between formal and informal credit markets. Cole and Patrick (1986) report that in Korea there is a widespread practice of re-lending by privileged borrowers in regulated markets to users in unregulated markets (and hence profit from arbitrage). This fact invalidates the notion that the state can effectively monitor the behaviour of borrowers. In addition to fallibility, the state regulators are likely to be influenced by corruption. In such circumstances, a legitimate question is 'who monitors the monitors'? The experience of Bangladesh's Grameen Bank shows that a system of peer monitoring can perhaps overcome some of the associated problems (Calomiris and Himmelberg, 1994; Stiglitz, 1989, 1990).

Finally, the widespread scepticism about the financial liberalisation hypothesis can be seen as a reaction to the popular perception that financial reform is synonymous with a *laissez-faire* approach. As reviewed in Chapter 4, current developments in the literature, as well as the experience of a wide range of countries with financial reforms, have brought to the fore the issue of prudential regulation of the financial system (Long and Vittas, 1991; Park, 1991). In order to avoid the recurrence of financial scandals, prudential regulations which entail, *inter alia*, enforceable measures such as audits and disclosures are necessary. Thus the choice is not between a *laissez-faire* approach and a dirigiste system, but for a competitive financial sector within the institutional context of prudential regulation.

SUMMARY AND CONCLUSION

This chapter has reviewed the major theories of money and finance in economic development. The core question in monetary growth theory is whether money has any effect on real variables in a growing economy either in the steady state or in the transition towards the steady state. In the literature such questions have been examined within the context of neutrality and superneutrality of money. The review of the literature on neutrality of money reveals that both the Keynesians and the monetarists accept that money is non-neutral in the short run. The short-run non-neutrality of money originates from workers' expectational errors or imperfect information. Closely related to the neutrality of money is the concept of superneutrality of money. The core question with respect to the superneutrality of money is whether any change in the growth rate of nominal money has an effect on the growth paths of real economic variables with the exception of real balances. The review of the literature on superneutrality of money reveals that the superneutrality condition does not hold in strict sense, but it can be considered as a reasonable approximation.

While the neutrality and superneutrality of money has been the focus of growth analysis in developed countries in the context of a fully employed economy, an important branch of the money-growth literature has been concerned with the role of inflationary finance in economic growth in developing countries. The review of the literature on inflationary finance and growth reveals that any money creation to finance public investment may have some influence on economic growth, but it is unlikely to be a major source of growth. Experience of Latin American countries suggests that inflationary finance is in fact a hazardous means of economic growth.

The earlier discussions of financial factors in developing countries were primarily concerned with their role in mobilising savings. The predominantly Keynesian school believes that investment is the constraining factor for growth and prescribes financial repression characterised by low nominal interest rate and high inflation. While a low interest rates is expected to encourage investment, inflation is used to create forced savings.

On the other hand, the followers of the classical school hold the view that prior savings and financial development are key elements in economic development. According to this view, financial reform enhances the aggregate savings rate, induces financial deepening and improves investment efficiency. These salutary effects in turn contribute to rapid economic growth.

However, the empirical foundation of the financial liberalisation paradigm has not been so robust. The lack of robustness has been compounded by burgeoning arguments that directly challenge the doctrine of financial liberalisation. A stronger critique of the financial liberalisation hypothesis maintains that a repressed financial system would facilitate rapid economic growth. It is also argued that earlier studies of the adverse effects of financial repression were influenced by large repressions. The large repressions themselves may be symptoms of government failures, making it difficult to conclude whether the adverse growth effect is due to repression *per se* or to government mismanagement.

It is now increasingly realised that financial markets do much more than mobilise savings – whether 'forced' or 'voluntary'. Financial markets not only deal with intertemporal decisions but also with risk and information, and 'how well they perform these functions may affect not only the extent to which they can mobilise savings but, more broadly, the overall efficiency and rate of growth of the economy' (Stiglitz, 1994: 23). Because of endemic nature of market failures in the financial sector due to information asymmetry, moral hazard, and the high transaction costs of monitoring and information transfer, a consensus now seems to be emerging that small repression is perhaps growth promoting. Even the World Bank, which vigorously preached the financial liberalisation programme, itself appears to have accepted the emerging view (World Bank, 1993).

Furthermore, after the initial euphoria with the financial liberalisation programme, it is now realised that financial liberalisation is not synonymous with a *laissez-faire* approach. Current developments in the literature as well as the experience of a wide range of countries with financial reforms have brought to the fore the issue of prudential regulation of the financial system. In fact, the choice is not between a *laissez-faire* approach and a dirigiste system, but for a competitive sector within the institutional context of prudential regulation.

NOTES

1. Per capita real income is commonly used as a measure of economic progress. However, it is an imperfect measure of economic welfare. There are other complementary performance criteria which are used in developing countries. For a detailed discussion on this issue, see Adelman and Morris (1973), Sen (1988), and Streeten (1981).

2. For example, the Harrod–Domar model shows that economic growth rate equals the rate of investment multiplied by the reciprocal of the capital–output ratio. When the capital-output ratio is assumed constant, investment becomes the determinant of growth (Domar, 1946, 1947; Harrod, 1939). However, an increase in per capita physical capital may not be enough to raise per capita income because there is a need for both an effective use of physical capital (Stiglitz, 1988) and an increase in investment in human capital and intangible productivity-enhancing capital goods (King and Levine, 1993).

3. For a critical and detailed discussion on all major approaches to development finance, see Khatkhate (1972), and Thirlwall (1989).

4. It follows from the classical view that since in a fully employed economy the aggregate supply curve is vertical, any increase in investment demand without lowering consumption demand may generate inflation but no real income.

5. In general, financial repression represents the economic condition in which the government's discretionary policies indiscriminately distort financial prices, discourage saving, lower investment, and misallocate financial resources (Fry, 1988).

6. The notion of the quantity theory of money is found in early statements by David Hume (1752). For a historical discussion on the quantity theory of money, see also Friedman (1992), Hayek (1931), and Patinkin and Steiger (1989).

7. Individuals suffer from a money illusion if they change their economic behaviour after a currency conversion takes place (Patinkin, 1992). Fisher (1928: 4) defined money illusion as a 'failure to perceive that the dollar, or any other unit of money, expands or shrinks in value'.

8. Patinkin (1949) criticises the notion of money illusion as implied by the homogeneity postulate on the grounds that it does not take into account the real balance effect. He defines the absence of money illusion as a condition in which the demand functions of goods are homogeneous of degree zero in money prices and in the initial quantity of financial assets, including money (Patinkin, 1989). Howitt (1989) points out that the absence of money illusion in Patinkin's sense is operationally equivalent to the assumption of rational behaviour of utility-maximising economic agents. The inclusion of the real balance effect in the

Walrasian monetary model ensures that Say's identity does not hold, for a change in the absolute price level affects the excess demands for all goods. Money is however neutral in the sense that a change in the money supply does not change any of the real variables in the general equilibrium system of the economy (Harris, 1985; Patinkin, 1989).

9. Early quantity theorists, such as Hume (1752), also emphasised that prices do not immediately rise proportionately to the increase in the quantity of money and that in the intervening period it may stimulate production.

10. This presupposes that there is no liquidity trap and investment pessimism. In an open economy, it would also require that the exchange rate is sensitive to interest rate changes and net export responds to exchange rate changes.

11. Levhari and Patinkin (1968) also argue that the dropping of the assumption of a constant saving ratio rather than the different definition of disposable income yields their qualitatively different results from those of the Tobin model. Bandyopadhyay and Ghatak (1990) however show that it is neither the dropping of a constant saving ratio nor the different definition of disposable income but the form of the money demand function that produces different results.

12. In the original neoclassical model, any decline in the quantity of per capita real balances does not affect real output. It implies that the marginal productivity of real balances is zero. Most monetary economists argue that, while it is difficult to treat real balances as a productive service in the same way as labour and capital are treated in the production function, it is an oversimplification to ignore the role of real balances in the production function and to assume that per capita output is a function of only the capital–labour ratio. Stein (1970) argues that the marginal effect of inflation on per capita output $[(\delta y/\delta m)(\delta m/\pi)]$ may be substantial in a developing economy where financial institutions are not fully developed.

13. There is a subtle difference between inflation tax and seigniorage. Inflation tax refers to capital losses by moneyholders as a result of inflation. Inflation tax revenue (R^π) is measured as $R^\pi = \pi m$, where π is the inflation rate and m is the stock of real money. Seigniorage (S^μ) is the revenue collected by the government by exercising its monopoly power to print money. It is measured by the purchasing power of the money which is created and put into circulation in a given period, that is, $S^\mu = \mu m$, where μ is the growth rate of nominal money. At the steady state, since the rate of inflation equals the growth rate of nominal money, inflation tax revenue equals the size of seigniorage. For details, see Sachs and Larrain (1993).

14. For a detailed derivation and the working of the model, see Mundell (1971).

15. See Fry (1988) for several extensions and modifications of the basic McKinnon–Shaw model. Also see Roubini and Sala-i-Martin (1992) for a theoretical model of the relationship between financial repression and economic growth.

16. McKinnon (1973) suggests that households and firms maintain a portfolio balance by holding stocks of monetary assets at a certain proportion of current income. Stocks of monetary assets will be higher relative to income when the real return on holding money is high. Starting from a stationary state with zero net saving, a rise in economic growth will affect households' desired ratio of money to income and induce them to save from their incremental income to raise their asset position and establish the ratio of money to income. The portfolio effect of growth on saving is pronounced the higher the desired ratio of money to income and the higher the rate of growth. Because of the portfolio effect of growth on saving, the propensity to save instead of being constant is considered a function of the rate of economic growth.

17. This section draws heavily on Chowdhury and Islam (1993, Ch. 8).

18. Stiglitz (1994) lists seven market failures in financial markets. They are: monitoring as a public good; externalities of monitoring, selection and lending; externalities of financial disruption; missing and incomplete markets; imperfect competition; Pareto-inefficiency of competitive markets; and uninformed investors. Monitoring can be regarded as a public good because if one lender takes action that reduces the risk of default, all other lenders benefit. As with any other public good, there will be undersupply of monitoring. Externalities with regard to monitoring, selection and lending arise due to the presence of a large number of 'bad' firms seeking to raise equity, making it more difficult for investors to sort out. On the other hand, if another lender is willing to supply funds, the second lender finds it reassuring without compensating the first. As the macroeconomic consequences of disruptions in financial markets are quite serious, governments cannot sit idly when faced with an impending collapse of a major financial institution. This creates a moral-hazard problem in the sense that financial institutions tend to take more risks. The missing and incomplete markets refer to the fact that in many countries there are either no security (equity) markets or they are very weak. In most countries, the banking sector is dominated by a few large banks and there is limited competition. The absence of some markets and the endogeneity of information invalidate the fundamental theorem of welfare economics and the economy cannot be regarded as Pareto optimal. The uninformed investors refer to the fact that many individuals do not possess information correctly. For example, quite often the consumers do not understand the various conditions in insurance or loan documents even if written in plain language.

19. The term constrained is used to indicate that the costs of information or of establishing markets have been taken into account.

20. When transaction costs and corresponding information asymmetries between borrowers and lenders are high and pervasive, lenders cannot efficiently monitor the activities of borrowers (Mishkin, 1992: Stiglitz, 1989). A predictable outcome is credit rationing (Stiglitz and Weiss, 1981). It implies that in a freely functioning capital market, firms relying on external finance may find that investment projects entailing high *ex ante* social rates of return are crowded out as credit is rationed due to monitoring problems arising from asymmetry of information between borrowers and lenders. Under such circumstances, reliance on the internal capital market (reliance on finance generated through retained earnings or out of depreciation charges) can minimise transaction costs.

21. While the government in such circumstances employs relatively simple rules, the market, by contrast, converts the subjective judgements of a large number of participants into an objective standard (see Stiglitz, 1984: 28).

3

MONEY AND FINANCE IN
ECONOMIC GROWTH
A review of empirical evidence

In the previous chapter, we explored the possible theoretical links between monetary expansion, financial factors and economic growth. It has been observed that, at the theoretical level, there are considerable uncertainties regarding the supposed growth-promoting role of monetary expansion as well as that of financial liberalisation. This chapter surveys the empirical evidence on the link between money, finance and economic growth. Although the empirical evidence on the roles of monetary and financial factors in economic growth are examined separately, as Drake (1980) pointed out, there is a close synergy between them.

INFLATION AND ECONOMIC GROWTH

Monetary expansion affects economic growth, positively or negatively, through inflation; that is, money affects output via its impact on the price level. Figure 3.1 plots the mean values of monetary growth and inflation rates for 48 developing countries over the period of 1960–89. It shows that, except for two outlying observations for Indonesia and Myanmar, the relationship between monetary growth and inflation is almost linear. Although no causality is implied, the correlation coefficient between the two is high (0.98).

Figures 3.2–3.4 plot the mean values of inflation rates and growth rates for the same set of countries during the period 1960-89. From these scatter diagrams, we can see that, unlike the monetary-growth–inflation relationship, the relationship between inflation and economic growth is much more complex. To begin with, economic growth appears to be negatively related to inflation until the average annual inflation rate reaches around 10 per cent. It becomes mildly positive when the average annual inflation rate is moderate (between 10 and 15 per cent). If the extreme values of Brazil and Guyana are omitted, the relationship between the rates of inflation and economic growth again becomes negative for inflation rates above 15 per cent. Thus, there seems to be an inverted U-shaped relationship between the rates of inflation and economic growth when the average annual inflation rate exceeds 10 per cent.

45

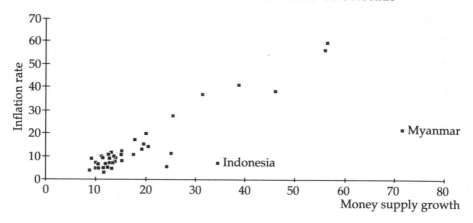

Figure 3.1 Money supply growth and inflation rate (mean values 1960–89)
Source: IMF, *International Financial Statistics*, various issues

Just as there are uncertainties about the supposed relationship between inflation rates and economic growth, there are controversies regarding the causality. As Friedman has put it:

> Sometimes the relationship is supposed to be that economic develop-ment causes inflation. Sometimes the relation is supposed to be that inflation promotes development.
>
> Friedman (1973: 41)

The neoclassical and Kalecki–Keynesian schools both believe that the causality runs from inflation to growth. The Kalecki–Keynesian 'forced savings' school holds that inflation increases the overall levels of savings and investment by transferring income from wage-earners with a low propensity to save to profit-earners who have a higher propensity to save if prices rise faster than wages (Taylor, 1979; Thirlwall, 1974). Furthermore the operation of inflation tax transfers resources from the private sector to the government sector where they could in principle be used to finance real investment (Aghevli, 1977; Johnson, 1969; Mundell, 1965). In the 'Tobin effect' the causality also runs from inflation to growth. This happens via the capital intensity effect as inflation makes rates of return from real investment more attractive than the returns on financial investment.

As opposed to the Kalecki–Keynesian view, economists of classical persua-sion believe that inflation retards economic growth (Baer, 1967; Bhagwati, 1978; Campos, 1967; Dornbusch and Reynoso, 1989; Mundell, 1971). The argument rests on several planks. First, inflation lowers returns to savings and hence discourages the act of saving. Second, it is argued that the high and variable inflation rates have the potential to raise the cost and riskiness of productive investment. The high variability of inflation may induce the

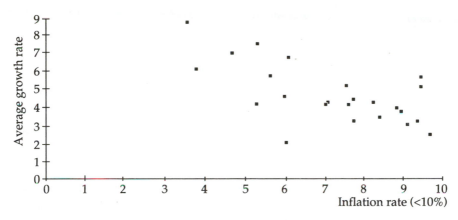

Figure 3.2 Inflation rate (< 10 per cent) and economic growth (mean values 1960–81)

Source: IMF, *International Financial Statistics,* various issues

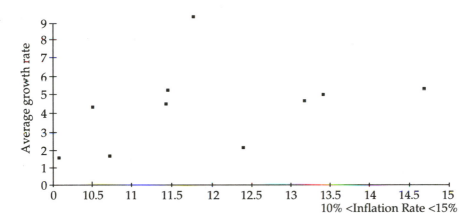

Figure 3.3 Inflation rate (< 15 per cent and > 10 per cent) and economic growth (mean values 1960–89)

Source: IMF, *International Financial Statistics,* various issues

private sector to invest in quick-yielding financial assets rather than in longer-term projects. Third, high inflation can generate 'rent-seeking' and directly unproductive activities as pressures mount on government to impose various price controls. Fourth, contrary to Tobin's conclusion, high inflation may make investment in unproductive real assets (for example, real estate, gold) more attractive. Fifth, if resources transferred to the government through 'inflation tax' are not invested, the net increase in aggregate investment will be lower. Finally, in an open economy, if domestic inflation exceeds world

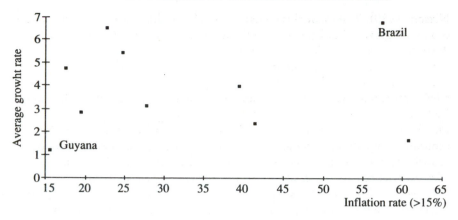

Figure 3.4 Inflation rate (> 15 per cent) and economic growth (mean values 1960–89)

Source: IMF, *International Financial Statistics,* various issues

inflation, and if the exchange rate is not fully flexible, then inflation will worsen the balance of trade. This will make the foreign exchange constraint more severe than the savings constraint (Findlay, 1984; Johnson, 1974, 1984; McKinnon, 1964). Moreover, hyperinflation can induce capital flights as it causes balance of payments problems and generates speculation about exchange rate devaluations.

The 'structuralist view' of inflation can be seen as reversing the causality. The structuralist argument relies on the inelasticity of supply with respect to changes in prices and various rigidities, especially downward rigidity of factor prices and factor immobility. Due to these rigidities and supply inelasticities prices will tend to rise in sectors experiencing excess demand but will not fall (or will move slowly) in sectors experiencing excess supply. Thus, there will be an initial rise in the overall or average price level *even when aggregate demand and supply are in balance* and inflationary pressure will build up which will need to be accommodated by an expansionary monetary policy if potential economic growth is to be realised (Baer, 1967; Canavese, 1982; Cardoso, 1981; Georgescu-Roegan, 1970; Lewis, 1964; Olivera, 1964; Seers, 1962, 1964; Taylor, 1983). The situation is exacerbated if various interest groups in the society attempt to maintain their relative position and thereby cause a self-propagating mechanism for inflation through a wage–price spiral (Sunkel, 1960). Thus the process of growth causes inflationary pressure.

Inflation causing growth

The empirical evidence on the relationship between inflation rates and economic growth is equally inconclusive (Johnson, 1984; Kirkpatrick and

Nixson, 1989). The inconclusive nature of relationship between inflation and economic growth has been succinctly summarised by Friedman (1973: 41): 'historically, all possible combinations have occurred: inflation with and without development, no inflation with and without development'.

Friedman has cited Great Britain's development in the eighteenth and nine-teenth centuries, that of the US and the recent experience of Hong Kong, Malaysia and Singapore as examples of economic growth without inflation. On the other hand, in India and South America inflation occurred despite economic stagnation. Israel and Korea are examples of the case of economic growth with inflation, whereas inter-war India and many European coun-tries experienced the co-existence of no inflation and stagnation.

Given the historical facts, it is not surprising that the earlier empirical works (for example, Bhatia, 1960–1) on inflation and growth failed to estab-lish any meaningful relationship between the two. The following quotes are indicative of the general view derived from earlier empirical works

> the economic indicators do not in themselves provide satisfactory expla-nation of either the causes or the consequences of inflation.
>
> Mikesell (1969: 150)

> it is abundantly clear from the available evidence that there is no close relation between the rate of inflation and the rate of economic growth.
>
> Harberger (1964: 320)

The general lack of empirical support for either positive or negative rela-tionship between inflation and economic growth led Seers (1962: 191) to conclude that 'it is meaningless to set up a hypothesis that inflation helps or hinders growth'.

Later works, therefore, shifted focus on various aspects of inflation and their impact on economic growth. These aspects include the pattern and variability of inflation, predictability of inflation, and whether or not infla-tion is too high. For example, in his study of 48 developing and developed countries for the period of 1953–61, Dorrance (1966: 94) found that 'declining prices or unduly low price increases appear to be associated with low rates of growth'. That is, a relatively mild inflation might have a stim-ulating effect. He also found that once inflation exceeded a certain unspecified rate, 'rising prices tended to discourage economic development and rapid inflation seriously inhibits growth' (ibid.). However, he qualified his findings by stating that 'it is not possible to conclude that the rate of price change will determine the rate of economic growth' (ibid.). None the less, this finding is broadly consistent with the inverted U-shaped pattern detected in Figures 3.3–3.4 and also similar to an earlier work by Tun Wai (1959). Although Tun Wai did not find any conclusive evidence in his study of 31 developing countries covering the period of 1938–54, in the small number of countries (mostly Latin American) in which the rates of inflation differed significantly

his study indicated that the rate of growth was higher when the rate of inflation was lower. We may, therefore, conclude that a rapid price increase retards
economic growth.

Thirlwall (1974) and the International Monetary Fund (IMF, 1982) also
reported similar findings. Thirlwall, for example, found that in a cross-section
of 15 Latin American countries over the period of ten years (1958-68), the
rates of inflation and economic growth were positively related at the lower
spectrum of inflation rate. As the rate of inflation accelerated beyond 10 per
cent, economic growth declined. This inverted U-shaped relationship between
the rates of inflation and economic growth suggests that the 'optimum' rate
of inflation is perhaps below 10 per cent. In an earlier work, Thirlwall and
Barton (1971) also reported a similar finding when they subdivided the countries with per capita income less than US$800 into below and above 10 per
cent of average annual inflation rate. The IMF (1982: 134) study of 112
non-oil developing countries for the period of 1969-81 concluded that, for
the most part, 'relatively low inflation have been associated with an improvement, or relative improvement, in growth rates'.

Thus these findings are in broad agreement with empirical observations
that inflation retards growth when inflation rate exceeds certain level as plotted
in Figures 3.3–3.4. Based on their observations of Latin American countries,
Dornbusch and Reynoso (1989: 209) also concluded that 'we emphasise that
the scope for deficit finance as an engine of economic development is
extremely limited and extraordinarily hazardous. When overdone, inflationary
finance acquires a dynamics of its own that can set back the development
effort by a decade or more.'

Among the studies which examined the impact of anticipated versus unanticipated inflation, Hanson (1980) found a stronger positive correlation
between unanticipated inflation and output growth in five Latin American
countries (Brazil, Chile, Colombia, Mexico and Peru) during the period
1950–74 than what was reported in Barro (1979). He used a variant of the
Phillips curve and found that ten percentage points of unexpected inflation
produced about one extra percentage point of economic growth. However,
Edwards (1983) disputed this '10 per cent rule of thumb' result by arguing
that it might disappear if the open economy aspects (for example, the terms
of trade shock) and the role of fiscal deficits were introduced into the analysis.
Using the extended model, Edwards found no significant effect of an unexpected expansion of money supply on output growth for Brazil and Chile,
while he found some evidence of a positive effect for Colombia, Mexico and
Peru. He also concluded that inflation tended to have a negative impact on
output growth in these countries. However, based on his study of 40 developing countries over the period 1953-68, Glezakos (1978) concluded that
the unpredictability of inflation is more detrimental to growth than inflation
per se. He argued that the losses from an allocative inefficiency arising from
hedging into unproductive assets against an anticipated inflation might not

be excessive because of a limited degree of monetisation in developing countries. However, if the rate of inflation cannot be anticipated, the wage- and profit-earners' ability to successfully hedge against inflation could be reduced considerably. This together with the discouragement of long-term investment because of an increased risk from future uncertainty would impair economic growth. However, like Edwards, Johnson (1984) found that both anticipated and unanticipated inflation had a negative effect on economic growth.

There are also studies which examined the investment effect of inflation on growth. For example, on the basis of his study of 43 countries, which included 25 developing countries, for the period 1956–65 Wallich (1969) concluded that a very small part of the negative effect of inflation on growth was due to its detrimental effect on the volume of investment. Other factors, such as quality, distribution and cost of investment, accounted for the larger part. Thirlwall (1974) found a negative relationship between inflation rate and the aggregate investment. However, Galbis (1979) did not find any significant relationship between inflation and investment in his cross-country study of 16 Latin American countries during 1961-73. This was primarily due to differences among country performances. For example, the relation- ship was found to be positive in nine countries (three significant) and negative in the other seven countries. Blejer and Khan (1984) found in their study of 24 developing countries covering the period 1971–9 that public sector investment significantly crowded out private sector investment. Thus, to the extent that inflation transfers resources from private sector to public sector (via inflation tax), the net increase in investment is likely to be lower than the inter-sectoral resource shift.

Cuddington (1986) examined the causes of capital flights from selected Latin American countries and Korea. He found mixed results in terms of the explanatory power of inflation. The increase in public sector deficits in Argentina in the 1970s accelerated price increases to the verge of hyperin- flation. The downward crawl of the exchange rate in the mid-1970s and later the floating of the peso failed to offset the acceleration of inflation. This led to a severe overvaluation of the peso, and the increasing probability of deval- uation caused capital flight in the early 1980s. The story is similar in other Latin American countries. However, the regression analyses did not produce any uniform results. For example, while the exchange rate was found to be significant, the inflation rate was not significant in explaining capital flight from Argentina. In the case of Mexico and Venezuela, the regression analysis with quarterly data found inflation and overvaluation of the exchange rate has the two important determinants of capital flight. The coefficient of the inflation rate had a positive sign but was found to be marginally significant in the Brazilian equation. In the case of Uruguay, the inflation rate was found to be negatively related to capital flight, while no correlation could be estab- lished in Peru. For the only non-Latin American country included in the study, Korea, inflation was found to be significant and negatively related to capital flight.

Cuddington attributed the mixed results and the failure to find a significant correlation between inflation, currency overvaluation and capital flight to the difficulty in measuring capital flights and the existence of various regulations that might have restricted capital flights. He concluded:

> Inflation rates and the degree of variability in real exchange rates differed markedly among the eight countries . . . Nevertheless, Brazil, Chile, and Peru which has less acute problems with capital flight than Argentina, Mexico, Uruguay, or Venezuela, suffered sufficiently from inflation and overvaluation to have experienced capital flight. . . . The presence of capital controls greatly reduced the amount of capital flight that would otherwise have occurred given the movements in inflation rates and the real exchange rates between 1974 and 1982.
>
> Cuddington (1986: 32)

Economic growth causing inflation

The hypothesis that some rise in general price level is the unavoidable companion of economic growth was tested within the context of a structuralist-monetarist debate on inflation, especially in Latin America. The seminal work in this area by Harberger (1963) covering the period 1939–58 did not find much support for the structuralist hypothesis in Chile. Rather, inflation was found to be caused by monetary factors. Argy's (1970) study of 22 countries for the period of 1958–65 also found little support for various aspects of the structuralist hypothesis. Vogel's (1974) extension of Harberger's (1963) work to 16 Latin American countries for the period 1950–69 also failed to establish structural causes for inflation. According to Vogel (1974: 113), 'the substantial differences in rates of inflation among these countries cannot under the present model be attributed to structural differences, but must rather be attributed primarily to differences in the behaviour of the money supply'.

On the other hand, on the basis of his study of Mexico, Brazil, Chile, Colombia, Mexico, Peru, Uruguay and Venezuela, Edel concluded that

> the direction of the relationship is the one indicated by the structuralist theory that less adequate food production means more inflation, as well as relative rises in food prices, more food imports, and slower growth in other sectors of the economy.
>
> Edel (1969: 135–6)

Although Kahil's (1973) findings on Brazil for the period 1946–64 are more monetarist in nature, he attributed inflation to the rapid industrialisation policy of the 1950s and the government's attempt to win the support of the urban masses while at the same time serving the interests of other groups. Thus, his conclusion comes very close to the structuralist position when he concluded that inflation was the outcome of the attempt by the state to promote growth and grant privileges to mutually antagonistic interest groups.

Wachter (1976), Aghevli and Khan (1978) and Bhalla (1981) attempted to integrate both monetarist and structuralist models in their works. Although these studies found stronger support for the monetarist hypothesis, there was also some evidence supporting particular aspects of structural factors. For example, Wachter (1976: 137) concluded that 'the reformulated structuralist model is also substantially supported by the finding . . . of a significant and positive coefficient for the rate of change in the relative price of food'. Similarly, the explanatory power of Bhalla's (1981) hybrid model increased considerably when food supply bottlenecks and import price changes were introduced. Aghevli and Khan (1978) found that government fiscal deficits played the dual role of the original force and the propagating mechanism in the inflationary process.

Bi-directional causality between inflation and growth

The preceding discussion indicates that the relationship between inflation and growth is complex and could be bi-directional; that is, inflation and growth can cause each other. Paul *et al.* (1992) have examined the nature of causality between inflation and growth for 70 countries covering the period 1960–89. The sample included 45 developing countries from Africa, Asia and Latin America and three from Europe (Cyprus, Malta and Turkey). As expected, one major conclusion emerging from their study is that the pattern of causality varies across countries. For example, no causal relation between inflation and growth was found in 25 developing countries. The causality was found to run from inflation to growth in Indonesia, Cyprus, Madagascar, Rwanda and Venezuela. While inflation was found to have a negative impact on growth in Indonesia and Cyprus, the relationship was found to be positive in the other three countries. On the other hand, for Korea, Colombia and Honduras growth was found to accelerate inflation. For four Latin American (Bolivia, Brazil, Dominican Republic and Panama), three Asian (Nepal, Pakistan and the Philippines) and two African (Tanzania and Zaire) countries, economic growth was found to reduce inflation. A bi-directional causality was found in Mauritius, Turkey, Barbados, Costa Rica, Haiti and Peru. The relationship was found to be negative in both directions in Turkey, Costa Rica and Peru while for Barbados and Haiti both inflation and growth affected each other positively. In the case of Mauritius, inflation affected growth negatively, but growth accelerated inflation.

In sum, there is general support for an inverted U-shaped relationship between inflation and economic growth. While low inflation may promote growth, the empirical evidence tends to support the view that high and variable inflation adversely affects economic growth. There is also some evidence in favour of the 'structuralist' view that inflation is a necessary evil caused by growth. It is also found that, in some countries, both inflation and growth interact to generate a bi-directional relationship.

FINANCIAL CONDITIONS AND ECONOMIC GROWTH

Figures 3.5–3.6 graphically depict two stylised facts about the relationship between financial condition and economic growth. Figure 3.5 shows a close link between economic growth and average financial size, measured by the ratio of quasi-liquid liabilities (liquid liabilities minus M1) and gross domestic product (GDP). Countries with faster growth rates tend to have larger financial systems. The second stylised fact as demonstrated in Figure 3.6 is that countries with initially larger financial systems enjoy faster subsequent growth.

From these two stylised facts it can be argued that the absence of a developed financial sector, which is largely the result of financial repression, is an impediment to growth. Financial repression is one of the most widely cited reasons for the failure to raise the savings rate, channel investible funds properly and invest them efficiently. Since most developing countries are capital-scarce, the interest rate is expected to be high. However, in the past it was believed that any high interest rate might discourage investment and adversely affect economic growth. As a result, most developing countries imposed ceilings on interest rates, much below their market-clearing levels. This is regarded as financial repression because the market is prevented from playing its role in allocating investible funds. Rapid and excessive monetary expansion and the consequent high inflation may make the real interest rate low, and in most cases negative. It may exacerbate the impact of financial repression on economic growth via its adverse effect on the rates of savings and investment.

A repressed financial sector and negative or low real interest rate are believed to have a number of growth-inhibiting impacts. First, it encourages people to hold their savings in unproductive real assets such as real estate, gold and other precious metals. This hampers the growth of the financial sector due to inadequate demand for financial assets. The 'shallow' financial sector itself adversely affects the savings rate due to lack of alternative financial assets and hence reduces financial resources for investment. Second, the non-market allocation of investible funds encourages rent-seeking and directly unproductive activities because the government seeks to pick 'winners' or 'priority' activities. Third, the low and negative real interest rate encourages potential investors to be indulgent. This results in an inefficient investment profile and a capital-intensive industrial structure which is out of line with the country's factor endowment.

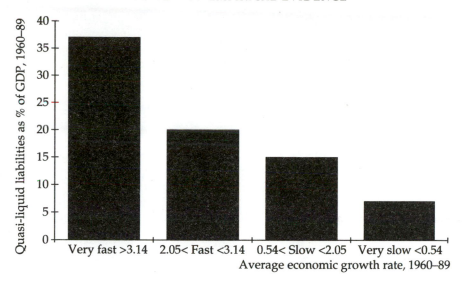

Figure 3.5 Average size of the financial sector and economic growth
Source: King and Levine (1992)

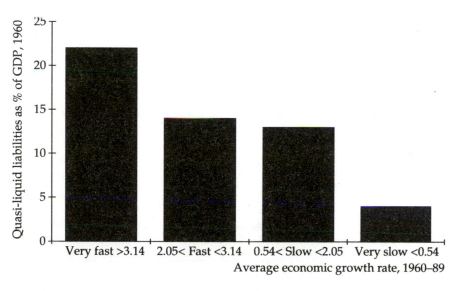

Figure 3.6 Initial size of the financial sector and economic growth
Source: King and Levine (1992)

Thus, it is a fairly widely held view that financial liberalisation and development enhances economic growth by facilitating capital accumulation and its efficient use. It also facilitates trade and specialisation by providing a stable and widely acceptable medium of exchange and thereby reducing transactions costs (World Bank, 1989; Fry, 1988; McKinnon, 1973; Shaw, 1973). In particular, financial liberalisation entails four testable hypotheses:

(a) the real deposit rate of interest and the savings rate are positively related (volume effect);
(b) the real deposit rate of interest and financial deepening are positively related (composition and efficiency effect);
(c) the positive and high real interest rates enhance efficiency of investment;
(d) financial deepening enhances economic growth (trade and specialisation effect).

The spectacular financial development and growth performance of East Asian newly industrialising economies (NIEs) and some other countries (for example, Turkey) are regarded as vindicating the financial liberalisation hypothesis. However, as will be shown in the subsequent sections, the evidence on the link between financial liberalisation and economic growth is not overwhelming (Chowdhury and Islam, 1993; Dornbusch, 1991).

Real deposit interest rates and savings

Table 3.1 presents average real deposit interest rates and private savings rates in selected countries. It shows that there is little or no relation between deposit interest rates and private savings. There are countries (Japan and Philippines) with high savings rates but without high positive real deposit interest rates. On the other hand, in Chile a high real deposit interest rate did not produce a high private savings rate. In contrast, despite a massively negative real deposit rate of interest, the private savings rate in Ghana was found to be nearly three times that of Chile. Malaysia and Thailand are two other countries with contrasting combinations of real deposit interest rates and private savings rates. These heterogeneous observations imply that there are other variables which influence the household savings behaviour. In fact, in the literature a large number of variables other than the interest rate have been identified as possible determinants of the household savings behaviour. They include socioeconomic factors such as economic growth, macroeconomic environment, family structure, social security system, retirement practices, the self-financing nature of investment due to borrowing constraints, population growth and dependency ratio, attitude towards education, income distribution, and so on (Fry, 1984, 1991; Scitovsky, 1985).

Hence, it is not surprising that attempts to verify empirically the impact of real interest rate on savings failed to establish any significant positive relationship between the two. Fry (1984, 1985, 1988), for example, noted that

Table 3.1 The deposit real interest rate and private saving in selected countries

Country	Average real deposit interest rate (%)		Private savings rate (%)	
Japan	−1.12	(1953–1991)	16.0	(1955–1988)
Malaysia	2.77	(1976–1991)	18.9	(1961–1990)
Thailand	4.41	(1977–1990)	9.7	(1980–1987)
Philippines	0.45	(1976–1991)	12.8	(1980–1987)
Chile	31.84	(1965–1991)	1.5	(1980–1987)
Ghana	−28.31	(1978–1988)	4.1	(1980–1987)

Source: World Bank (1993: tables 5.5 and 5.6)

the real deposit rate coefficient was not significantly different from zero in the saving rate functions and the magnitude of real interest rate effect was not large enough to warrant policy significance. McKinnon (1986), concluded that any positive link between real interest rates and personal savings is much less apparent. According to the World Bank (1993: 27), '[w]hether financial variables affect the savings rate is still an open question. . . . Empirical estimates range from a large positive effect to no effect at all.'

The apparent high interest elasticity of savings found in East Asian NIEs can be attributed to outliers. Giovannini (1985) showed that once the outlying observations for Korea (1967–8) were removed, the coefficient of the real interest rate became negative and insignificant. The increase in private savings following interest rate reforms can in fact be attributed to the shift of savings from the informal to the formal financial sector.

The failure to find a strong relationship between national savings and interest rates is in line with theoretical predictions. The rise in the real interest rate has two effects – income effect and substitution effect. When the interest rate rises, it induces intertemporal substitution of savings for consumption. But at the same time a rise in the real interest rate represents an increase in income and induces more consumption. The theory suggests that 'at least at the household level, income and substitution effects go in opposite directions' when the interest rate changes (Stiglitz, 1994: 40).

Real interest rates can be low or high depending on inflation rates. Perhaps what affects household savings behaviour more than the real deposit rate is the inflation rate. If the inflation rate is high and variable, it not only lowers the real deposit rate, but also introduces uncertainty. The private sector responds to this situation by adjusting its savings behaviour. Thus, any observed relationship between the real deposit rate and savings may actually be the result of inflation affecting both.

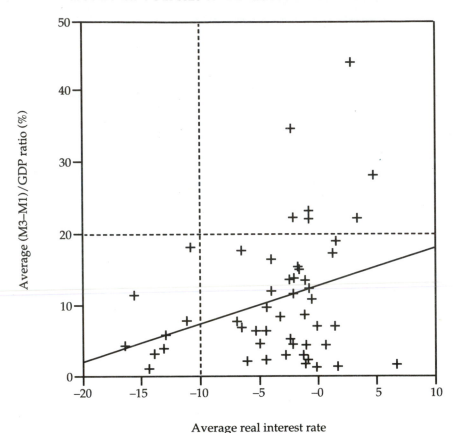

Figure 3.7 Financial deepening and real interest rates, 1965–89
Source: Ghani (1992: Figure 2)

Real interest rate and financial deepening

Here, too, empirical results are not robust. For example, Hong Kong has the 'deepest' financial sector among the successful East Asian NIEs (Arndt, 1983). Its M_2/GDP ratio reached nearly 90 per cent in the 1960s and now stands in excess of 100.[1] Yet Hong Kong had persistently negative real deposit interest rates during 1970–80 (Fry, 1985: table 11.2). Figure 3.7 plots real deposit interest rates and the ratio of total assets of the financial system to GDP – both averaged over the period 1965–89 – for 52 developing countries, as reported in Ghani (1992). Although this shows some sort of positive relationship between real deposit interest rates and financial deepening, the relationship is weak. The correlation coefficient is only 0.28 and would probably be even lower if the extreme values were eliminated. As a matter of fact, if we draw lines to exclude real interest rates below –10 per cent and the

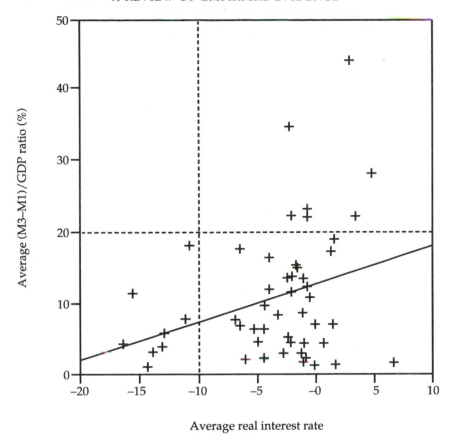

Figure 3.8 Financial intermediation and real interest rates, 1965–89
Source: Ghani (1992: Figure 3)

ratio between financial assets and GDP above 50 per cent, the whole relationship would disappear.

If the real deposit rate does not play a strong role in financial deepening,
it is likely that it would be a minor factor in financial intermediation. This
is confirmed by a low correlation coefficient of 0.31 between real deposit
interest rates and financial intermediation (M3–M1) as a ratio of GDP –
both averaged over 1965–89. The plot of the data (Figure 3.8) indicates that
the correlation is also affected by extreme values. Ghani's (1992) study shows
that factors such as reserve requirements and the structure of financial sector
are more closely related to financial deepening than are real deposit rates.
Both reserve requirements and the size of the central bank in the financial
system are negatively associated with financial deepening.

Real interest rates and efficiency of investment

The evidence on this channel linking financial reforms and economic growth, too, is weak. Considerable doubts can be cast on studies (for example, Fry, 1991; World Bank, 1993) which reported a negative relationship between real interest rate and incremental capital–output ratio (ICOR), and a positive relationship between real interest rates and total factor productivity (TFP). To begin with, none of the studies showed how the real interest rate affected TFP or technical progress and we cannot conclude causality from an observed correlation between the real interest rate and the growth contribution of TPF. Moreover, the observed correlation could be coincidental if neutral technological progress were occurring due to some other reasons such as government's increased expenditure on R&D and human capital development during the same period (Chowdhury and Islam, 1993).

The World Bank (1993) study shows that countries which have been classified as having either strongly or moderately negative real interest rates have above average productivity of investment. More interestingly, we find that investment in Singapore, which has strongly positive real interest rates is less productive, as measured by deviations from average productivity, than Algeria, Ecuador, Mexico and Turkey, which have been classified as having strongly negative real rates.

The classification of countries according to deposit interest rate can also be misleading as the relevant rate for the investors should be the lending or loan rate. The use of the deposit rate can be justified if the lending rate is above the deposit rate, as we might expect in a liberalised financial market. However, in many of these countries, including Korea and Taiwan, there exist widespread credit rationing and subsidised credit schemes. As a result the real lending rate may turn out to be negative (or very low) despite positive (or high) deposit real rates.

Financial deepening and economic growth

In a seminal work, Patrick (1966) raised the possibility of a 'supply-leading' and 'demand-following' relationship between financial development and economic growth. In the case of the former, the expansion of the financial system precedes the demand for its services and, by facilitating intermediations, promotes growth. The demand-following expansion of the financial sector occurs as demand for financial services for transaction purposes grows with economic expansion. It is, thus, the supply-leading phenomenon that is implied by the financial liberalisation hypothesis.

Jung's (1986) study of 56 developing and developed countries found only moderate support for the supply-leading relationship. According to him, the financial sector is more important in facilitating transactions (demand-following) than intermediations (supply-leading). King and Levine

(1992) in their study of 119 developed and developing countries found that the average financial size indicator was significantly correlated with average growth rate over the period 1960–89 in a simple regression through both the investment and the efficiency channels. However, the pooled cross-country and time-series regression revealed that the average size of the financial system did not enter with a significant coefficient. More interestingly, 'the average size of the financial system is *negatively* and significantly correlated with the efficiency part of growth' (King and Levine, 1992: 13).

Dornbusch and Reynoso (1992), on the basis of their study of 84 developing countries, noted that the correlation of growth and financial deepening was not tight. The apparent correlation between financial deepening and growth disappears once extreme values are omitted, and 'by judicious choice of sample any partial correlation can be generated' (Dornbusch and Reynoso, 1989: 205). They further noted that 'the empirical support for the growth effects of liberalised financial system is episodic' (p. 206). In a separate study, Dornbusch observed:

> Most of the evidence about the harmful consequences of misdirected capital market policy comes from the outlier–countries that have vastly negative asset returns. Once these outliers are isolated, the evidence no longer supports the claim that positive real interest rates help growth.
>
> Dornbusch (1991: 37)

The real interest rate and economic growth

The failure to find strong evidence on the channels through which financial reforms, in particular real interest rate changes, affect growth led many, notably Fry (1984) and Gelb (1989), to examine directly the relationship between real interest rates and growth. Although both Fry and Gelb have found evidence in favour of a significant positive relationship between real interest rates and economic growth, there are a number of shortcomings in their estimation (World Bank, 1993). First, they have failed to distinguish between large and small repressions. Second, they have not considered other factors, such as inflation. In many developing countries, both low economic growth and large negative real interest rates are the results of high and volatile inflation rates. Failure to take account of this fact may produce a spurious relationship between real interest rates and economic growth. Third, neither Fry nor Gelb included any demand shift variable in their regression analysis. Changes in investment opportunities affect real interest rates and may not necessarily imply changes in repression. Fourth, both used the ordinary least square (OLS) technique, which produces biased results if the independent variable is related with the error term.

In the light of the above shortcomings, the World Bank study (1993) used a two-stage estimation method and included inflation as a second independent variable. For a sample of 20 countries, the study found that when the inflation rate was included in the regression, the real interest rate no longer remained statistically significant. However, when the same exercise was repeated for the countries with positive real interest rates only, both the inflation rate and the real interest rate were found to affect economic growth negatively. This suggests that lower real interest and inflation rates, may have a positive impact on economic growth.

A CASE FOR MILD FINANCIAL REPRESSION

If the empirical evidence in favour of the financial liberalisation paradigm is dominated by large repressions, then can a case be argued in favour of mild financial repression? The experience of high performing Asian economies (HPAE)[2] indeed provide some evidence to support the hypothesis of mild repression. Although these countries have introduced financial reforms at various times and are widely cited as a vindication of the financial liberalisation paradigm, these reforms were counteracted by protected periods of financial repressions. As pointed out by Park (1994: 57), '[a]lmost every financial activity in Korea, including access to the banking sector, the determination of interest rates, and the allocation of credit, has been heavily regulated by the government'.

However, a recent World Bank study (1993) shows that financial repression in the HPAEs, as opposed to many other countries, has been mild and was not the unintended consequence of rapid inflation. The study also concludes that a policy of moderate financial repression may have actually promoted economic growth in these economies.[3] When the interest elasticity of household savings is low and the corporate sector has a higher propensity to save then low interest rates, by transferring income from depositors to the corporate sector, may increase overall savings and investment. Furthermore, lower costs of funds boost corporate profit and enable the firms to increase their equity through reinvestment. Firms with higher equity–debt ratio (less leveraged) tend to take a more cautious approach to their investment plans and are likely to select good projects as their own capital is at stake.

The experience of Korea and Malaysia during the 1980s also shows that selective financial repressions can minimise the impact of external shocks and aid recovery. For example, highly leveraged Korean firms were squeezed simultaneously by high interest rates and sluggish sales during the international recession of 1980–1. The consequent rise in company bankruptcies created instability in the domestic banking sector. The Korean government responded to the situation by sharply lowering deposit and loan rates. This helped both banks and firms to ride over the difficult time. Similarly, when the international tin market collapsed and commodity prices plummeted in 1985, Malaysia responded by lowering the real interest rate to bring stability in the economy.

SUMMARY AND CONCLUSION

This chapter has provided a survey of empirical evidence on the two aspects of the relationship between monetary factors and growth. It shows that in both cases the relationship is much more complex than it is theoretically perceived. To begin with, in the case of the inflation–growth relationship, extreme values, that is very high inflation, dominate the empirical evidence. While low or moderate inflation is found to be positively correlated with economic growth, very high or hyperinflation is generally found to affect growth negatively mainly because it increases the variability of inflation and hence uncertainty, and causes capital flight. However, there is also some support for the structuralist hypothesis that inflation is a necessary companion of growth. In some cases, a bi-directional causality between inflation and growth cannot be ruled out.

Thus the empirical evidence on the relationship between monetary factors and growth is not different from that observed by Johnson more than twenty years ago:

> Does inflation hamper economic growth? This is a difficult question, . . . [A]n observed relation between inflation and slow growth is not sufficient to establish an adverse causal connection between inflation and slow economic growth. In fact, there is frequent evidence (especially for underdeveloped countries) that the causal connection runs the other way, from slow growth to inflationary policies. For what such evidence is worth, it tends to show that if inflation is mild . . ., the rate of inflation does not affect the rate of growth, but that either rapid inflation or deflation is associated with slower rates of growth. This evidence, though frequently interpreted by central banks as argument for price stability, seems to argue for mild inflation as the best environment for economic growth.
>
> Johnson (1969: 136)

Also in the case of financial factors, large repressions are found to dominate empirical results. Careful scrutiny of empirical evidence shows that only persistently large negative real deposit rates are found to misdirect savings. Similarly, random and non-price allocation of investment negatively affect productivity of resources. The nature of the relationship between financial liberalisation and economic growth is at best 'episodic'. On the other hand, the experience of HPAEs shows that mild repression promotes rather than retards growth. More specifically, selective interventions in the form of forced savings, directed credits, restrictions on the outflow of capital and repression of interest rates appear to have succeeded in accelerating economic growth in HPAEs. However, this does not mean that these policies can be readily replicated elsewhere. These policies can have very high costs if misapplied in terms of deadweight loss in both consumer and producer surpluses due to 'rent-seeking' activities. The success of selective intervention policies depends largely on a strong institutional framework pertaining to monitoring and prudential regulations – a topic discussed in greater details in the following chapter.

NOTES

1 Hong Kong's M_2/GDP ratio should, however, be interpreted with caution. This may well be due to the fact that Hong Kong does not make any distinction between local residents' and non-residents' bank deposits. See Cole (1988).
2 HPAEs, led by Japan, are identified by several common features, such as very rapid export growth. They include Hong Kong, Korea, Singapore, Taiwan, Malaysia, Indonesia and Thailand.
3 The World Bank study has found that in a sample of twenty countries, inflation rates were far more important than real interest rates in explaining growth.

4

ISSUES IN FINANCIAL
LIBERALISATION REFORM

After a period of more than two decades of financial repression in the 1950s and 1960s, a large number of developing countries in Africa, Asia and Latin America have undertaken financial liberalisation reform of one form or another since the mid-1970s. The impetus to financial liberalisation reform came from a number of economic and political factors. The main aim of the reform has been to develop a market-oriented, world-integrated financial system for the mobilisation of savings, an efficient allocation of investible resources from domestic and foreign sources and an acceleration of economic growth (World Bank, 1989).

The pace and scope of financial reform differed from one country to another. It was extensive and rapid in Southern Cone of Latin American countries (Corbo, 1985; Diaz-Alejandro, 1985; Edwards and Edwards, 1987), selective and slow in Asian developing countries (Fry, 1990; Tseng and Corker, 1991) and limited in African countries (Seck and Nil, 1993). The implementation of financial reform in the various countries was against the background of different degrees of economic stress. Argentina, Chile, Turkey and Uruguay started financial reform against the background of high and unstable inflation of between 50 and 500 per cent per annum in the five years prior to financial reform. By contrast, Asian developing countries, such as Indonesia, South Korea, Malaysia, Nepal, the Philippines, Singapore, Sri Lanka and Thailand, started financial reform against the background of moderately low and stable inflation (World Bank, 1989).

Financial reform has not been an outright success or failure[1] in developing countries. There are cases where financial reform experiments went badly and there are other cases where they had a considerable success. Argentina, Chile and Uruguay are the most publicised examples of financial reform failures because they partially reversed their liberalisation reform measures after financial crises in the early 1980s (Corbo and de Melo, 1987; Diaz-Alejandro, 1985; Edwards, 1984). By contrast, Hong Kong, Indonesia, South Korea, Malaysia, Singapore, Sri Lanka and Taiwan are examples of financial reform success (Athukorala, 1992; Tseng and Corker, 1991), although they also experienced financial crises of various degrees of intensity. African countries had limited success with financial reform, and some of them, including Ghana, Kenya, Tanzania and West African Monetary Union countries, experienced banking distress (World Bank, 1989).[2]

Financial reform experience in developing countries, and the Southern Cone countries in particular, has led to a reassessment of the financial liberalisation reform exercise. There are two broad explanations of reform failures in Latin America. Neo-structuralist economists consider these failures as a vindication of their view that financial liberalisation is essentially a theoretical aberration unrelated to objective conditions of financial markets in developing countries (Taylor, 1988). By contrast, the protagonists of financial liberalisation blame macroeconomic instability, the lack of prudential regulation and supervision, and the incorrect order of liberalisation for Latin American financial reform failures (McKinnon, 1989a, 1991). The lack of adequate regulation and prudential supervision is also held responsible for financial crises in some Asian developing countries (Fry, 1990). High inflation, directed credit programmes, and the existing controls over interest rates are held responsible for a limited financial reform success in African countries (Seck and Nil, 1993).

This chapter reviews financial reform issues in developing countries with a view to shedding further light on individual countries' financial reform experiences. Financial reform issues are examined here in a broader, global context. In order to emphasise the point that not all developing countries have undertaken financial reforms voluntarily and many of them were less than enthusiastic in undertaking or implementing reform measures, some background information is provided at the outset on factors which may have acted as a catalyst in developing countries' undertaking financial reforms.

FACTORS BEHIND FINANCIAL REFORMS IN DEVELOPING COUNTRIES

The 1950s and 1960s were the heyday of financial repression in developing countries. Many leading development economists favoured financial repression because it was believed to promote economic growth (Fry, 1988). The governments of developing countries actively promoted it because they found it economically attractive and politically convenient. However, any consensus that might have existed on the role of financial repression in economic growth broke down in the early 1970s. It was not financial repression alone but the whole strategy of state-led, import-substituting industrialisation (ISI), and foreign-aid-based economic development came under challenge for economic and political reasons.[3]

Questions were asked in both aid donor and recipient countries on the efficacy of foreign aid in economic development. After experimenting with foreign aid since the early 1950s, most developing countries began to realise that it does not necessarily promote faster growth but may retard it by substituting for, rather than supplementing, domestic savings and investment and by exacerbating balance of payments deficits because of increasing debt-repayment obligations and the linking of aid to donor country exports. By the late 1970s there was also growing disquiet over foreign aid in donor countries as domestic issues such as inflation, unemployment, fiscal, and balance of payments deficits gained increasing priority over international cold war politics (Todaro, 1989).

The post-colonial paradigm of development, in which the state took the role of promoting economic growth through a wide range of controls and intervention in private sector activities, was essentially a political response to economic aspirations of long-neglected and exploited common people of developing countries. Despite some early success stories, by the mid-1960s the state-led ISI development paradigm had lost its credibility as the promises of rapid economic growth and poverty alleviation remained unfulfilled in most developing countries. Beginning from the early 1970s most developing countries began to encounter serious macroeconomic problems, including inflation, current account deficits and external debt, when the oil shocks and consequent recessions engulfed all the industrialised countries. By the early 1980s there was a general disenchantment among economists and policy-makers with the efficacy of controls over external trade, capital flows, domestic credits and interest rates in economic development. Therefore, most developing countries began to restructure their development strategies by shifting emphasis from ISI to export orientation and by financial liberalisation reform. And the spectacular success of Asian newly industrialising economies also created growing support for financial liberalisation reform on the lines suggested by McKinnon (1973) and Shaw (1973).

In addition, the effective impetus to financial reform came from the World Bank and IMF (Long, 1993). Facing serious macroeconomic problems in the 1970s and early 1980s, many developing countries approached the World Bank and IMF for financial and other development assistance, which was provided only when they agreed to undertake stabilisation and structural reform measures as a binding condition. Financial liberalisation reform was one major component of stabilisation and structural adjustment programmes designed for developing countries.

FINANCIAL SECTOR REFORM AND FINANCIAL CRISIS

Many developing countries have experienced financial crises following the introduction of financial reform programmes in the mid-1970s. The *World Development Report 1989* examined financial crises of various intensities in Argentina, Bangladesh, Bolivia, Chile, Colombia, Costa Rica, Egypt, Ghana, Kenya, South Korea, Kuwait, Madagascar, Malaysia, Nepal, Pakistan, the Philippines, Sri Lanka, Tanzania, Thailand, Turkey, West African Monetary

Union countries and Uruguay. As all these countries undertook financial liberalisation reform of one sort or another, the question has been raised whether there is a linkage between financial reform and financial crisis.

Two major studies on this issue are by Fry (1988) and Sundararajan and Balino (1990) for Asian and Latin American countries. Both studies conclude that there is no necessary relationship between financial reform and financial crises. For example, Fry makes the following comments for eleven Asian developing countries:

> Far from being the result of financial liberalization, fraud in Korea's unorganized money market over the period 1982–1984 produced an outcry for financial liberalization. After its 1985–1986 recession, Malaysia experienced a wave of failures among its finance companies which was also unconnected with financial liberalization. In 1985, the two largest banks in the Philippines carrying half the banking system's assets went bust long after the financial liberalization measures of 1980. In Sri Lanka, six finance companies failed in 1987–1988. In Taiwan, the Cathay Group collapsed in 1985 causing a run on Taiwan's unorganized money market. In 1983 five banks and 50 finance companies failed in Thailand ... None of these cases was immediately preceded by any substantial liberalization ... [Thus] the evidence suggests that financial liberalization by itself has not been responsible for financial crises [in Asian developing countries]. In almost all cases, however, lack of adequate regulation and supervision can be held responsible.
>
> (Fry, 1988: 36, 40)

Although Sundararajan and Balino (1990) did not find a relationship between financial reform and financial crises in seven Asian and Latin American countries,[4] they have identified a number of channels through which financial liberalisation reform may increase the degree of fragility of financial and non-financial firms and set the stage for a financial crisis:

(a) Financial liberalisation reform may lead to excessive risk-taking by financial institutions by increasing freedom of entry into the financial sector and freedom to bid for funds through both interest rates and new financial instruments unless such a freedom is tempered with regulation and prudential supervision. An implicit or explicit guarantee of government bailout of depositors and bankers may also encourage unsound lending patterns and trigger excessive risk-taking by financial institutions following financial deregulation. As financial deregulation often facilitates the growth of financial institutions, it is possible for unqualified and inexperienced people to enter into financial business.

(b) Financial deregulation is often accompanied by changes in the institutional structure of the financial system in which the new structure may lead to concentration of power in banking, interlocking ownership and lending patterns. Such a financial structure may create market failures because of moral hazard, adverse risk selection, and oligopolistic pricing (Velasco, 1988).

(c) Financial deregulation excessively raises the interest rates when euphoric expectations generate an artificial demand for credit. For non-financial firms whose debt–equity ratios are high, any initial rise in the real interest rate may lead to distress borrowing by such firms; this, given the inelastic nature of demand for credit, may raise the interest rates further. High debt–equity ratios of non-financial firms in developing countries are often the consequences of pre-reform negative real interest rates and directed credit programmes.

(d) After the interest rates are deregulated the monetary authority may either lack adequate and effective instruments of monetary control to influence the interest rates or follow a hands-off policy in the belief that domestic interest rates will automatically converge to foreign interest rates through arbitrage. Moreover, the monetary authority may target monetary and credit aggregates as in the past even though the money demand function may have become unstable or the money multiplier process may have changed because of financial innovation and financial deregulation. Such an action may raise the real interest rates and precipitate a financial crisis.

(e) Any sharp increase in demand for credit following financial reform may lead to credit rationing if interest rates above a certain level are considered risky by financial institutions because of potential adverse risk selection and moral hazard problems. Credit rationing can cause bankruptcies of firms which in turn may affect the banks.

(f) Financial deregulation often takes place before the supervisory authority is fully prepared to handle the new issues and problems that crop up in a deregulated financial system. Lack of effective supervision is often one major cause of financial crisis.

(g) The deregulation of interest rates may adversely affect banks and other financial institutions if they have large exposure to long-term assets at fixed interests funded by short-term liabilities.

Therefore, it is apparent that even though financial reform does not necessarily lead to a financial crisis, there are several channels through which financial reform may increase the degree of fragility of financial and non-financial firms and set the stage for a financial crisis.

EXPERIENCE WITH FINANCIAL REFORM IN DEVELOPING COUNTRIES

Most developing countries which have undertaken financial reforms have experienced financial crises of various degrees, therefore an examination of their individual experiences with financial reform may provide country-specific information on factors which could have triggered these crises. This section reviews the experiences of major developing countries with their financial reform over the past two decades.[5]

Latin American 'Southern Cone' countries

Although a large number of developing countries have undertaken financial reform of one form or another since the early 1970s, financial reform experiments in the Southern Cone countries of Argentina, Chile and Uruguay have remained the focus of debate and controversy about financial liberalisation. Indeed, in some respects they have become the laboratory of financial reform experiments for the developing countries.

Chile and Uruguay started economic reform in 1974 and Argentina in 1977. Chile went furthest in its economic reform, Uruguay was in the middle, and Argentina moved the least (Corbo, 1988). Financial reform was a major component of economic reform in all these countries. It was carried out in the spirit of the McKinnon–Shaw proposition that financial liberalisation reform promotes saving, investment and economic growth. Since a group of Chicago-trained economists, often called the 'Chicago Boys', played the key role in the design of economic reform measures, these were treated as test cases for monetarism. The financial crises that erupted in these countries during the early 1980s drew international attention and publicity. Critics interpreted financial crises in Southern Cone countries as a failure of monetarism as well as its reincarnation in the form of financial liberalisation. Their judgement was perhaps a bit harsh and premature. Post mortem examination by Latin American specialists (Corbo and de Melo, 1985, 1987; Diaz-Alejandro, 1985; Edwards and Edwards, 1987) found that financial reform experiments in Southern Cone countries were more complex than the popular media portrayed and that they had both successes and failures in their reform experiments.

Argentina

The Argentine financial system was heavily regulated prior to financial reform in 1977 (Corbo and de Melo, 1987). A military government implemented financial reform but in an unstable macroeconomic environment characterised by large budget deficits and high inflation. The major financial reform measures which were undertaken during 1977–81 included the elimination of controls over interest rates, the easing of bank branching and entry regulations, the abandonment of selective credit controls, the liberalisation of foreign borrowing and foreign exchange transactions on capital account, the pronouncement of a schedule of devaluation of domestic currency, and the strengthening of prudential regulation and supervision (Sundararajan and Balino, 1990). The main aim of such a financial reform was to liberalise

Table 4.1 Argentina: key macroeconomic variables

Year	Budget deficit[a]	Inflation rate[b]	Real exchange rate[c]	Real lending rate[d]	Current account[a]
1975	−15.6	335.1	36.9	−9.0	−3.5
1976	−10.6	347.5	46.4	−7.8	1.7
1977	−5.0	160.4	50.7	−0.6	3.0
1978	−6.7	169.8	64.7	0.1	4.0
1979	−6.7	139.7	83.4	−0.2	−1.0
1980	−8.6	87.6	100.0	0.5	−7.6
1981	−18.0	131.3	69.5	2.6	−7.4
1982	−18.9	209.7	48.9	−2.0	−3.8
1983	−17.8	433.7	58.8		−3.8
1984	−13.8	688.0	58.4		−3.5

Sources: Balino (1987); Dornbusch (1993).

Notes
 [a] Per cent of GDP
 [b] Per cent per annum
 [c] Index 1980 = 100
 [d] Per cent per month.

the domestic capital market with a view to linking Argentina effectively with the world capital market (Dornbusch, 1993).

Financial reform was blamed for the Argentinian financial crisis which erupted in March 1981. It began with the failure of a large private bank. The crisis spread rapidly to other banks and non-bank financial institutions. Over 70 financial institutions were liquidated or intervened, accounting for 16 per cent of total assets of commercial banks and 35 per cent of total assets of finance companies (Sundararajan and Balino, 1990). High real interest rates, loans of dubious quality, inadequate and ineffective supervision, and overvalued real exchange rates were identified as the factors which caused the Argentinian financial crisis.

Inflation data in Table 4.1 reveal that Argentina started financial reform in an unstable macroeconomic environment, and it was not able to attain price stability after financial reform. Inflation was reduced from about 350 per cent in 1976 to about 88 per cent in 1980, but any further reduction in inflation was not possible without lowering budget deficits. Fernandez (1985) points out that despite high inflation the Argentinian government was concerned about the political consequences of unemployment, which limited its stabilisation efforts. Moreover, instead of looking into fiscal problems, the government focused on the inflation–depreciation spiral and the role of expectations, and decelerated the rate of depreciation of the exchange rate. It made the real exchange rate excessively overvalued and unsustainable because inflation consistently outpaced the rate of depreciation of the exchange rate (Dornbusch, 1993). In anticipation of a major devaluation in the presence of excess demand for credit and uncertainty over government economic policies, the real interest rate increased sharply. High real interest rates and overvalued real exchange rates, which led to large scale capital flight, lowered investment and exports. They caused recession and the collapse of many firms, resulting in a deterioration of the quality of loan portfolios of the financial system. As Dornbusch (1993: 389) points out, the overvaluation of the exchange rate had 'sown the seeds of financial destruction' in Argentina. Inadequate and ineffective supervision also contributed to the crisis.

Chile

Until the early 1970s the financial sector in Chile was underdeveloped and distorted. It had all the other symptoms of financial repression as well. After the Allende government's nationalisation measures in 1973, all major banks and financial institutions came under government control. The Allende government was overthrown by the military, which took power in late 1973. After the takeover of power the military government began to implement stabilisation and liberalisation reform measures to reduce inflation and to transform 'an isolated and tightly government controlled economy into a world integrated market-oriented society' (Edwards and Edwards, 1987: 9). The government was particularly keen to liberalise the financial sector with a view to creating a dynamic capital market.

Chile initiated its financial reform in early 1974 by allowing the operation of new non-bank financial institutions. The central bank allowed such non-bank financial institutions to determine freely the short-term interest rates in May 1974. The government started denationalising commercial banks in April 1975. A number of such banks were acquired by private conglomerates (or *grupos*). Interest rates charged and paid by commercial banks were freed in October 1975. The government also abolished selective credit controls, removed bank entry and branching restrictions, and facilitated the development of a multipurpose banking system by eliminating any distinction between commercial, investment, mortgage and development banking. Controls over capital flows were, however, removed gradually. Quantity and term controls were relaxed between 1979 and 1980. Limits on bank borrowing from abroad were abolished in 1980, and the minimum maturity requirements were abolished in 1982. The consequence of such a comprehensive financial sector reform was a rapid increase in both the number of financial institutions and the volume of intermediation (Corbo and de Melo, 1987; Edwards and Edwards, 1987; Velasco, 1988).

Chile's financial sector problems started during late 1976 and early 1977 when a number of minor non-bank financial institutions went bankrupt. The government undertook remedial measures and the problem was contained. However, it became apparent that financial deregulation was undertaken without adequate and effective supervision and regulation. In fact the lack of a supervisory system became evident as early as 1974 and 1975 when

Table 4.2 Chile: key macroeconomic variables

Year	Budget deficit[a]	Inflation rate[b]	Real exchange rate[c]	Real lending rate[d]	Current account[a]
1975	−1.7	340.7	97.9	164.9	−4.5
1976	3.7	174.3	79.9	176.4	0.9
1977	1.7	63.5	90.0	92.9	−3.7
1978	2.1	30.3	100.0	55.0	−5.3
1979	4.8	38.9	92.4	23.1	−5.5
1980	5.5	31.2	79.8	15.7	−7.8
1981	0.8	9.5	70.5	42.4	−14.3
1982	−3.4	20.7	99.4	42.4	−9.5
1983	−2.8	23.1	93.4	15.9	−5.4
1984	−4.4	23.0	106.1		−10.7

Source: Velasco (1988).

Notes
[a] Per cent of GDP
[b] Per cent per annum
[c] Index 1978 = 100
[d] Per cent per month.

a number of informal financial institutions started to operate with only the implicit approval of the government, but with no control. Importantly, the government allowed the *grupo*-owned commercial banks to channel a large proportion of loans to firms owned or controlled by the *grupos* themselves. Such loans were 'bad loans', but were rolled over. Since an excessive 'false demand' for credit was generated in the euphoria of the boom during 1977–80, the rolling over of bad loans raised the interest rates sharply. The economic boom collapsed during 1981–2. High real interest rates and over-valued exchange rates were much to blame.[6]

Following the increase in company bankruptcies, the financial crisis erupted in November 1981 when the government intervened and assumed control of three banks and four non-bank financial institutions that together accounted for one-third of the loan portfolio of the financial system. The whole of 1982 was plagued with rumours about bank problems, which were confirmed in January 1983 when the government placed seven banks and one non-bank financial institution under temporary government management (Velasco, 1988). Three of which were liquidated immediately and central bank inspectors were placed in seven other financial institutions (Sundararajan and Balino, 1990).

One major objective of financial reform in Chile was the improvement in savings and investment performance. The Chilean data suggest that the average savings rate for the liberalisation period (1974–81) rose only marginally to 12.6 per cent from 12 per cent during 1960–73 (Velasco, 1988). There was, however, an increase in private investment during 1974–81 despite the high real loan rates of interest. Another feature of Chilean financial reform was the rapid growth of financial assets and the change in the composition of financial assets towards short-term, highly liquid, interest-bearing assets. The demand for financial assets, however, did not reflect any shift in private portfolio holdings from real estate and land to interest-bearing financial assets (as expected in the McKinnon–Shaw model); rather, the perceived increase in private wealth due to higher prices of land and real estates spilled over into higher demand for financial assets. Another weakness of the Chilean financial experiment was a rapid accumulation of external debt by the private sector after the removal of controls over foreign capital flows and private borrowings. The rapid increase in demand for credit induced private banks to seek dollar-denominated loans from overseas. Much of the increase in demand for credit, however, originated from an increase in demand for consumer durables (Velasco, 1988).

Uruguay

The Uruguayan economy was stagnant from the late 1950s to the early 1970s (Corbo and de Melo, 1987). As it had been suffering from structural problems in the real and financial sectors, the government launched a reform programme of stabilisation and liberalisation during 1974-82. However, like Argentina and Chile, Uruguay started liberalisation reform against the background of macroeconomic instability characterised by high inflation, large budget deficits, deteriorating terms of trade and falling foreign exchange reserves (Hanson and de Melo, 1985).

During the first phase of liberalisation reform (1974–8) restrictions on capital flows were eliminated, domestic residents were allowed to hold foreign exchange, ceilings on interest rates for peso loans and deposits were substantially raised, guidelines for sectoral credit allocation were eliminated, and barriers to entry into banking were lifted. Such a financial sector reform was carried out concurrently with reforms in the commodity market and the foreign trade sector. Financial liberalisation was completed during the second phase of the reform (1979–82) with the removal of legal reserve requirements and banking tax (Corbo and de Melo, 1987; Hanson and de Melo, 1985)

Financial reforms, particularly the removal of the prohibition on holding dollar assets and the progressive increase in interest rate ceilings, sharply increased the growth of financial assets, especially assets denominated in foreign currencies. Part of the increase in the financial portfolio was due to inflows of capital from Argentina (Hanson and de Melo, 1985)

Uruguay used monetary and exchange rate policies to control inflation during the reform period. During 1974 and 1978, it tried to control inflation by lowering the money growth rate, but its efforts to control money supply were not successful because of short-term foreign capital inflows. When the government failed to control inflation by lowering money growth, it was

Table 4.3 Uruguay: key macroeconomic variables

Year	Budget deficit[a]	Inflation rate[b]	Real exchange rate[c]	Real lending rate[d]	Current account[a]
1973	−1.4	97.0	117.3	−30.2	1.3
1974	−4.5	77.2	100.0	−21.9	−3.1
1975	−4.4	81.4	117.7	−13.6	−5.2
1976	−2.6	50.6	126.3	−1.5	−1.9
1977	−1.2	58.2	124.3	−8.4	−3.9
1978	−1.3	44.5	122.0	3.6	−2.5
1979	0.1	66.8	106.7	−21.0	−4.9
1980	0.0	63.5	87.5	4.5	−7.0
1981	0.1	34.0	88.6	13.3	−4.1
1982	−8.7	19.0	107.5	19.6	−2.5
1983	−4.0	49.2	201.4	−1.5	−1.1
1984	−5.2	55.3			−2.5

Sources: *International Financial Statistics Yearbook* (1992); Hanson and de Melo (1985).

Notes   [a] Per cent of GDP
            [b] Per cent per annum
            [c] Index 1978 = 100
            [d] Per cent per month

believed that the business sector was increasing prices in a less-liberalised commodity market with the expectation that the government would devalue the currency to maintain external competitiveness; therefore, the government used the exchange rate to control inflation by preannouncing a declining rate of devaluation of the currency. Such an exchange rate policy appreciated the currency when inflation did not fall much. The real lending rate gradually increased as the nominal interest rate remained high, although inflation at last fell in 1981 (table 4.3).

The Uruguyan financial crisis began in 1982 when most banks were incurring losses and had liquidity problems. Three banks were rescued by the central bank in 1982. Banking distress became pronounced from 1984 onward. One bank was liquidated in 1984 and the central bank intervened to take over the two largest private banks.

Other Latin American countries

Several other Latin American countries, including Brazil, Colombia and Mexico, started financial reform more cautiously than Southern Cone countries. They built balanced and diversified institutional structures. However, as they were not able to control inflation and maintain macroeconomic stability, their financial reforms were not so successful in achieving their goals (World Bank, 1989).

Asian developing countries

In the midst of pervasive financial repression all through in the 1950s and 1960s, three Asian developing countries – Indonesia (1968), South Korea (1965) and Taiwan (1950s) – broke rank and undertook financial reforms. However, the scope of reform was limited and consisted of raising the nominal deposit rate of interest above the prevailing inflation rate. The loan rate of interest was also increased, but not as much as the deposit rate of interest.

Table 4.4 Taiwan: real deposit rate of interest and financial deepening

Period	Real deposit rate[a]	Financial deepening[b]
1953–60	10.1	15.8
1961–65	10.0	30.8
1966–70	5.1	n.a.
1971–80	0.9	58.1
1981–90	4.6[c]	110.2

Sources: McKinnon (1973, table 8.10) for the period 1953–65; Chowdhury and Islam (1993, tables 8.2 and 8.3) for the period 1966–90.

Notes [a] period average (%)
[b] period average: M2/GNP (%)
[c] 1981–83

Table 4.5 Taiwan: financial indicators in 1980 and 1990

Indicator	1980	1990
Budget deficit[a]	–0.2[b]	0.1[c]
Inflation	7.4[b]	1.3[c]
Real effective exchange rate (1980=100)	100.0	115.3[d]
Percentage of domestic credit to public sector	6[e]	1[f]
Selective credit controls		
subsidised loan rates for priority sectors	yes	scope reduced
preferential rediscount rates	yes	scope reduced
Reserve requirements (%)		
sight deposits	25	
time deposits	13	

Sources: Fry (1990); *Asian Development Outlook*, 1990.

Notes: [a] per cent of GNP
[b] 1979–84
[c] 1984–9
[d] 1989
[e] December 1979
[f] December 1988

Along with the increase in interest rates, efforts were made to keep inflation low so that the real interest rates remain positive (Cole and Patrick, 1986). Based in large part on Asian experiences with financial reform, McKinnon (1973) and Shaw (1973) developed their theoretical models and demonstrated that financial repression retards, rather than promotes, economic growth.

Taiwan

Taiwan is perhaps the most publicised success story of financial liberalisation. Unlike other developing countries, it undertook financial reform in the 1950s when its banking system introduced a high interest rate policy. Since then it has made efforts to keep the real deposit rates of interest positive. It has been successful in doing so, except during some years in the 1970s.

One possible impact of the positive real deposit rate of interest has been a rapid growth of financial assets. Table 4.4 shows that the ratio of broad money (M2) to output has increased from 16 per cent during 1953–60 to 110 per cent during 1981–90.

Even though Taiwan has been able to maintain a positive real interest rate most of the time during the past few decades, its financial sector remains regulated and uncompetitive because of the dominance of state-owned banks which mainly carry out government policy directives. Moreover, half of these banks are specialised banks and they do not face any competition from other financial institutions (Fry, 1990). It explains why financial reform has not been able to lower the importance of curb markets as a source of business finance.[7] In the external sector Taiwan maintains a managed floating exchange rate system, and also controls capital flows. Although foreign banks have been allowed to operate in Taiwan since 1965, stringent conditions apply for their operations.

South Korea

The early financial reform programme in South Korea was initiated in the mid-1960s. Against the background of an annual inflation of about 35 per cent in 1964 and slow growth of the economy, South Korea substantially raised the ceilings on nominal interest rates at the recommendation of a US aid mission. The South Korean government accepted this recommendation because it was impressed by the Taiwanese success in mobilising increased financial savings after it raised the deposit rates of interest and stabilised inflation (Cho, 1989).

From the interest rate of 15 per cent per annum on one-year time deposits, South Korea raised the weighted average nominal interest rates on all classes of time and savings deposits to about 24 per cent in 1966. When its annual inflation rate declined from about 35 per cent in 1964 to about 10 per cent during 1965–70, the real rate of return on holdings of one-year time deposits

Table 4.6 Korea: financial indicators in 1980 and 1990

Indicator	1980	1990
Budget deficit[a]	−2.2[b]	−0.3[c]
Inflation	11.4[b]	4.1[c]
Deposit rate of interest	13.3[b]	10.0[c]
Lending rate	13.4[d]	10.2[c]
Real effective exchange rate (1980=100)	100.0	94.4[e]
Percentage of domestic credit to public sector	9[f]	1[g]
Selective credit controls		
subsidised loan rates for priority sectors	yes	scope reduced
preferential rediscount rates	yes	scope reduced
credit floors	yes	yes
credit ceilings	yes	yes
proliferation of specialised institutions	yes	yes
Reserve requirements (%)		
sight deposits	14	10
time deposits	10	7

Sources: Fry (1990); *International Financial Statistics Yearbook* 1991; *Asian Development Outlook*, 1990.

Notes:
  [a] per cent of GNP
  [b] 1979–84
  [c] 1984–9
  [d] 1980–4
  [e] 1989
  [f] December 1979
  [g] December 1989

increased from minus 15 per cent in 1964 to about 17 per cent during 1965–70. According to McKinnon (1973) and other proponents of the financial liberalisation hypothesis, such a turnaround of the real deposit rate of interest contributed to the improvement in the South Korean economy.

Despite the financial reform success in the the 1960s, South Korea reverted to a low interest rate policy and intensified controls over credit allocation in the 1970s. There were two major reasons for the adoption of repressive financial policies by the Korean government. First, many business firms, which borrowed heavily from domestic banks and abroad, encountered financial difficulties because of high real interest rates, the domestic recession, and the devaluation of the exchange rate at the end of the 1960s and during the early 1970s. The presidential decree of August 1972, which forced the introduction of the low interest rate policy in response to strong pressure on the government by business, was an across-the-board bailing out of troubled firms at the expense of depositors. Second, beginning from 1972 the Korean government introduced a new industrial policy which pushed for the promotion of capital-intensive heavy and chemical industries. Since large businesses were reluctant to invest in these industries at their own risk, the government provided them with preferential low-interest credits.

The Korean government's heavy industrialisation policy was not so successful and a broad consensus was reached by the end of the 1970s that the interventionist approach to industrialisation was retarding the growth of the financial sector and was causing misallocation of resources. Moreover, facing macroeconomic imbalances and a slow economic growth, the South Korean government changed the direction of its industrial policy and started financial deregulation along with stabilisation and structural adjustments in the early 1980s (Cho,1989; World Bank, 1989).

South Korea undertook a number of measures to encourage competition in the financial sector. They included the deregulation of non-bank financial institutions, the relaxation of barriers to bank entry, the approval of foreign bank branches, the privatisation of publicly owned commercial banks, the elimination of preferential lending rates, and a ban on the introduction of new directed credit programmes. Despite all these measures, the Korean financial sector has, however, remained regulated and under the control of the government. As Park writes,

> After almost ten years of liberalization attempt, Korea's financial sector is still under rigid and pervasive government control and largely remains closed to foreign competition . . . despite numerous and often confusing reform measures, deregulation of the financial sector has been slow, uneven, and most of all limited in scope and degree.
>
> (Park, 1990: 2, 30)

Amsden and Euh (1993) suggest that big businesses influenced the extent and nature of financial reform in South Korea. They wanted a liberalised financial system so that they could gain control over capital and investment, but at the same time they wanted the financial system to remain protected so that they could get cheap credits. Such a conflict of interests of the big businesses was instrumental in slowing down the pace of financial reform in South Korea.

Despite a limited type of financial reform, South Korea's is considered a success story of financial liberalisation and is often contrasted with financial crises in Southern Cone countries. However, South Korea's enviable record of economic growth over the past two decades, despite its half-hearted financial reform, casts doubt on the role of financial liberalisation in economic growth. The Korean experience led even a 'true believer' to conclude that 'full-blown financial liberalization is not a prerequisite for rapid economic growth' (Fry, 1993: 50).

Indonesia

Indonesia experienced a high rate of inflation during 1962–7. It was mainly caused by excessive money creation to finance large budget deficits (Sabirin, 1993). In 1968 Indonesia undertook financial reform, which included a sharp increase in the time deposit rate of interest. The high interest rate policy was a part of the Indonesian government's economic stabilisation programme which was designed to reduce inflation from the three-digit level through a balanced-budget policy. When inflation began to fall in 1969, the real time deposit rate of interest became positive. It increased the holding of real balances. Although Indonesian deposit holders were found to be sensitive to the real deposit rate of interest, the Indonesian financial system, which was dominated by state banks, could not make efficient use of increased real deposits. Therefore, monetary reform had no immediate impact on economic growth (McKinnon, 1973).

Indonesia's financial sector remained regulated throughout the 1970s. It was in 1983 that concerted efforts were made to deregulate the financial sector as part of a stabilisation and structural adjustment programme intended to correct the shortcomings of a repressed financial system. In the early stage of financial reform, a number of measures were undertaken. They included the removal of credit ceilings and controls over interest rates, the discontinuation of sectoral credit allocation requirements, and the introduction of a managed floating exchange rate system. In the second stage a set of new instruments of indirect monetary control were introduced, the managed floating exchange rate system was modified to permit a greater market determination of the exchange rate, and the controls over capital flows and the restrictions on short-term external borrowings by residents were removed. Since 1988 a number of additional financial reform measures have been undertaken. They include the move towards a uniform tax treatment of various financial assets, the introduction of a new private stock exchange, the strengthening of prudential regulations, the defining of capital and foreign exchange activities, the extending of capital adequacy requirements to all banks, and the establishment of a supervisory system to recommend corrective measures and sound banking practices (Tseng and Corker, 1991; Sundararajan and Molho, 1988).

Thus one feature of Indonesia's financial reform was that it was gradual and cautious. Indonesia did not experience any major financial crisis, although there were a few minor hiccups during reform. For example, the real lending rate of interest reached about 20 per cent per annum in 1986, which created financial distress. The sharp rise in the interest rate was due to expectations of Rupiah depreciation which raised inflationary expectations (Tseng and Corker, 1991).

Indonesia is considered a moderately successful example of financial liberalisation reform. Financial reform helped to achieve the external balance of payments objective and promoted the growth and integration of money and capital markets. The positive real interest rate policy contributed to financial deepening as measured by the ratio of broad money to output. Financial reform also encouraged competition and efficiency in banking and enhanced

Table 4.7 Indonesia: financial indicators in 1980 and 1990

Indicator	1980	1990
Budget deficit[a]	−4.0[b]	−5.7[c]
Inflation	10.9[b]	5.9[c]
Deposit rate of interest	6.0[d]	17.1[c]
Lending rate		20.9
Real effective exchange rate (1980=100)	100.0	44.8[e]
Percentage of domestic credit to public sector	38[f]	−2[g]
Selective credit controls		
subsidised loan rates for priority sectors	yes	scope reduced
preferential rediscount rates	yes	scope reduced
direct budgetary subsidies	yes	
credit floors	yes	yes
credit ceilings	yes	
proliferation of specialised institutions	yes	yes
Reserve requirements (%)		
sight deposits	15	2
time deposits	2.5–10	2

Sources: Fry (1990); *International Financial Statistics Yearbook* (1991)

Notes   [a] Per cent of GNP
           [b] 1979–84
           [c] 1984–9
           [d] 1979–83
           [e] 1989
           [f] December 1979
           [g] December 1989

the technical ability of the central bank to control reserve and monetary aggregates and to handle any potential financial crises.

Malaysia

Malaysia has undertaken a limited form of financial reform since the late 1970s. It formally removed controls over interest rates in 1978, although effective controls were removed only in 1982. In the external sector the exchange rate has been floated. However, it has not been a free float; rather, it is subject to intervention by the central bank which uses a set of indicators as a guide for intervention. Capital flows have been freed, except that foreign borrowings by private residents and the holding of foreign accounts abroad require approval from the monetary authority.

Although Malaysia strengthened prudential regulations and the supervision of financial institutions during reform, it experienced short-lived financial distress in July 1985 when there were runs against some branches of a large domestic bank following rumours of the collapse of a related bank in Hong Kong. Sporadic runs persisted against other weak financial institutions

Table 4.8 Malaysia: financial indicators in 1980 and 1990

Indicator	1980	1990
Budget deficit[a]	−14.0[b]	−7.8[c]
Inflation	5.7[b]	1.4[c]
Deposit rate of interest	8.1[b]	6.2[c]
Lending rate	9.2[b]	9.8[c]
Real effective exchange rate (1980=100)	100.0	68.4[d]
Percentage of domestic credit to public sector	−5[e]	6[f]
Selective credit controls		
subsidised loan rates for priority sectors	yes	yes
preferential rediscount rates	yes	yes
credit floors	yes	
Reserve requirements (%)		
sight deposits	10	
time deposits	10	

Sources: Fry (1990); *International Financial Statistics Yearbook* (1991); *Asian Development Outlook*, 1990.

Notes [a] per cent of GNP
   [b] 1979–84
   [c] 1984–9
   [d] 1989
   [e] December 1979
   [f] = December 1989.

throughout 1985–6. The central bank intervened in 24 deposit-taking co-operatives, and injected capital into three ailing banks. Economic recovery, changes in monetary policy, regulatory adaptations, and the provision of support measures to ailing businesses have since restored the health of financial institutions (Sundararajan and Balino, 1990).

Like South Korea, Malaysia is considered a success story of financial liberalisation despite its limited reform efforts. It has maintained macroeconomic stability during reform, and its economy, along with the financial sector, has grown rapidly over the past decade or so.

The Philippines

Until the early 1980s the Philippines had all the symptoms of financial repression, including negative deposit rates of interest and rationing of bank credits (Cabalu, 1993). It started financial reform in 1981 by deregulating all interest rates, except short-term lending rates. Ceilings on the deposit rates of interest were lifted in October 1981, while ceilings on short-term lending rates were eliminated at the end of 1982. Along with the deregulation of interest rates, entry barriers to banks were removed and commercial banks were allowed to provide a wide range of financial services. Capital flows were also freed. During reform prudential regulation and the supervisory apparatus were

Table 4.9 The Philippines: financial indicators in 1980 and 1990

Indicator	1980	1990
Budget deficit[a]	−2.3[b]	−2.7[c]
Inflation	17.9[b]	9.9[c]
Deposit rate of interest	13.9[b]	12.8[c]
Lending rate	18.1[b]	18.9[c]
Real effective exchange rate (1980=100)	100.0	67.8[d]
Percentage of domestic credit to public sector	16[e]	14[f]
Selective credit controls		
subsidised loan rates for priority sectors	yes	yes
preferential rediscount rates	yes	yes
direct budgetary subsidies	yes	yes
credit floors	yes	yes
credit ceilings	yes	yes
proliferation of specialised institutions	yes	yes
Reserve requirements (%)		
sight deposits	20	21
time deposits	20	21
Interest paid on required reserves		yes

Sources: Fry (1990); *International Financial Statistics Yearbook* (1991)

Notes   [a]   per cent of GNP
         [b]   1979–84
         [c]   1984–9
         [d]   1989
         [e]   December 1979
         [f]   December 1988

strengthened, but the enforcement of such regulations remained weak (Sundararajan and Balino, 1990).

The Philippine financial sector experienced a major financial crisis during 1981–7. The first episode began in 1981 when the commercial paper market collapsed and created a crisis of confidence. The number of rural bank failures accelerated during 1981–3, while the failures of thrift banks accelerated during 1984–5. Three private banks were liquidated during 1985–6. In total, between 1981 and 1987, 126 rural banks, 32 thrift banks, and three commercial banks were closed down. In addition, during 1985–6 two large state-owned banks and five private commercial banks received financial support and subsidies and were restructured, and two government-owned banks were liquidated and bailed out (Sundararajan and Balino, 1990).

Macroeconomic and political instability and the lack of effective prudential regulation and supervision were the main reasons for financial crisis in the Philippines. The lack of prudential regulation and supervision was responsible for widespread risky lending and for bank fraud and mismanagement. Political uncertainty and corruption reinforced the loss of confidence in the economy. Capital began to flow abroad and the supply of foreign finance dried up. It increased the financial fragility of corporate and non-corporate institutions, and a set of factors which were largely endogenous to the financial sector provoked and exacerbated the bank crisis (Nascimento, 1990; World Bank, 1989).

Sri Lanka

Sri Lanka had a regulated and repressed financial system until the mid-1970s. It started a wide range of structural and financial reforms in 1977, albeit at a slow pace. The major reform measures included the liberalisation of trade, the adjustment of exchange rates, the removal of controls over bank credits, interest rates and prices, and the discontinuation of subsidised sectoral credit allocation programmes. Foreign banks were also allowed to operate in the country to increase competition and efficiency in the banking system.

Despite these changes, the Sri Lankan financial sector has remained regulated. For example, capital flows and current account transactions are restricted and the exchange rates are only periodically adjusted. Moreover, selective credit control programmes have been reimposed recently. Nevertheless, Sri Lanka is considered a success story of financial liberalisation. Its financial reforms have had some positive impact on financial intermediation, savings and investment (Athukorala, 1992; Cho and Khatkhate, 1989).

Table 4.10 Sri Lanka: financial indicators in 1980 and 1990

Indicator	1980	1990
Budget deficit[a]	−15.6[b]	−11.4[c]
Inflation	15.7[b]	8.1[c]
Deposit rate of interest	16.1[b]	15.1[c]
Lending rate	16.7[b]	12.3[c]
Real effective exchange rate (1980=100)	100.0	75.4[d]
Percentage of domestic credit to public sector	54[e]	55[f]
Selective credit controls		
subsidised loan rates for priority sectors	yes	yes
preferential rediscount rates	yes	yes
direct budgetary subsidies	yes	yes
credit floors		informal
credit ceilings	yes	yes
Reserve requirements (%)		
sight deposits	12	15
time deposits	5	15

Sources: Fry (1990); *International Financial Statistics Yearbook* (1991); *Asian Development Outlook*, 1990.

Notes   [a] per cent of GNP
      [b] 1979-84
      [c] 1984-9
      [d] 1989
      [e] December 1979
      [f] December 1988

Turkey

Against the background of balance of payments crises, high inflation and slow economic growth, Turkey embarked on a comprehensive stabilisation and liberalisation programme in 1980. It reduced fiscal deficits and lowered annual inflation from about 100 per cent to about 25 per cent within two years. It also allowed the domestic currency to depreciate in real terms. Such a stabilisation programme was able to raise Turkey's economic growth and was therefore considered a success (World Bank, 1989)

The stabilisation programme in Turkey was accompanied by some financial reform measures, which included the removal of controls over interest and exchange rates. Controls over capital flows, however, remained in force between 1980 and 1982. Since late 1983 the central bank has periodically reviewed and set ceilings on the domestic bank deposit rates by taking into account fluctuations of inflation and the expected yields on foreign currency deposits which are determined freely. In 1987 the one-year deposit rate of interest was fully freed (Kopits and Robinson, 1989).

The overall macroeconomic changes in Turkey affected its corporate sector profits and forced business enterprises to adjust to a new environment. However, as not all businesses were able to cope, financial problems did crop up in the corporate sector; it caused banking distress and bankruptcies of brokerage houses. The government intervened in mid-1982: it merged insolvent banks with bigger ones, imposed ceilings on deposit interest rates and increased monitoring of banks (World Bank, 1989).

Other Asian developing countries

A number of other Asian developing countries, such as Bangladesh, India, Myanmar, Nepal, Pakistan and Thailand, have adopted stabilisation cum financial reform measures since the early 1980s. The main features of financial reforms in these countries are the maintenance of positive real interest rates, the removal of controls over credits, and the enhancement of competition and efficiency in the banking system. However, the scope and pace of reform has differed from one country to another. Although Bangladesh, Nepal, Pakistan and Thailand experienced financial distress of various intensities, they did not experience any major financial crises during reform because of the gradual, phased and continuing nature of their reform processes.

African countries

In recent years several African countries have undertaken financial reforms. They were carried out as a part of structural adjustment programmes, rather than as financial liberalisation *per se*. Table 4.11 reports a summary of financial reform measures undertaken by major African countries.

Table 4.11 Summary of financial reform measures by African countries

Country	Public sector share of credit[a]	Legal reserve requirements ratio[b]	Real deposit rate[c]	Interest rate deregulation[d]	Competitively priced financial securities[e]
Botswana	-117 (-122)	n.a.	-1.4 (-3.0)	DF,LF,LP	S,BP
Egypt	67 (72)	25/15 (15/15)	-4.6 (9.0)	DF, LF, LP	S,TB,CD,GB
Gambia	61 (-223)	15 (15)	-2.6 (1.1)	DF, LF	TB
Ghana	91 (59)	25 (15)	-56.4 (-9.1)	DF, LF	TB, GB
Kenya	31 (31)	20 (24)	1.1 (0.6)	DF, DL	S,TB,GB,FXC
Malawi	63 (41)	10 (20)	-5.1 (-3.0)	DF, DL	TB, GB, BP
Nigeria	52 (52)	n.a. (30)	4.1 (-9.4)	DF, DM, LF, LC	S, TB, GB
Tunisia	14 (12)	0 (2)	-3.3 (0.2)	DF, DM, LF, LC, LP	S, TB, CD, CP
Zimbabwe	49 (41)	n.a. (10)	0 (n.a.)	DR, LR	S, TB, CD

Source: Seck and Nil (1993)

Notes
a Figures refer to the starting year of the reform programme; figures in brackets refer to end of 1990.
b Figures refer to the starting year of the reform programme; figures in brackets refer to the situation as of June 1991.
c Figures refer to the average of the two years before programme started; figures in brackets refer to the average of the two most recent years for which data are available.
d DF = deposit rates fully liberalised; LF = lending rates fully liberalised; LP = directed credit to priority sectors at below market rates; DM = minimum deposit rates enforced by central bank; LC = maximum lending rates enforced by central bank; DR, LR = fully or partially regulated deposit/lending rates.
e S = stocks; TB = treasury bills; CD = certificate of deposit; GB = government bonds; FXC = foreign exchange certificates; BP = central bank paper; CP = commercial paper.

Seck and Nil (1993) reviewed the financial reform measures in Africa and examined their effects on African economies. They concluded that

> African countries' limited success with financial liberalization can be explained to some extent by the following factors. Real deposit rates have failed to remain consistently positive because (a) inflation is high and unstable which, given the need for banks to operate large interest spreads, tends to keep nominal rates at a low level, (b) banks have a low demand for deposits owing to their credit rationing policy motivated by the potential for adverse risk selection, (c) the implicit tax that government extracts from the banking system through enforcement of below-market lending rates on behalf of priority sectors is passed on by banks to their borrowers and depositors.
>
> (Seck and Nil, 1993: 1877)

WHAT ARE THE LESSONS?[8]

The campaign for financial liberalisation reform by McKinnon, Shaw, Fry and others has been a success, in the sense that the message that financial repression does not promote economic growth has reached the policy-makers in developing countries. It was, however, not a one-sided triumph for the proponents of financial liberalisation. Indeed, the early missionary zeal of the protagonists of financial liberalisation has now subsided as most of the reforming developing countries have experienced financial crises of various degrees. It is widely acknowledged that financial reform is much more complex than was earlier thought. McKinnon (1991:x) himself admits that 'liberalizing a highly repressed economy has been likened to walking through a minefield: your next step might be your last'.

A large number of studies have revealed the potential pitfalls of financial reform. Some sceptics have also challenged the benefits of financial liberalisation.[9] Nevertheless, an overwhelming view is that financial reform is desirable for developing countries with indiscriminate credit controls and large negative real interest rates. Even the highly publicised Southern Cone countries do not necessarily constitute cases against financial reform. Rather, they indicate that financial liberalisation 'is a formidable task that requires careful and, many times more pragmatic policy decisions ... [and requires] particular attention to the evolution and supervision of the financial system after its liberalization' (Edwards and Edwards, 1987: 206).

It is now increasingly realised that whatever benefits financial reform may bring for the liberalising countries, they are unlikely to automatically follow reform. The success of financial reform would depend on a host of pre-conditions, including the initial conditions of the economy, the sequence of reform, the accompanying macroeconomic policies, the credibility and political sustainability of reform, and the international economic environment during reform. Therefore, most strategists of economic reform suggest that it should be carried out by stages, because when all reform measures are carried out simultaneously they may create adverse consequences and halt the reform process.

Cautious approach to financial reform

The first lesson to learn from the experience of liberalising countries is that it requires extreme caution because of the links between the financial sector and other sectors of the economy. Any crisis in the financial sector has the potential to destabilise the whole economy as the crisis spills over to other sectors. Similarly, instability in other sectors can also cause distress in the financial sector. Therefore, the financial reform process must be planned and sequenced with other reform measures. As Zahler (1993: 49) has put it, 'one of these causes [of financial crisis] resulted from a hasty and unorganized liberalization for which these countries were not prepared'. Financial reform must be accompanied by macroeconomic policies which are consistent with financial liberalisation. It also requires the establishment of adequate regulatory and supervisory institutions to ensure the solvency and stability of the financial system. It is further realised that complete liberalisation of interest rates may create moral hazard and adverse selection problems, leading to bankruptcy and instability. Each of these issues are discussed below in greater details.

First stabilise, then liberalise

One of the lessons learnt from past reform experiments is that financial reform is unlikely to succeed in isolation and that any reform which is carried out against an unstable macroeconomic background may make that instability worse (World Bank, 1989). One of the factors that contributes to a government's budgetary problems and macroeconomic instability is the black holes of state enterprises which absorb resources. There must be some action programmes in place either to make these enterprises profitable or to close them down before the financial reform programme commences.

Macroeconomic stability entails a reasonable domestic relative price structure. High and unstable inflation, balance of payments crises, external debt, expectations of devaluation of the currency and capital flight are all symptoms of macroeconomic instability, and they all increase the real interest rates. Genberg (1991) points out that the idea that stabilisation should be carried out before liberalisation is based on two judgements: first, high inflation reduces the information content of prices and therefore makes resource allocation decisions difficult; and second, the external consequences of excessive demand, including current account deficits and a sharp rise in the real exchange rate, lower the credibility of liberalisation measures.

High real interest rates, overvaluation of domestic currency and financial distress were the features of financial reforms in Southern Cone countries. High real interest rates and financial distress moved closely, and the premature opening of the capital account and the pegging of exchange rates against an inflationary background caused an unsustainable appreciation of their currencies. The exchange rates did not crawl sufficiently to close the gap between domestic and foreign inflation rates. In addition, expansionary monetary and fiscal policies caused high and unstable inflation, which encouraged capital flights as uncertainties with respect to returns on domestic assets increased and investors lost their confidence in the domestic financial system.

Inflation tax replacement

High inflation is often caused by large monetised budget deficits. Therefore, McKinnon (1991) suggests that budget control must precede financial

Table 4.12 The size of revenue from financial repression

Country	Sample	Revenue from financial repression	
		% of GDP	% of tax revenue
Algeria	1974–87	4.3	11.4
Brazil	1983–87	0.5	1.6
Colombia	1980–84	0.2	2.1
Costa Rica	1972–84	2.3	12.8
Greece	1974–85	2.5	7.8
India	1980–85	2.9	22.4
Indonesia	1976–86	0.0	0.0
Jamaica	1980–82	1.4	4.7
Jordan	1978–87	0.6	2.4
Korea	1975–87	0.3	1.4
Malaysia	1974–81	0.1	0.3
Mexico	1984–87	5.8	39.7
Morocco	1977–85	2.3	8.9
Pakistan	1982–83	3.2	20.5
Panama	1977–87	0.7	2.5
Papua N. G.	1981–87	0.4	1.9
Philippines	1975–86	0.5	3.9
Portugal	1978–86	2.2	6.9
Sri Lanka	1981–83	3.4	19.2
Thailand	1976–86	0.4	2.6
Tunisia	1978–87	1.5	4.8
Turkey	1980–87	2.2	10.9
Zaire	1974–86	0.5	2.5
Zimbabwe	1981-86	5.5	19.1

Source: Giovannini and de Melo (1993: 859)

liberalisation. When budget deficits are the cause of monetary expansion, and monetary expansion is the cause of inflation, any control of inflation requires a reduction in government expenditure or an increase in government revenue from other than inflation tax. However, as most developing countries have only limited access to other forms of taxation, there is a difficulty in finding other sources of taxation or replacing inflation tax (Corden, 1988). External borrowing is not a solution because, when a government decides to borrow abroad to finance budget deficits, it may end up with an unsustainable current account deficit or external debt problem.

Financial repression: a source of government revenue

In a repressed financial system, governments finance budget deficits at domestic interest rates which are much lower than the rates that prevail in world capital markets. Thus, financial repression itself is a source of government revenue as is the inflation tax. Therefore, any attempt to liberalise the financial sector would require the government to give up a substantial source of revenue. Giovannini and de Melo (1993) have estimated the size of tax revenue from financial repression by multiplying the size of the government debt with the difference between foreign and domestic interest rates and found that it could be substantial.

Table 4.12 reports the size of revenue from financial repression in selected developing countries. It shows that the size of revenue from financial repression ranges from zero in Indonesia to 6 per cent of GDP in Mexico and Zimbabwe. In seven countries it exceeds 2 per cent of GDP and in five countries it exceeds 3 per cent of GDP. When expressed as a percentage of government revenue, financial repression provides as high as 40 per cent of government revenue in Mexico and about 20 per cent in India, Pakistan, Portugal, Sri Lanka and Zimbabwe. Therefore, it is apparent that financial liberalisation may generate budgetary problems for many developing countries. It indicates that financial reform needs to be accompanied by fiscal reform with the objective of raising government revenue to avoid any budgetary problems.

Financial reform may also create problems for financial intermediaries when the deposit rates of interest are liberalised but there is no corresponding increase in interest rates on government securities which the deposit banks and other institutions are forced to hold. Under such circumstances, financial intermediaries may risk bankruptcy, which may require public bail-out. Therefore, the likely budgetary impact of financial liberalisation may include the cost of bailing-out of financial intermediaries or the increased cost of debt servicing.

High real interest rate, adverse risk selection, and moral hazard

Although the interest rate is an important relative price, it is now increasingly realised that it cannot be liberalised fully or too rapidly. If the interest rate is allowed to rise to a very high level, it will discourage safe borrowers and encourage riskier borrowers – a phenomenon that Stiglitz and Weiss (1981) called 'adverse risk selection'. High real loan rates of interest also cause 'moral hazard', in the sense that once loans are made available to borrowers, they have incentives to undertake riskier investment projects than they might have submitted to banks before loans were granted. Rapidly rising interest rates also cause insolvency problems for many firms and exacerbate macroeconomic instability.

The Stiglitz–Weiss model suggests that, expecting adverse risk selection and moral hazard problems, banks voluntarily put a limit on loan rates so that they can maximise their expected profits. However, it may not be the case when banks themselves suffer from moral hazard in an unstable macroeconomic environment in which the government implicitly or explicitly commits itself to providing deposit insurance. It may happen because, in an unstable macroeconomic environment, any one bank can undertake risky lending at unnaturally high real loan rates of interest on the presumption that favourable outcomes, where the non-bank borrowers succeed in repaying their high interest loans, provide large profits to the bank's shareholders, whereas unfavourable outcomes, with highly correlated defaults among the non-bank borrowers, leading to massive losses by the bank in question, are borne by the government. It means that the bank can effectively become a beneficiary of an unfair bet against the government and suffer from moral hazard by extending risky loans (McKinnon, 1991).[10]

The order of liberalisation of the external sector

Macroeconomic instability is often blamed for the failures of financial liberalisation in developing countries, including Argentina, Chile and Uruguay. However, the strategy of financial liberalisation itself may add to macroeconomic instability and compound the problem. It is generally believed that any premature opening of the capital account in the balance of payments during economic reform may generate macroeconomic instability and destabilising capital flows. McKinnon (1973, 1982) and Dornbusch (1983, 1984) suggest that any early opening of the capital account may result in large destabilising capital outflows when the domestic capital market is repressed and the interest rates are fixed at low levels.

On the other hand, Edwards (1984) has developed a partial adjustment model to demonstrate that, after restrictions on capital inflows are lifted, there may be rapid inflows of capital because of the accumulated large gap between the desired level of external debt and actual debt (Figure 4.1). His

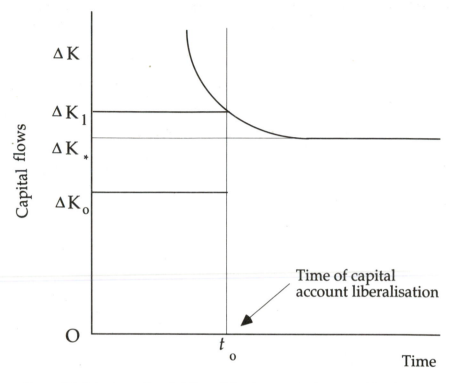

Figure 4.1 Behaviour of capital flows following a capital account liberalisation

capital flow equation is given by: $\Delta K = \min [\gamma(D^* - D_{-1}), \Delta K_0]$, where ΔK are capital inflows, D^* is desired external debt, D_{-1} is actual external debt in the previous period, γ is the partial adjustment coefficient, and ΔK_0 is the maximum amount of net capital inflows allowed by the authority in every period. Over time the amount of capital flows will decline to the equilibrium level ΔK^*.

Massive inflows or outflows of capital have substantial effects on domestic inflation, exchange rates and interest rates, depending on whether the country operates under a fixed or a flexible exchange rate system. Under a fixed exchange rate system, if capital inflows after financial reform are monetised, they may generate inflation and appreciate the real exchange rate. Under a floating exchange rate system, capital inflows may appreciate both the nominal and real exchange rates. When financial markets adjust faster than goods market, there may be an abrupt appreciation of the real exchange rate.[11]

Finding that any large capital inflows following financial reform create macroeconomic instability, a commonly held view is that the capital account should be opened only after both liberalising the domestic financial sector and opening the current account in the balance of payments. However, the

World Bank Report (1989) suggests that even though the capital market should not be opened prematurely, freer capital movements may promote better alignment of domestic interest rates with international rates, increase the availability of funds from abroad, and provide more opportunities for risk diversification.

Private overseas borrowing

As financial reform includes the opening of the capital account in the balance of payments, it may create an external debt problem when the private sector takes the opportunity to borrow excessively from overseas at interest rates which are often lower than domestic interest rates. It has been observed in many developing countries that following financial reforms the private sector borrowed heavily when foreign financial institutions were eager to lend without properly evaluating the credit risk and not charging interest rates which include a risk premium. Hanson and de Melo (1985) found that financial liberalisation and the opening of the capital account contributed to increased indebtedness in Uruguay which, after generating two asset bubbles, led to widespread default when the loan rates rose. Following the opening of the capital account and the removal of controls over private borrowing, Chile also encountered an external debt problem. Foreign banks were eager to lend to Chilean banks when the latter encountered an excess, or false, demand for credit. In the early stage of financial reforms the official view in Chile was that the private sector debt should not be a matter of concern because any debt-servicing difficulty would be solved through bankruptcy procedures. But in the end any distinction between private and public debt became artificial when the Chilean government had to nationalise a large proportion of non-guaranteed private debt (Edwards and Edwards, 1987).

Following McKinnon (1991), the private overborrowing syndrome after financial reform can be explained by a simple model (Figure 4.2). When the government of a borrowing country explicitly or implicitly guarantees foreign loans by the private sector, an individual borrower in the foreign capital market faces a horizontal (S_F) rather than an upward-sloping supply curve for finance (ACF). An upward-sloping supply curve captures the increase in riskiness of any private borrower as it increases its exposure. As Figure 4.2 shows, the horizontal supply curve of finance allows the private borrower to borrow more than is optimal in the absence of any guarantee by the government. It has also been pointed out by Edwards and Edwards (1987: 17) that '[t]o the extent that private sector knows that it will be bailed out by the government, moral hazard type behaviour becomes highly likely'. An implication is that to avoid any external debt problem there should be an indirect form of control of private foreign borrowing by phasing out implicit or explicit official guarantees of private loans. Any government policy or declaration in this regard must be time consistent, otherwise it will not be credible and effective.

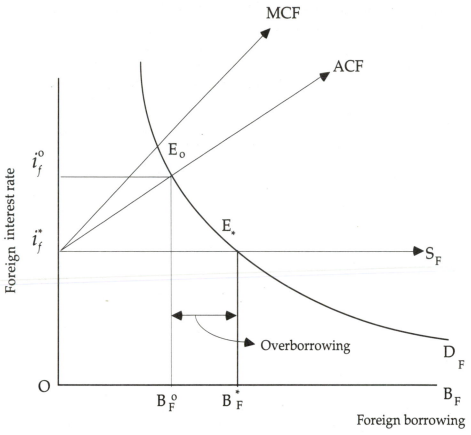

Figure 4.2 Private sector overborrowing

Prudential regulation and supervision

The success of financial reform is partly dependent on the establishment of a sound structure of prudential regulation and supervision. A weak regulatory and supervisory framework can be a barrier to financial liberalisation because financial liberalisation may place a different, and heavier, demand on the regulatory body than does a directed credit system. The human skills required for the smooth functioning of financial institutions in a deregulated financial environment may also be different from those needed where interest rates and credits are controlled (Diaz-Alejandro, 1985; Dooley and Mathieson, 1987).

The lack of adequate and effective supervision was one reason for financial crises in Chile, the Philippines and Turkey. In fact an optimal check and balance system of regulation and supervision and market forces is required for the smooth functioning of financial institutions in a deregulated environment. Honohan makes the point within a broader perspective:

> prudential regulation, designed to ensure that intermediaries are operating in a safe and sound manner, is necessary as a general background of the smooth functioning of the financial system. It is further argued that even regulation of interest rates can be non-distorting to the extent that it merely serves to prevent speculative mispricing of financial assets. The appropriate policy stance thus becomes a question of balancing the need for establishing and policing the basic 'rules of the game' for the financial system, with the need to give financial intermediaries the freedom to do that for which they are uniquely specialized, namely credit and risk appraisal and pricing. This perspective provides a bridge between those who criticize financial repression and those who caution against reckless financial liberalization.
>
> (Honohan, 1992: 90)

Therefore, financial liberalisation should not be understood as a *laissez-faire* approach to financial markets. It should aim at regulatory reforms rather than simply deregulation. Many developing countries have laws and regulations and financial practices that have not kept pace with changing financial needs and innovations in financial technology. Therefore, developing countries need to undertake a variety of reforms so that they can develop their financial systems with a view to financing the private sector efficiently. Reliable information is essential for sound investment choices and to improve monitoring of firms' behaviour after funding so that corrective action can be taken, if needed, to avoid crises. This entails overhauling accounting, auditing and information disclosure rules. The various laws governing companies, banks, financial institutions and bankruptcies must also be updated and enforced to protect both debtors and creditors. Thus the focus of bank supervision should shift from the implementation of government directives, such as credit allocation, to the quality of loan portfolios, the adequacy of capital and the soundness of bank management. In other words, regulatory reforms should aim at enhancing the safety and efficiency of the financial system. However, as Long and Vittas point out,

> The line between economic and prudential regulation is thin. Any specific aspect of regulation may ... and most do ... have components of both. But the focus is different between using regulation to control credit allocation and pricing and using regulation to maintain a healthy and efficient financial system. It is not a matter of a complete reorientation of focus, but rather a reweighting of the importance of economic and prudential regulation. The rules of the game need to change. This does not suggest a *laissez-faire* approach ... but a different orientation to regulation.
>
> (Long and Vittas, 1991: 6)

Political sustainability of economic reform

Recent research on economic reform has been concentrated on issues relating to aspects of the political sustainability of reform. Economic reform is essentially a political decision and no reform takes place in a political vacuum. Politicians and policy-makers ask whether the economic reform package in question has sufficient political support for it to be carried out to its completion. Political support in a democratic country comes in various forms, such as the re-election of the government which starts economic reform, an adequate parliamentary support for reform, and a sufficient degree of social acceptability (Asilis and Milesi-Ferretti, 1994). Some structural features of reforming countries often determine whether their reforms are economically, socially and politically sustainable. Initial economic conditions, the institutional structure and the nature of the political system are important structural features that determine whether reforms can be successfully carried out.

Macroeconomic imbalances, microeconomic distortions, per capita income and income distribution are some of the initial economic conditions that affect the sustainability of macroeconomic policy reform. The question of whether economic reform is essential comes from macroeconomic problems, such as inflation and current account deficits. High or hyperinflation often creates a condition which is conducive to the design and implementation of stabilisation and reform programmes because such reforms are expected to benefit all sections of the people. However, while most stabilisation and structural adjustment programmes carry adjustment costs, not all sections of the people share the burden equally; but it is desirable that all sections carry these adjustment costs during reform on an equitable basis in order to make it a success. The level of development of the reforming country is an important determinant of reform success, because the people of a rich country with high incomes and a low degree of income inequality are able to withstand adjustment costs better than the people of a poor country with low incomes and a high degree of income inequality. Moreover, a high degree of income inequality makes it difficult for any government to reach a consensus on economic reform because it imposes costs disproportionately on different sections of the people.

Economic reform is also influenced by the institutional structure of the country. The system of property rights, the flexibility of the labour market, the degree of centralisation of expenditure centres and the degree of independence of the central bank are some of the institutional factors that determine the degree of effectiveness of economic reform. The nature of the political system may itself play a critical role in the reform process. For example, a coalition government finds it difficult to reach a consensus on economic reform; such a government often suffers from what is known as 'a status quo bias'. As financial reform may affect the interests of the powerful groups in the society, the latter find it easier to influence the decision of a coalition government and to halt the reform process itself. As Gelb and Honohan make the point:

> A highly regulated banking system is typically a cartelized and potentially profitable one. Opening the system up to competition will erode high profits and allow new institutions and markets to flourish at the expense of the old. In anticipation of such effects, therefore, there will be strong lobbying against liberalization. There are losers as well from the establishment of tighter prudential regulation. Uncreditworthy borrowers who received loans from badly managed banks will no longer have access to credit. That they have received loans in the past, however, suggests that they will form a powerful lobby against reform. In most developing countries, extensive ties exist between major banks and borrowers; moving them to an 'arms-length' relationship attacks the basis of the economic power structure and is therefore a slow and difficult process.
>
> (Gelb and Honohan, 1991: 89–90)

Political sustainability of economic reform is also dependent on the supply response to the reform. To be successful all reforms must deliver expected results at some stage, but the sooner the better. When the supply response is slow, any enthusiasm for reform may fade away, particularly when the adjustment costs begin to hurt the people. No democratic government finds it politically easy to continue with any reform which fails to deliver tangible benefits to the people.

Finally, the success of economic reform is dependent on policy credibility. Experience of Southern Cone countries suggests that economic policies with respect to reform or economic management must be credible and time consistent, otherwise they would be ineffective. For example, although the Chilean government repeatedly warned the public that their deposits, except small deposits with banks, were not guaranteed and that banks and other financial intermediaries could go bankrupt, it intervened when one important bank was in trouble in 1977 because it was feared that its bankruptcy would tarnish external and internal confidence in the Chilean financial system.

SUMMARY AND CONCLUSION

Financial liberalisation was not the overwhelming success that had been predicted by its protagonists. The Southern Cone Latin American countries faced serious macroeconomic problems following reform. However, detailed examination of Asian and Latin American experience does not suggest any causal relationship between the two, although financial liberalisation reform may increase the degree of fragility of financial institutions.

The experience of developing countries with financial reform suggests that financial liberalisation reform is more complex than most economists thought.

The success of financial reform depends on a host of factors, including the existing macroeconomic conditions, the optimal level and appropriate sequencing of reform, the accompanying economic policy reforms, prudential regulation and supervision and, above all, the political sustainability of the reform process (Asilis and Milesi-Ferretti, 1994; Edwards and Edwards, 1987; McKinnon, 1992; World Bank, 1989).

Some specific lessons have been learnt from financial reform experiences in developing countries.

(a) The introduction of a financial reform programme requires careful planning and sequencing with other reforms. It cannot be rushed through before appropriate institutional arrangements are in place. A gradual and phased reform may be appropriate in countries where there are difficulties in bringing about monetary and financial discipline and in creating appropriate institutions and human skills for prudential regulation and supervision of financial institutions.

(b) Financial liberalisation should start only after macroeconomic stability is established. Countries that attempted financial liberalisation before undertaking stabilisation measures suffered destabilising capital flows, high interest rates, and corporate and financial distress, which in turn led to monetary expansion, inflation and capital flight.

(c) A market-based financial system is not the panacea for all success. If, for example, interest rates that are allowed to rise too rapidly to a very high level create moral hazard and adverse selection problems. A very high and rapidly rising interest rate also exacerbates macroeconomic instability by causing financial insolvency.

(d) Financial reform should be accompanied by a prudential regulatory and supervisory body, particularly to counter any pervasive moral hazard problem resulting from deposit insurance (Fry, 1988).

(e) To avoid any destabilising capital flows, care must be taken in opening the capital market. In fact it should be delayed to a point at which the effects of internal financial liberalisation on the domestic economy have settled down (Genberg, 1991; World Bank, 1989).

(f) The authority must create credibility on the question of financial reform. If the public believes that the reform attempt is not genuine and will be reversed, it may act accordingly and frustrate the reform process. The implementation of a consistent and credible policy package may prove to be more important than any order of liberalisation (Edwards and Edwards, 1987).

(g) Financial liberalisation does not guarantee competition in the financial sector because of the uncompetitive and oligopolistic nature of the financial system in many developing countries.[12] Therefore, financial reform program should be supplemented with competition policy.

(h) Government reform programmes must receive political support. This may require devising a feasible programme of compensation for losers.

Even though the complexities of financial reform are evident and the pitfalls of reform are acknowledged by the proponents of financial liberalisation, the short run-effects of financial reform have attracted disproportionate attention. As little time has passed since the implementation of financial liberalisation reform in most developing countries (except those of the Southern Cone), it is premature to make a final judgement on the efficacy of financial liberalisation reform in economic development. Moreover, as financial reform in most developing countries has been carried out simultaneously with stabilisation policies in an unstable macroeconomic environment, it has become difficult to disentangle the net effect of financial reform from that of stabilisation policies. Given the complexities of financial reform and its linkage with stabilisation and structural adjustment programmes, the effectiveness of financial reform has to be judged in the long-run context and after allowing adequate time after the reforms. The emphasis on the long run often gives a different perspective and a different picture. For example, even in the case of Chile, McKinnon sees a better future:

> Chile's excellent economic position in the early 1990s seems to be at least as good as, or better than, that of any of the other major Latin American countries, none of which has succeeded in implementing such thoroughgoing trade, fiscal, and financial reforms.
>
> (McKinnon, 1991: 82)

NOTES

1 There is no standard definition of success or failure of financial reform policies. Michaelly (1982) defines the failure of a liberalisation attempt as the reversal of reform policies. Edwards and Edwards (1987) consider failure as a significant deviation between expected (and publicised) results and actual results of reform policies. However, such a definition of success or failure does not mention the time span that should be allowed for the reform policies to work. Financial reforms may adversely affect the economy in the short run, but they improve the economy in the medium or long run.

2 See World Bank (1993), table A5.5 for a summary of the nature, causes and resolution of banking system crises in Hong Kong, Japan, Malaysia, Singapore, Taiwan, Thailand, Chile, Ghana, Philippines, Turkey, Norway and the United States.

3 Little (1982) regards this phenomenon as the 'resurgence of neoclassical economics' in development economics.

4 The selected countries are Argentina, Chile, Malaysia, Philippines, Spain, Thailand and Uruguay.

5 See S. Faruqi (ed.), *Financial Sector Reforms in Asian and Latin American Countries: Lessons of Comparative Experience*, Economic Development Institute of the World Bank, 1993, for a comparative study of Chile, Indonesia, Malaysia, Thailand, Korea, Colombia, Brazil, Japan, Mexico and the Philippines.

6 Corbo (1985) and Dornbusch (1993) provide the following explanations for high real interest rates and overvalued real exchange rates in Chile:

The real cause [of a high real interest rate] was the lack of adequate regulations for the financial system ... the deregulation of domestic financial markets gave commercial banks and financial institutions too much freedom. The financial intermediaries took undue risks by inadequate evaluation of their loans as well as by concentrating their loans in clients connected to the banks through cross-ownership. And without appropriate supervision, intermediaries in financial difficulty were able to increase interest rates just to attract new deposits and make up the shortfall on interest payments to depositors created by their nonperforming loans.

(Corbo, 1985: 909)

Following the coup in 1973 and a period of fiscal stabilization, the Chilean currency was placed on a *tablita* (schedule), and in 1978, when inflation was still above 20 percent, the currency was fixed to the dollar. As a result, the real exchange rate appreciated steadily and vastly. Inflation did come down over the next two years, but not fast enough to avoid a dramatic overvaluation.

(Dornbusch, 1993: 40)

7 Fry (1990) reports that the share of borrowings of private business enterprises from curb markets was 48 per cent in 1964 which fell to 27 per cent in 1986 but increased to 48 per cent in 1993.

8 For an excellent summary of issues and lessons, see A. Roe 'Seminar Proceedings: a Summary', and M. Long 'Financial Reforms: a Global Perspective', in Faruqi (ed.) (1993).

9 Collier and Mayer do not share the view that financial liberalisation has beneficial effects on the economy. They have reached the following conclusion:

The basis for supporting financial liberalization is weak. The benefits of financial liberalization can at best be described as unproven. The relation of savings to interest rates is questionable and the benefits of improved resource allocation at higher interest rates seems to have more to do with the role of financial institutions than interest rates *per se*.

(Collier and Mayer, 1989: 10)

10 McKinnon (1991) cites the experiences of Argentina and Chile in the 1970s and the American banking experiences in the 1980s and 1990s as test cases of the moral hazard problem in the banking system itself.

11 The rapid inflows of capital produce a large current account deficit. As McKinnon (1976) and Harberger (1982) point out, whenever a fraction of the additional foreign funds is spent on non-tradable goods, the relative price of non-tradables will rise and the real exchange rate will appreciate.

12 Fry (1993) finds that even after financial deregulation, there was a lack of competition in the financial sector in most reforming developing countries. He suggests that competition is essential to ensure that banking cartels do not take over the interest-rate-setting role relinquished by the government in the process of financial liberalisation.

5

MONETARY POLICY AS A TOOL OF ECONOMIC STABILISATION

Although monetary policy can play both a growth-promoting and a stabilisation role, its primary objective in developing countries has been to promote economic growth largely through inflationary means, interest rate ceilings and directed credit programmes. The review of both theoretical and empirical literature on money, inflation and economic growth in Chapters 2 and 3 shows that the empirical relationship between inflation and economic growth is more complex than is theoretically perceived. The literature on inflationary finance reveals that monetary expansion to finance public investment is a hazardous means of economic growth. The review also shows that although the relationship between financial liberalisation and economic growth is much more complex, large repressions of the financial sector severely retard economic growth.

Therefore, activist monetary policy either in the form of inflationary financing or financial repression (subsidised directed credit) is more likely to hinder economic growth. The lacklustre growth performance of most Latin American countries since the 1950s in an environment of macroeconomic instability indicates that high and unstable inflation retards economic growth. On the other hand, relatively low and stable inflation has played a positive role in economic growth in newly industrialising economies of Asia during the past two decades or so.

Although the role of macroeconomic stability in economic growth is understood, there is controversy as to whether monetary policy should be used as a tool of economic stabilisation in developing countries. The experience of many developing countries reveals that activist monetary policy may itself become a source of macroeconomic instability. However, the issue of the role of monetary policy and its relative efficacy has its origin in the monetarist–Keynesian debate. To examine the role of monetary policy in economic stabilisation in developing countries, it is therefore important to have an understanding of the broader debate on the need for stabilisation in a capitalist economy in a historical context.

MONETARIST–KEYNESIAN DEBATE ON STABILISATION[1]

The idea of economic stabilisation is at the heart of Keynesian economics. The Keynesian theory has provided an explanation of the great depression of the 1930s and has suggested policy measures that can be used to prevent any future depression. The basic Keynesian argument is that the great depression was the result of the drying up of investment opportunities and an autonomous downward shift in investment and consumption spending. It implies that the government could have undertaken expansionary fiscal policies to avoid the depression. Such a Keynesian explanation was widely accepted. Indeed, it has become an orthodoxy that countercyclical fiscal policy can smooth out economic fluctuations in an inherently unstable economy. Thus fiscal activism has become an integral part of Keynesian economics.

Keynes also believed that if there was no liquidity trap and/or investment pessimism[2] then an expansionary monetary policy could achieve full employment much quicker than waiting for market forces to reduce unemployment. This stems from the belief that wages and prices do not adjust downward. This makes the self-adjustment mechanism of the economy very weak.

Much has changed since the heyday of the Keynesian economics in the 1950s and 1960s. Since the early 1960s Friedman and Schwartz (1963), Friedman (1968) and others[3] have rehabilitated the classical/monetarist income determination model in which the money supply determines the level of nominal income.[4] Friedman and Schwartz argued that in the United States the depression of the 1930s was the result of contractionary monetary policy, instead of being caused by an autonomous downward shift in private spending, and that money growth leads business cycles. The monetarist reinterpretation of the great depression, and the difficulties in conducting activist economic policies in the face of the coexistence of inflation and unemployment have polarised the Keynesians and monetarists on a wide range of issues relating to stabilisation.

Although monetary policy has now become an important policy instrument in the armoury of policy-makers, the proper role of monetary policy has remained a contentious issue. The Keynesians want to assign to it a demand management role in the same way that they have assigned a stabilising role to fiscal policy (Modigliani, 1977). However, monetarists are not impressed with such a role for monetary policy because they do not see the need for activist policies to achieve stabilisation. Even if a case for activist policies for stabilisation can be made, monetarists argue that monetary policy is not capable of playing such a role. The main role of monetary policy, according to Friedman (1968), is to create a stable macroeconomic environment where real forces can operate rather than monetary policy itself becoming a source of economic disturbance.[5] Therefore, he expresses concern that policy-makers are in danger of assigning to monetary policy a larger role than it can perform, in danger of asking it to accomplish tasks that it cannot achieve, and as a result, in danger of preventing it from making the contribution that it is capable of making.

(Friedman, 1968: 5)

Despite the intense debate on the question of stabilisation in developed countries, it did not receive much attention in the developing countries themselves.[6] The reason is that whereas in developed countries instability in output or employment originates primarily from the demand side, in developing countries such instability originates mostly from the supply side, and neither fiscal nor monetary policy is effective in smoothing out fluctuations in output arising from the supply shock.

DEMAND SHOCK AND STABILISATION IN DEVELOPING COUNTRIES

There are two pertinent questions about economic stabilisation in developing countries. First, how prevalent are demand shocks in developing economies? Second, how sensitive are developing economies to demand shocks? The Keynesians believe that demand shocks are rampant and tend to persist, while monetarists suggest that demand shocks are infrequent and not persistent.

At a sophisticated level the Keynesian and monetarist views are presented in terms of economic relationships, such as the consumption function, the investment function, the money demand function, and the source and pattern of economic instability. Keynesians argue that instability in the capitalist economy originates from the autonomous shift in consumption and investment spending and that it requires intervention by the government for two main reasons. First, demand shocks persist over time; and second, wages and prices are not flexible enough to bring equilibrium to the system when it is disturbed by demand shocks. Therefore, the Keynesian theory predicts that a capitalist economy would experience either inflation or unemployment depending on whether the demand shocks are positive or negative. Schematically,

$$AD \uparrow \to i \uparrow \to (M^s - M^d) \uparrow \equiv (AD - AS) \uparrow \to P \uparrow$$

$$AD \downarrow \to i \downarrow \to (M^s - M^d) \downarrow \equiv (AD - AS) \downarrow \neq P \downarrow$$

where AD is aggregate demand, AS is aggregate supply, i is the interest rate, M^s is the nominal money supply, M^d is the nominal money demand, and P is the price level. It shows that a rise in aggregate demand raises the interest rate, which, by lowering the demand for money, creates an excess supply of money (or an excess demand for goods). This, in turn, raises the price level.

In contrast, a fall in aggregate demand, although it reduces the excess supply of money, does not lower the price level because of downward rigidities of prices and wages, and therefore raises unemployment. Both monetarists and new classical economists disagree with the Keynesian view on unemployment. They believe that wages and prices are flexible enough to bring the economy back to equilibrium when it is disturbed by demand shocks. Given the extreme positions of Keynesians and monetarists, mainstream economists believe that the question of rigidities in wages and prices is a matter of degree and not of kind and can only be resolved empirically.[7]

Sources and pattern of economic instability

Demand disturbances in a market economy may originate from a number of sources, including private expenditure demand shocks, such as a shift in private consumption or investment spending, and sharp changes in both budget deficits and net exports. In the early literature the debate on private sector instability centred on the question of whether consumption spending or investment spending or a combination of the two is stable. The Keynesian consumption function states that the level of consumption expenditure depends on current disposable income and on an autonomous component. It implies that any shift in the autonomous consumption component because of changes in consumer confidence or optimism may create instability in consumption expenditure.

The Keynesian consumption function was later found theoretically inadequate and inconsistent with actual observations. It was superseded by Friedman's permanent income hypothesis and by Modigliani's lifecycle hypothesis. Friedman's permanent income hypothesis suggests that consumption expenditure depends on permanent income and is stable. Modigliani's lifecycle hypothesis goes one step further and suggests that consumers tend to stabilise their consumption expenditures over their lifetimes. Thus these forward-looking consumption theories imply that consumption expenditure is stable. A broad consensus has now emerged that consumption expenditure on non-durable goods and services is stable, although the expenditure on durable goods is procyclical. An outburst of spending on durable goods is one likely source of instability in the private economy (Abel, 1990).

How stable is consumption expenditure in developing countries? It depends on two main factors; first, whether current or permanent income is the determinant of consumption expenditure; second, the share of durable goods in total consumption expenditure. Gersovitz (1988) has reviewed the literature on consumption behaviour in developing countries. He writes: 'the general sense of the literature on developing countries is that a permanent, or lifetime, notion of income . . . is an appropriate determinant of consumption, rather than current income' (p. 389). Nevertheless, current income has a role in consumption expenditure in developing countries. The high incidence of absolute poverty is one reason why current income is closely linked with consumption expenditure. Such a link becomes stronger when underdeveloped credit markets create liquidity constraints for various categories of consumers. The presence of liquidity constraints raises the value of the short-run marginal propensity to consume from what is implied by the permanent income–lifecycle hypothesis. Consumption expenditure on durable goods is procyclical in developing countries. However, the share of consumption expenditure on durable goods (monetised component) appears low in developing countries. Most poor people simply cannot afford to buy many durable consumer goods and most rural households produce various durable goods for their use rather than for purchase (Gersovitz, 1988).

Investment is the second component of private expenditure. Unlike consumption expenditure, investment expenditure is relatively unstable. Most Keynesians suggest that although the real interest rate may influence investment decisions, it is not very sensitive to changes in interest rates (a very low interest-elasticity of investment). Rather, investment spending depends on business confidence or optimism. In contrast, monetarists suggest that private investment expenditure is as stable as consumption expenditure and can be expressed as a function of the cost of borrowing (or the real loan rate of interest). Monetarists also believe that investment is highly sensitive to changes in interest rates.

There is a lack of consensus on factors which determine the rate of private investment in developing countries. The debate is centred on the question of whether the real loan rate of interest has any effect on the rate of private investment in developing countries, as the neoclassical theory suggests.[8] Empirical studies, such as Blejer and Khan (1984), Greene and Villanueva (1991), Khan and Reinhart (1990), Sundararajan and Thakur (1980), and Tun Wai and Wong (1982), suggest that the real interest rate, the inflation rate and economic growth are the primary determinants of private investment in developing countries. Therefore, the argument that private investment is autonomous or dependent on non-economic factors does not appear to be valid in these countries. However, it does not necessarily imply that the investment function is highly stable. The question is whether any variation in the rate of private investment can generate instability in the private economy. As the share of investment in private expenditure is small in most developing countries, changes in private investment are unlikely to create instability in the private economy. Moreover, even if private investment is unstable, when consumption expenditure and investment expenditure are aggregated the resulting private expenditure function may remain stable. This point is emphasised by both monetarists and new Cambridge economists. Unlike the Keynesians, they argue that private consumption expenditure and investment expenditure should be treated jointly (Godley and Cripps, 1983). The aggregation of consumption expenditure and investment expenditure into one category implicitly suggests the possibility that the interest rate affects consumption expenditure and that income affects investment expenditure; this conflicts with the spirit of Keynesian macro modelling (Laidler, 1971).

Although the early literature on demand shocks focused on fluctuations of private consumption and investment spending arising from domestic sources, there has been a shift in focus towards international sources of instability. In an open economy with a large external sector, autonomous changes in net exports can become a source of demand instability. As most developing economies are heavily linked with industrialised economies, any demand shocks to industrialised economies may affect the incomes and expenditures of developing countries. For example, the sharp rise in interest rates in the industrialised countries in the early 1980s was one of the principal factors that caused the debt crisis in many developing countries. The resultant payment difficulties was responsible for recessions in debt-ridden countries. Sharp changes in the terms of trade are also considered another external source of demand disturbance to developing economies.[9] Most of the developing countries, being net importers of oil, faced serious terms of trade shocks in the 1970s following two sharp oil price rises.

In sum, the possibility of demand shocks arising from the domestic source in developing countries is not very high. However, developing countries are more prone to demand shocks from the external source as they are mostly primary commodity exporters and importers of industrial machinery and oil. But how large is the impact of demand shocks, be it internal or external, is an empirical issue which is examined below.

Sensitivity of economy to demand shocks

How sensitive an economy is to demand shocks depends on the parameter values of key macroeconomic relations, such as the marginal propensity to consume, the interest elasticity of demand for money, and the interest sensitivity of investment spending. The higher the value of the marginal propensity to consume, the larger the degree of economic instability after a demand shock as it works through the multiplier process. The lower the interest sensitivity of investment spending, the lower the offsetting change in investment by changes in interest rates arising from the initial shock and therefore the greater the degree of instability. The higher the interest elasticity of demand for money, the higher the change in excess money supply from changes in interest rates and therefore the greater the degree of instability (Aghevli et al., 1979). Therefore, the sensitivity of a developing economy to demand shocks may be determined by estimating the parameter values of consumption, investment and money demand functions. Despite the lack of reliable time series data, a large number of studies have investigated each of these functions in developing countries during the past few decades. The findings of those studies can be used to gauge the degree of sensitivity of developing economies to demand shocks.

The main parameter value of interest in economic stabilisation is the marginal propensity to consume. It has been suggested earlier that for reasons of absolute poverty and because of liquidity constraints, the value of the marginal propensity to consume may be close to unity in some developing countries. Although empirical studies do not confirm this view, the marginal propensity to consume in developing countries is generally found to be higher. Kandil (1991), for example, has found that the mean value of the marginal propensity to consume for 21 developing countries is 0.60, with a minimum value of 0.32, a maximum value of 0.79 and a standard deviation of 0.11. On the other hand, the mean value of the marginal propensity to consume for 18 developed countries has been found to be 0.56, with a minimum value of 0.43, a maximum value of 0.67 and a standard deviation of 0.06.

Another parameter of importance for the conduct of monetary policy is the value of the interest elasticity of demand for money. Empirical studies suggest that the absolute value of the interest sensitivity of demand for money is low in developing countries. For example, Kandil (1991) has found that the mean value of the interest sensitivity of demand for money for selected developing countries is –0.58 compared with –0.66 for selected developed countries. He has also estimated the slopes of the LM curve for selected developed and developing countries. The slope of the LM curve for developing countries has been found to be steeper than that for developed countries. Like the empirical studies cited earlier, Kandil's study shows that investment spending in developing countries is sensitive to the interest rate. In fact, he finds 'a higher sensitivity of investment demand to changes in the interest rate' in developing countries compared with that in developed countries.

In sum, although a larger marginal propensity to consume indicates that developing countries are sensitive to demand shocks, the parameter values of the investment and money demand functions suggest otherwise. As a result, developing economies are not likely to be highly sensitive to demand shocks and the impact of demand shocks are unlikely to be very large. At the same time, whether or not the impact of demand shocks would persist and require policy intervention depends on the degree of flexibility of relative prices.

Flexibility of wages, interest and exchange rates

One of the themes of the Latin American structuralist literature is that there are structural rigidities in the product and factor markets which make wages and prices unresponsive to market conditions. As in the Keynesian model, the structural rigidities of wages and prices may prevent the product and factor markets from clearing after demand or supply shocks. However, most empirical studies do not support the view that wages and prices in

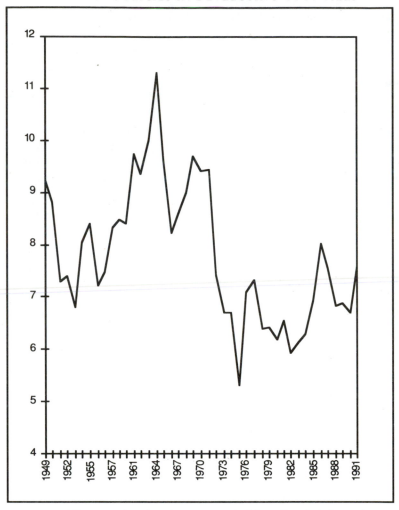

Figure 5.1 The agricultural real wage rate (*taka*) in Bangladesh, 1949–91

developing countries are rigid: agricultural wages and prices are particularly flexible in developing countries.[10]

The idea that agricultural real wages in developing countries are flexible contrasts with the implication of the traditional subsistence and nutrition-based efficiency wage theories that agricultural real wages are stable at a subsistence or an efficiency level. A number of empirical studies for developing countries, such as Bangladesh, Egypt and India, provide evidence that agricultural real wages show substantial variations and fluctuate between the peak and slack agricultural seasons. Consider Bangladesh, for example. Figure 5.1 shows that the agricultural real wage rate in Bangladesh during 1949–91

Table 5.1 Movements of the real time deposit rate of interest,[a] 1975–87

Country	Maximum	Minimum	Mean	Coefficient of variation[b]
Argentina	107.3	−74.3	−19.2	2.3
Bangladesh	1.2	−10.2	−3.4	1.1
Bolivia	41.7	−98.3	−25.3	1.7
Brazil	42.7	−46.8	−8.7	2.5
Chile	57.4	−3.5	17.1	1.0
Colombia	15.2	−5.6	6.1	1.1
Costa Rica	17.4	−36.1	2.2	6.6
Ecuador	−0.8	−23.9	−9.7	0.6
Guatemala	9.7	−20.4	−1.3	5.6
India	16.9	−5.0	0.7	8.1
Kenya	7.8	−9.7	−2.4	2.3
Korea	11.0	−7.8	3.6	1.4
Mexico	−4.3	−22.4	−10.2	0.6
Pakistan	7.9	−2.1	2.0	1.6
Peru	−7.5	−83.1	−28.0	0.6
Philippines	−18.4	−24.0	−0.2	39.7
Singapore	8.3	−1.5	3.7	0.8
Sri Lanka	12.3	−8.8	2.1	2.7
Thailand	12.0	−8.9	4.2	1.5
Tunisia	0.7	−8.5	−2.6	0.9
Turkey	14.2	−44.2	−7.6	2.4
Uruguay	23.4	−19.7	0.1	210.2
Venezuela	8.0	−15.9	−3.3	2.2
Zimbabwe	−2.6	−11.8	3.6	1.3

Sources: Nominal deposit rate of interest, except for Bangladesh: Greene and Villanueva (1991); inflation rate: *International Financial Statistics Yearbook 1993*. All data for Bangladesh are taken from *Economic Trends* (various issues).

Notes [a] The real interest rate is defined as: $[(1 + i)/(1 + \pi_{t+1}) - 1]*100$, where i is the nominal deposit rate of interest and π is the rate of inflation, which is computed from the consumer price index. Both the interest and inflation rates are divided by 100 (that is, a 5 per cent interest rate is expressed as 0.05). Following Greene and Villanueva (1991), π_{t+1} is used as a proxy for expected inflation.
[b] Coefficient of variation = standard deviation divided by mean.

fluctuated within a wide range rather than remaining stable at a subsistence or an efficiency wage level.

Market forces play a role in agricultural real wage determination in developing countries (Ahmed, 1981; Bardhan, K., 1977; Bardhan, P., 1979; Hansen, 1969; Hossain, 1989; Lal, 1984; Rosenzweig, 1980; Squire, 1981). In fact, P. Bardhan suggests that market forces play a fuller role in wage determination in developing countries:

In one respect, the market forces play a fuller (and harsher) role in a poor agrarian economy than in a developed country, as minimum wage

109

Table 5.2 Movements of the real effective exchange rate in Asian developing countries, 1981–90 (1980 = 100)[a]

Country variation	Maximum	Minimum	Mean	Coefficient
Bangladesh	97	69	83	0.11
Fiji	108	69	91	0.16
Hong Kong	137	100	115	0.10
India	104	64	89	0.16
Indonesia	113	44	71	0.37
Korea, Rep.	103	74	90	0.11
Malaysia	101	68	86	0.17
Myanmar	162	88	111	0.25
Nepal	114	81	96	0.13
Pakistan	110	57	80	0.25
Papua, N.G.	102	81	92	0.08
Philippines	102	81	92	0.08
Singapore	109	87	98	0.08
Sri Lanka	105	75	90	0.13
Taiwan	115	87	101	0.09
Thailand	103	72	86	0.16

Source: *Asian Development Outlook* (various issues).

Note [a] A fall in the index value indicates a depreciation of the real exchange rate.

legislation is much less effectively, if at all, implemented, unionization of rural labor is rare, and the state does not pay unemployment benefits. The agricultural labor force is also relatively homogeneous, and most operations are performed by illiterate and unskilled workers.

(Bardhan, 1979: 486)

Unlike agricultural wages, however, there are downward nominal wage rigidities in the manufacturing and public service sectors in developing countries. Organised unions, minimum wage laws, and the difficulties in hiring and firing of public sector workers create such wage rigidities (Amin, 1982). But there are no wage rigidities in the informal private manufacturing and services sectors as wages in these sectors are determined by market forces (Hossain, 1989).[11]

Besides the flexibility of wages, the flexibilities of real interest and exchange rates are important in the adjustment processes of the economy towards the equilibrium path after any demand shock. The nominal interest rates in developing countries are institutionally determined and are not often adjusted in response to money market conditions. Nevertheless, the real interest rates are flexible because of the flexibility of prices.

Table 5.1 reports the summary measures of the real deposit rates of interest for selected developing countries during 1975-87. It shows that the real deposit rates of interest in developing countries are highly flexible. This is reflected in the high value of the coefficient of variation of the real interest rate in most developing countries in the sample.

In an open economy aggregate demand is linked with the real effective exchange rate. A depreciation of the real exchange rate improves the competitiveness of exportable goods and induces a switch in domestic spending towards the domestically produced goods. Table 5.2 shows that the real effective exchange rate in Asian developing countries is reasonably flexible and has exhibited a smooth trend of depreciation since the early 1980s.

In sum, developing countries are less prone to demand shocks and these shocks are unlikely to be very large. Furthermore, given the flexibility of real wage rates and of real interest rates and exchange rates in developing countries, it is possible that any demand shock to developing economies would be adjusted through the price mechanism, so there may not be any need for active stabilisation by the government.

SUPPLY SHOCKS AND INFLATION: THE ROLE OF MONETARY POLICY

Although in developing countries demand shocks are not so prevalent, supply shocks originating primarily from the agriculture sector are frequently experienced. Droughts and floods are features of agriculture in developing countries. Because agriculture is the dominant sector, any supply shock to it does have macroeconomic consequences. However, supply shocks are not restricted to the agricultural sector, they also originate from the external sector. The OPEC oil shocks to non-oil developing economies in the 1970s can also be regarded as a supply shock because higher import prices reduce the marginal product (in terms of external output) of domestic resources. To the extent oil is used as a raw material, the rise in oil price shifts the production function inwards.[12]

Agricultural supply shocks and inflation

In developing countries, because of the high dependence of agriculture on weather and other natural factors, supply shocks to agriculture are frequent. Although such shocks are random (that is, they could be positive or negative in any particular year), the negative shocks get most of the publicity and often induce government intervention due to their adverse effect on output, employment and prices, in particular of food. In developing countries food prices are politically highly sensitive because of their dominance in the cost of living, especially for urban people. Hence the question of whether the monetary authority should adopt a hands-on or a hands-off policy after a supply shock has a considerable economic and political significance at the national level.[13]

111

In the literature on inflation in developing countries, crop failure is considered a cause of inflation. Food crop failure can increase the general price level when non-food prices are rigid downward. However, in the absence of any accommodative monetary expansion such price increases are unlikely to be sustained. Why, then, should the monetary authority increase the money supply in such a situation when there is a danger of sustained price increases (inflation)? This question was addressed in an early paper by Porter (1961). He argues for monetary expansion after an agricultural supply shock to lower the danger of, rather than to ignite, inflation. According to him, in a developing country any increase in the price level after a crop failure would remain at the high level whether or not the monetary authority increases the money supply. He then advocates an expansion of the money supply; otherwise, farmers may hoard foodgrain to balance the desired and actual levels of wealthholding because a disequilibrium in their wealth position is being created after the price increase. Such an action by farmers may increase the price level further because of the decline in food supply in the open market.

However, Porter's arguments become weak if the normal level of food supply in the market can be maintained from both domestic official stocks and imports. In that case, there may not be any significant increase in food price after any food crop failure. Even if there is an increase in the price level after the crop failure, it is unlikely to generate a self-sustaining inflationary process without the support of expansionary economic policies. The adoption of such policies remains at the discretion of the monetary and fiscal authorities. The question of whether farmers will hoard foodgrain after the food crop failure depends on the expected price of food. It is likely that any expansionary monetary and fiscal policies would increase expected inflation, which, contrary to Porter's view, would induce farmers to hoard more foodgrain rather than less.

Following the tradition of the modern monetary theories of aggregate demand and aggregate supply, a theoretical model is developed below to explain the above contention. The two building blocks of the model are the monetary theory of aggregate demand and the expectations-augmented aggregate supply functions.

The monetary theory of aggregate demand shows the relationship between output demand and the price level when the money market is in equilibrium. To derive such a relationship, an aggregate money demand function is specified below.

Demand for money

Assume that the demand for money is derived in the same way as the demand for any other durable good. Real money balances are considered a type of real asset, a form of wealth with the additional property of higher liquidity, providing a flow of non-observable services that enter into individuals' utility functions. All individuals are assumed to maximise their utility functions subject to budget constraints. The demand for real money balances, derived by the utility maximisation principle, will then depend on real income and the opportunity cost of holding money instead of other financial and real assets.

Let M^d be the demand for nominal money balances, P the price level, y the real income or output, and π^e the expected inflation. Then the demand for money can be expressed in the following semi-logarithmic form:

$$\ln (M^d/P) = \alpha \ln y - \beta \pi^e \qquad (5.1)$$

where α and β are structural parameters and ln represents the natural logarithm.

It shows that the demand for money increases with the increase in real income and decreases with the increase in expected inflation.[14]

Money market equilibrium

Equilibrium in the money market refers to a situation where the demand for real money equals the supply of real money, so that at equilibrium, $\ln (M^d/P) = \ln (M^s/P)$. Any discrepancy between the demand for and supply of money indicates that the money market is in disequilibrium. Any excess money supply (or excess money demand) is expected to spill over to the commodity market. In a closed economy it changes the price level and brings equilibrium in the money market. In a completely open economy where there are no non-traded goods, any disequilibrium in the money market adjusts itself through changes in foreign exchange reserves. When an economy is neither completely closed nor completely open, any disequilibrium in the money market adjusts itself through changes in both the price level and foreign exchange reserves.

An aggregate demand function

The money market equilibrium condition yields the following aggregate demand function

$$\ln y = \delta_1 \ln (M^s/P) + \delta_2 \pi^e \qquad (5.2)$$

where $\delta_1 = 1/\alpha$ and $\delta_2 = \beta/\alpha$.

It shows that when M^s and π^e remain constant, the demand for output is inversely related to the price level. The downward-sloping demand curve shifts to the right with the increase in both the money supply and expected inflation and shifts to the left with the reduction in both the money supply and expected inflation.

An aggregate supply function

An expectations-augmented aggregate supply function can be specified in the form of a single reduced form equation:

$$\ln y_t = \ln y_{nt} + \gamma_1 \ln (P_t/P_t^e) \qquad (5.3)$$

where y is measured output, y_n is natural output, determined by factors such as capital, labour and technology, P is the price level, and P^e is the price level expected by workers, given the information available at time t, and γ_1 is the elasticity of output with respect to any discrepancy between the current and expected price levels.

The specified supply function is called the Lucas supply function, although Gordon (1981) prefers to refer it as the Friedman supply function. In terms of Friedman's labour supply analysis, the demand for and supply of labour depend on the real wage rate. Employers calculate the real wage rate by evaluating the nominal wage rate in terms of the current price level, but workers calculate the real wage rate by evaluating the nominal wage rate in terms of the expected price level. Therefore, employment and output changes only if the monetary authority can adopt such a policy which moves the actual price level while not simultaneously moving the expected price level for workers. According to Milton Friedman, it is possible that in the short run, due to imperfect information on the part of workers, they can be 'fooled' temporarily but not in the long run. If it is assumed that the price expectations are formed rationally in the sense of Muth (1961) as an unbiased estimator of the actual price level, such output fluctuations do not arise and the aggregate supply curve becomes vertical – its position being determined uniquely by the production function and the conditions of equilibrium in the labour market.[15]

Any supply shock that shifts the production curve downward and the marginal productivity of labour curve leftward would shift the aggregate supply curve leftward. Therefore, the leftward shift of the aggregate supply curve is the combined effect of the downward shift of the production curve and the lower level of employment because of the decline in the marginal productivity of labour (Branson, 1989).

An application of the model in a closed economy

In Figure 5.2 the aggregate demand and aggregate supply functions are brought together to examine the effects on the price level and output of both a hands-off and a hands-on policy by the monetary authority following a supply shock. The D_0 (LM_0^s, π_0^e) line represents aggregate demand with the given money supply M_0^s and expected inflation π_0^e. The S_0 line represents aggregate supply which corresponds to a specific production function with equilibrium in the labour market. It actually represents the

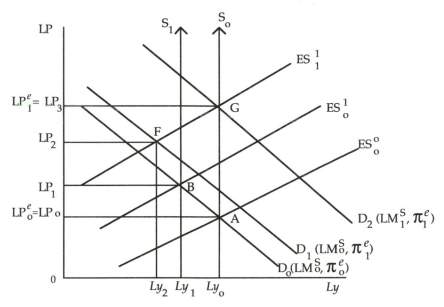

Figure 5.2 The effects on the price level in a closed economy of a hands-off and a hands-on policy by the monetary authority following a supply shock

full capacity output. The ES^o_o line represents the expectations-augmented aggregate supply. It cuts the long-run aggregate supply line at the level at which the actual and expected price levels are equal ($LP^e_o = LP_o$). The point A is the initial equilibrium position of the economy with output Ly_o and the price level LP_o.

Assume that the economy unexpectedly experiences a supply shock and the aggregate supply line S_o shifts to the position S_1, which represents a less than full capacity output. As the supply shock is unexpected, the expected price level will remain at LP^e_o and the ES^o_o line will shift to the position ES^1_o. The subscript o in ES^1_o indicates the level of demand represented by $D_o(LM^s_o, \pi^e_o)$ and the superscript 1 indicates that the aggregate supply line has unexpectedly moved to the position S_1. After the supply shock the economy will settle at the temporary equilibrium position B with output Ly_1 and the price level LP_1.

Assume that the supply shock discussed here is a negative agricultural supply shock. Such shocks are random and do not usually persist. Therefore, it is expected that after the one-period supply shock is over, there will be normal production in the next period. It will shift the aggregate supply line S_1 to the right and settle at the original position S_o. When that happens, the ES^1_o line will move to the original position ES^o_o and the price level will fall from LP_1 to LP_o. It shows that the impact of any agricultural supply shock on the price level would be temporary if the monetary authority does not intervene and if there is no change in price expectations.

A complex situation may however arise if there is a policy intervention by the monetary authority. If the economic agents change their price expectations after the supply shock, any policy intervention by the monetary authority will create a complex and uncertain situation. Consider the case when the expected price level increases from LP_o^e to LP_1^e. The ES_o^o line will then shift to the position ES_1^1. Since the demand for money depends on expected inflation, an increase in the expected price level will shift the aggregate demand line rightward to the position D_1 (LM_o^s, π_1^e). Changes in the expected price level thus shift both the aggregate demand and aggregate supply curves. Given the expected price level LP_1^e, the temporary equilibrium position of the economy is not B but F with the price level LP_2 and output Ly_2. But F does not represent a stable equilibrium because the actual and expected price levels are not equal. Whether the economy will remain at the position F or move towards the position A after the normal production during the next period will depend on how economic agents form their price expectations. Any action by the monetary authority after the supply shock may provide vital information which may influence economic agents in forming their price expectations. Even the monetary authority's behaviour in the past in such circumstances could become the guide to economic agents in forming their price expectations. If the norm is such that the monetary authority adopts a hands-off policy following the supply shock, then it is possible that the one-shot increase in the price level will fall from the peak level after normal production during the next period. When the expected price level falls, wealth-holders would substitute money for goods which would shift the aggregate demand curve to the left. The expectations-augmented supply curve is also likely to shift to the right after the normal production. The economy may then return to the original position A. In contrast, if the monetary authority increases the money supply after the supply shock, the aggregate demand curve will shift to a further right position, say, D_2 (LM_1^s, π_1^e), which will increase the price level to LP_3. If the expected price level remains at LP_1^e, G may be a stable equilibrium because at this point $LP_3 = LP_1^e$. However, if the monetary expansion becomes a source of price expectations, the aggregate supply curve may shift to the left and cause a further increase in the price level.

An application of the model in an open economy

The model discussed above can be extended to the case of an open economy under both fixed and flexible exchange rate systems. For simplicity, ignore the international trade in financial assets and capital flows so that the capital account in the balance of payments disappears.

The balance of payments and the monetary sector

In an open economy the national income identity can be written as

$$\text{gnp} = \text{con} + \text{inv} + \text{ge} + \text{ex} - \text{im} \qquad (5.4)$$

where gnp = gross national product, con = consumption spending, inv = investment spending, ge = government spending, ex = exports, and im = imports. All variables are at constant prices.

Total spending or absorption by domestic residents can be expressed as:

$$\text{abs} = \text{con} + \text{inv} + \text{ge} \qquad (5.5)$$

Equations (5.4) and (5.5) give:

$$\text{abs} = \text{gnp} - \text{ex} + \text{im} \qquad (5.6)$$

Following the monetary approach to the balance of payments theory (discussed in detail in Chapter 8), the absorption function can be specified as:

$$\text{abs} = y + \epsilon(M^s/P - M^d/P) \qquad (5.7)$$

where ϵ is the adjustment coefficient of monetary disequilibrium, whose value lies between zero and unity. Equations (5.6) and (5.7) yield:

$$\text{ex} \quad \text{im} - \epsilon(M^s/P - M^d/P) \qquad (5.8)$$

Taking the exponent of both sides in equation (5.1) yields:

$$M^d/P = \exp(\alpha \ln y - \beta \pi^e) \qquad (5.9)$$

where exp denotes the exponentiation operator.

Substitution of equation (5.9) into equation (5.8) yields:

$$\text{im} - \text{ex} = \epsilon[M^s/P - \exp(\alpha \ln y - \beta \pi^e)] \qquad (5.10)$$

It shows that the trade balance deteriorates with the increase in both the money supply and expected inflation and that it improves with the increase in income.

Supply shock and inflation under the fixed exchange rate system

In an open economy the effect of supply shock on the price level can be examined by taking into account the possibility that any change in each of fiscal and trade deficits due to a supply shock will change the money supply. However, whether the net effect of a supply shock on the money supply will be positive or negative will depend on the possibility of any increase in the money supply from increased fiscal deficits exceeding any decline in the money supply from the reduction in foreign exchange reserves due to increased trade deficits.

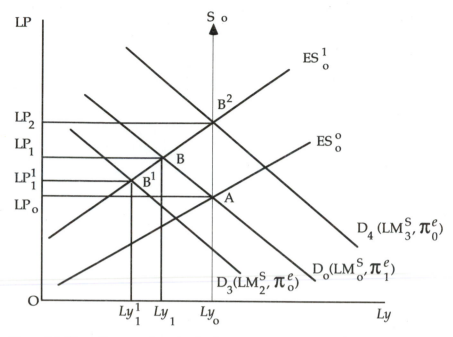

Figure 5.3 The effects on the price level in an open economy of a hands-off and a hands-on policy by the monetary authority following a supply shock

Consider the case when there is a decline in the money supply because of the reduction in foreign exchange reserves at a given level of central bank credit. In Figure 5.3 the decline in the money supply shifts the aggregate demand curve to D_3 (LM_2^s, π_0^e). The temporary equilibrium is at B^1 with the price level LP_1^1 rather than LP_1 and the income level Ly_1^1 rather than Ly_1. It shows that in an open economy the decline in output is larger than that in a closed economy.

Given that the government revenue is dependent on income, the supply shock which reduces income may lower the government revenue and increase the size of the fiscal deficit at a given level of government expenditure. When the government finances fiscal deficits by borrowing from the banking system, it increases the level of the central bank credit component of the money base at a given level of foreign exchange reserves. Assume that such an increase in the money base (or money supply) shifts the aggregate demand curve to the position D_4 (LM_3^s, π_0^e).

As indicated earlier, the net effect of supply shocks on the money supply is determined by the combined effect of the reduction in foreign exchange reserves and any increase in the central bank credit because of monetisation of fiscal deficits. Therefore, the aggregate demand curve is likely to lie some-

118

where between $D_3(LM_2^s, \pi_o^e)$ and $D_4(LM_3^s, \pi_o^e)$. It shows that even if the government does not increase the money supply, the supply shock has a net effect on the money supply – the direction of which cannot be predicted *a priori*. The movement of the price level will depend on the movement of the money supply. When such an uncertainty is associated with changes in price expectations, the monetary authority may create complex forces by adopting an active monetary policy, and the effect of which on the price level cannot be predicted *a priori*.

Supply shock and inflation under the flexible exchange rate system

Consider the following aggregate demand function:

$$y = \tau[b_0 + b_1 \ tb \ (rer) - b_2 \ rir] \tag{5.11}$$

where y is real output; b_0 is autonomous expenditure, tb is trade balance; rer is the real effective exchange rate, defined as: rer = ner.P*/P where ner is the nominal exchange rate of the domestic currency, P* is the foreign price level and P is the domestic price level; and rir is the real interest rate.

It shows that, given the real interest rate, the demand for domestic output is dependent on the real effective exchange rate. A depreciation of the real

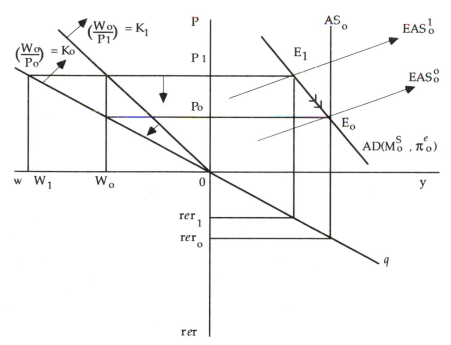

Figure 5.4 The adjustment of an economy following an adverse supply shock under a flexible exchange rate system

119

exchange rate[16] makes the domestic exportable goods competitive in the world market and induces a switch of domestic demand of residents from imports and increases the demand for domestic goods. In contrast, an appreciation of the real exchange rate makes the domestic exportable goods uncompetitive in the world market and induces a switch of domestic demand of residents from domestic to foreign goods and lowers the demand for domestic goods. In the lower part of Figure 5.4, the relationship between the real exchange rate and output is shown as an upward-sloping curve.

Assume that the negative supply shock shifts the supply curve EAS_0^0 to EAS_0^1. It increases the price level from P_0 to P_1 and the real exchange rate appreciates from rer_0 to rer_1. The appreciation of the real exchange rate is the result of the increase in the price level due to supply shock[17] which has not been associated with an instantaneous depreciation of the currency. However, at the price level P_1 the real wage rate has declined because the nominal wage rate has remained unchanged, say, because of short-term wage contracts. The fall in the real wage rate will increase employment and output and the economy will move from E_1 to E_0 and will be associated with a depreciation of the real exchange rate as the price level declines.

The adjustment process discussed above rules out any active government intervention in the form of monetary policy. An alternative to automatic adjustment is the adoption of an expansionary monetary policy to expedite the adjustment process so that the adverse costs of supply shock are minimised. However, any expansion of the money supply will shift the demand curve rightward and ignite inflation because of the expectations-induced leftward shift of the supply curve and the rightward shift of the demand curve. Therefore, if inflation is a concern to policy-makers, any accommodating monetary policy would be undesirable after the supply shock.

SUMMARY AND CONCLUSION

This chapter has examined the role of monetary policy in stabilisation in developing countries. The main question addressed is whether monetary policy should be, and can be, used for the stabilisation of developing economies. The role of monetary policy in stabilisation has been examined in the context of economic disturbances originating from both the demand and the supply sides.

A review of the sources of demand disturbances suggests that although there are possibilities of demand disturbances in developing economies originating from both domestic and foreign sources, they are unlikely to be rampant and persistent. The parameter values of the consumption, investment and money demand functions suggest that developing economies are also not highly sensitive to demand shocks. Indeed, as the real wage rate and the real interest and exchange rates in developing countries are flexible, it is possible that any demand shocks to developing economies would be adjusted

Table 5.3 Money growth, fiscal deficit and inflation in Bangladesh

| Year | Growth rate of | | Government | Fiscal | Rate of |
	$M1^a$	$M2^a$	expenditure[b]	deficit[b]	Inflation[c]
1973	43.5	44.9	20.5	−15.5	49.0
1974	21.9	25.2	11.4	−6.3	54.8
1975	10.2	15.2	8.6	−3.5	21.9
1976	1.4	4.1	12.8	−3.8	2.3
1977	13.3	21.1	17.3	−8.4	4.8
1978	17.5	21.9	15.4	−7.9	5.3
1979	24.4	25.0	15.4	−6.2	14.7
1980	16.3	20.4	16.9	−9.3	13.4
1981	12.8	22.4	16.6	−9.0	16.2
1982	8.6	16.6	16.2	−6.5	12.5
1983	14.0	18.5	14.8	−4.8	9.4
1984	33.5	38.9	11.8	−4.9	10.5
1985	27.9	33.4	17.5	−8.7	10.7
1986	11.2	15.9	16.8	−8.6	11.0
1987	7.8	18.1	16.1	−7.5	9.5
1988	−0.5	16.0	14.4	−5.7	9.3
1989	7.4	16.0	15.1	−6.6	10.0
1990	9.7	16.6			

Sources: Various issues of: *Economic Indicators of Bangladesh, Economic Trends* and the *Statistical Yearbook of Bangladesh.*

Notes
[a] the money growth rate (%) is calculated from 12 monthly average figures
[b] per cent of GDP
[c] inflation rate is defined as a percentage change in the consumer price index for the middle-class people at Dhaka

through the price mechanism and there may not be any need for active stabilisation by the government.

Although demand shocks are not so prevalent in developing countries, they frequently experience supply shocks originating from the agricultural sector. However, agricultural supply shocks are random and they do not persist. The question of whether the monetary authority should adopt a hands-on or a hands-off policy has been analysed by applying a model. It is found that the conduct of active monetary policy after a negative supply shock has the danger of igniting inflation. Therefore, when the danger of inflation is real after a negative supply shock, the monetary authority may even think of adopting a contractionary monetary policy to dampen inflationary expectations (Barro, 1981; Rivera-Batiz, 1985).

APPENDIX. CROP FAILURE AND INFLATION: THE CASE OF BANGLADESH

Bangladesh is predominantly an agricultural country. It frequently experiences droughts and floods that cause substantial crop losses. Food crop losses to droughts and floods are often believed to be a cause of inflation in Bangladesh (Ahmed, 1984).

The first major supply shock to the Bangladesh economy after independence came in August 1972 when the country was gripped by a severe drought. It damaged all major crops and the estimated loss in 1973 was about 20 per cent of agricultural output. The second shock came in the wake of floods during the last quarter of 1973. The climax was reached during June–September 1974 when the country was afflicted by major floods which damaged food crops. The situation became worse in 1973 when the oil shock fully impacted on a war-ravaged economy.

Table 5.3 shows that Bangladesh's inflation during 1973–5 was about 42 per cent per annum. Data for money growth, government expenditure and fiscal deficit also suggest that the Bangladesh government adopted expansionary monetary and fiscal policies during 1973–4. Therefore, even though it is difficult to make any distinction between the primary and secondary sources of inflation in Bangladesh during 1973–5, it appears that expansionary monetary and fiscal policies during and after the supply shocks generated an explosive inflationary situation.

Figure 5.5 explains the inflation episode in Bangladesh during 1973–5. Assume that the Bangladesh economy during 1969–70 was at point A

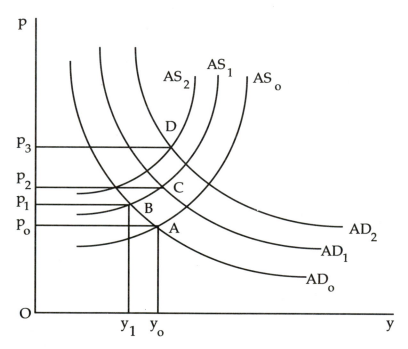

Figure 5.5 The crop failure and inflation episode in Bangladesh, 1973–5

with the price level P_0 and output y_0. The supply shocks, such as the liberation war-related destruction of productive capacity of the economy and the subsequent floods in 1973 and 1974, shifted the supply curve from AS_0 to AS_1. It moved the economy from A to B, which increased the price level from P_0 to P_1 and lowered output from y_0 to y_1. The adoption of expansionary monetary and fiscal policies, which began early in 1972, shifted the demand curve from AD_0 to AD_1 and caused a further increase in the price level to P_2. With the acceleration of inflation, the inflationary expectations of the people built up. The result was the shift in both the aggregate supply curve to AS_2 and the demand curve to AD_2, which increased the price level to P_3. Therefore, it appears that if the Bangladesh government did not adopt expansionary monetary and fiscal policies, the supply shock might have increased the price level only to the level P_1 but not to the level P_3.

Consider the fact that Bangladesh did not experience any sustained inflation in the 1950s and 1960s, although weather and weather-related factors lowered agricultural output and increased agricultural prices on some occasions. Such a price increase was reversed within a short period of time after a good harvest. There were not even two years in a row with high inflation. It was because inflationary expectations did not build up in the minds of the people and the government maintained conservative monetary and fiscal policies. As Papanek points out:

> The civil servants and military, who dominated decision making for most of the twenty years, were inclined to conservative fiscal and monetary policies. They had a pre-Keynesian abhorrence of deficits. An attitude of 'a gentleman does not incur debts he cannot meet' was carried over from family to national budgeting.
>
> (Papanek, 1981: 401)

Since the mid-1970s Bangladesh has experienced a number of major floods and droughts. For example, in 1979 a major drought caused food shortage and in 1988 a devastating flood hit the economy. On both occasions it was possible to keep inflation under control through both emergency imports of foodgrain and conservative monetary and fiscal policies. The 1988 floods were particularly severe as were those in 1974, but they increased the relative price of food only marginally and this rise was reversed quickly (Chadha and Teja, 1989).

The Bangladesh case suggests that conservative monetary and fiscal policies during and after supply shocks can keep inflation under control. When the supply shocks are random and one-off affairs, the government's hands-off policy may dampen inflationary expectations. However, when the damage is substantial, the government may need to take measures such as the importation of foodgrain and releasing stocks of foodgrain to stabilise food prices. Such measures should be taken on an emergency basis. In contrast, any cash handouts to the affected people and wild promises may worsen the inflationary situation.

NOTES

1 One standard definition of stabilisation is given in the *Economic Report of the President of the United States* (1962: 68):

> Stabilization does not mean a mere levelling off of peaks and troughs in production and employment. It does not mean trying to hold over-all demand for goods and services stable. It means minimizing deviations from a rising trend, not from an unchanging average.

2 Liquidity trap refers to a situation where the interest rate is very low and is not expected to fall any further. At that interest rate, money and bonds become perfect substitutes, and the demand for money infinitely elastic.

Investment pessimism refers to a situation where investment is not very sensitive to changes in the interest rate. It happens when the general economic environment and profit expectations are weak.

The existence of any one of these can make monetary policy ineffective.

3 Along with the works of Milton Friedman and his collaborators, the works of Brunner and Meltzer (1963, 1968) have been important.

4 Bomhoff (1983) has reported empirical evidence on the monetarist contention that the growth rate of money matters for short-term fluctuations in economic growth and for longer-term trends in inflation.

5 Monetarists consider economic policy as the design of institutions and rules which, they believe, would lower uncertainty and variability for society as a whole. They also believe that activist monetary-fiscal policy may destabilise an otherwise stable economy. If minimising fluctuations is the goal of fiscal activism, monetarists even claim that in this respect they are closer to Keynes. As Meltzer writes (1981: 62):

> Keynes's main concern in the General Theory and after is to reduce the instability of the economy by eliminating fluctuations in the most volatile elements, not to substitute one source of variability for another. Keynes, the probabilist, appreciated that variable policies affect expectations and can increase uncertainty.

6 The major studies in this area are by Aghevli *et al.* (1979); Bottomley (1965); and Park (1973). Coates and Khatkhate (1980) also contain a collection of papers on stabilisation. Moreover, the question of stabilisation in developing countries with respect to inflation and balance of payments has received attention in the IMF and World Bank studies. For details, see Ahmed (1986) and Khan (1987a, 1987b) and the references therein.

7 Following Argy (1992), the degree of wage flexibility can be estimated from the relationship: $Lw = \psi(Ly - Ly_f)$, where Lw is the real wage rate, Ly and Ly_f are actual and full employment levels of real output (all are in logs) and ψ is the degree of wage flexibility which would take a value between zero and ∞. He cites a list of empirical studies which provide empirical evidence on the relationship between real wage flexibility and unemployment performance in industrialised countries.

8 Both McKinnon (1973) and Shaw (1973) believe that the neoclassical investment model is not appropriate for developing countries. They developed a model of finance in economic development in which the real deposit rate of interest

has a positive effect on savings and investment.

9 Depending on whether the terms of trade shock is transitory or permanent, the effect of it on consumption expenditure will differ.

10 Agriculture is the dominant sector in most developing countries. It produces more than 50 per cent of GDP and employs about two-thirds of the labour force.

11 Chowdhury and Islam (1993) have examined the wage behaviour in East Asian countries. They found that the real wage rates in those countries are determined by market forces, although countries like Singapore and South Korea pursue various forms of wages and incomes policies.

12 See Bruno and Sachs (1985).

13 Economists of the Keynesian persuasion suggest that an active monetary policy should be adopted after a supply shock to neutralise its adverse effects on output and employment. In contrast, monetarists suggest that the monetary authority should not adopt an active monetary stabilisation policy after a supply shock because its hands-off policy may force prices to fall from a higher level when the shock is over.

14 Expected inflation, rather than the interest rate, is used in the specification to represent the opportunity cost of holding money. Such a specification is suitable for developing countries where money and capital markets are underdeveloped so that asset substitution takes place between money and real assets and not between money and financial assets. However, the interest rate can be included in the specification, which will not change the structure of the model.

15 Note that even if price expectations are formed rationally, the actual price level may vary independently of the expected price level to the extent that there are random (hence unexpected) demand shocks. This implies a non-vertical, positively sloped AS curve and thus output fluctuates *for any given expected price level.*

16 A rise in real exchange rate is depreciation while a fall is appreciation.

17 For the real exchange rate to remain unchanged, any increase in the price level must proportionately depreciate the domestic currency. It follows from the definition of the real effective exchange rate. That is, $r\hat{e}r = n\hat{e}r + \hat{P}^* - \hat{P}$, where $\wedge$ denotes percentage change of a variable. When $\hat{P}^* = 0$, $n\hat{e}r$ must equal $\hat{P}$ to keep $r\hat{e}r = 0$.

6

MONEY SUPPLY
AND THE CONDUCT OF
MONETARY POLICY

Monetary policy entails manipulation of the stock of money or interest rates to achieve some specific objectives. It presupposes the controllability of the money supply and the reliability of the relationship between money supply and the ultimate goal. However, both controllability and reliability are contentious issues in the debate about the effectiveness of monetary policy. The reliability of monetary policy crucially depends on the stability of the money demand function and this issue is examined in the next chapter. The focus of this chapter is the controllability of the money supply.

However, before examining the issues pertaining to controllability, it is useful to review conceptual distinctions among variables in terms of their roles as instruments, intermediate targets and goals in the conduct of monetary policy. An instrument variable is one that can be directly controlled by the relevant policy authority. Instruments are needed because the monetary authority cannot directly control the stock of money. As the term indicates, the intermediate targets are variables that are more directly related to both instruments and goals in a two-stage process whereby the policy-maker first chooses a time path for a target variable, such as narrow money or the interest rate, that promises to lead to desirable outcomes for the goal variable. In the second stage, the policy efforts are devoted to the achievement of a target path for the target variable by way of manipulating instruments. The goal variables represent the ultimate objectives of monetary policy, such as the stability of the price level and economic growth.

The survey of evidence in Chapter 3 revealed that there is a weak or no correlation between money supply growth and economic growth in the long run. It was also demonstrated in Chapter 5 that money supply affects real output only in the short run so long as there are rigidities in the system. On the other hand, there is overwhelming evidence showing that monetary expansion has been an important influence on inflation. Thus there is a broad consensus that the stability of the price level should be the ultimate goal of monetary policy.

A MONEY MULTIPLIER MODEL OF THE MONEY SUPPLY PROCESS

This section specifies a simple model of the money supply process to examine the controllability of monetary aggregates in developing countries.[1] The model is based on the fractional reserve system in which commercial banks are required by law to keep a fraction of their deposit liabilities as reserves with the central bank.

Monetary aggregates can be defined either narrowly or broadly. The narrow money (M1) comprises currency in circulation (Cp) and demand deposits (Dd)

$$M1 = Cp + Dd \qquad (6.1)$$

The broadly defined money (M2) is

$$M2 = Cp + Dd + Dt = M1 + Dt \qquad (6.2)$$

where Dt = time or fixed deposits.

Assuming that total deposits are divided into demand and time deposits in a fixed ratio (e), then

$$e = Dt/Dd \qquad (6.3)$$

Substitution of equation (6.3) in equation (6.2) yields

$$M2 = Cp + (1 + e) Dd \qquad (6.4)$$

While the currency held by the non-bank public (Cp) is the central bank's liability, deposits (Dd and Dt) are the liabilities of commercial banks. Thus M1 and M2 represent the liabilities of the banking system and it is essential to examine the balance sheet of the banking system for an understanding of the process of money creation. The central bank's balance sheet is given as

$$NF + CG + CB = Cp + Rb \qquad (6.5)$$
$$\text{(Assets)} \qquad \text{(Liabilities)}$$

where NF = net foreign assets; CG = credit to government; CB = credit to banks; Cp = currency held by non-bank public; and Rb = commercial banks' reserves with the central bank.

The central bank's liabilities which include currency held by public (Cp) and reserves held by commercial banks (Rb) are known as monetary base (MB), so that

$$MB = Cp + Rb \qquad (6.6)$$

The reserves–deposits ratio (rd) is defined as

$$rd = Rb/(Dd + Dt) \qquad (6.7)$$

Substitution of equation (6.7) in equation (6.6) yields

$$MB = Cp + rd\,(Dd + Dt) \qquad (6.8)$$

Dividing equations (6.1) and (6.4) by (6.8):

$$M1/MB = (Cp + Dd)/[Cp + rd\,(Dd + Dt) \qquad (6.9a)$$

$$M2/MB = [Cp + (1 + e)\,Dd]/[Cp + rd\,(Dd + Dt)] \qquad (6.9b)$$

Dividing both the numerators and the denominators on the right-hand side of equations (6.9a) and (6.9b) by Dd, we obtain

$$M1/MB = (cd + 1)/[cd + rd\,(1 + e)] \qquad (6.10a)$$

$$M2/MB = (cd + 1 + e)/[cd + rd\,(1 + e)] \qquad (6.10b)$$

where $cd = Cp/Dd =$ the currency–demand deposits ratio. Rearrangement of equations (6.10a) and (6.10b) yields

$$M1 = mm_1\, MB \qquad (6.11a)$$

and
$$M2 = mm_2\, MB \qquad (6.11b)$$

where $mm_1 = (cd + 1)/[cd + rd\,(1 + e)] > 1$ and $mm_2 = (cd + 1 + e)/[cd + rd\,(1 + e)] > 1$.

Both mm_1 and mm_2 are greater than one and thus equations (6.11a) and (6.11b) imply that M1 and M2 exceed the central bank's monetary liabilities (MB). The reason for money supply to exceed base money is the fractional reserves system. It allows commercial banks to keep only a fraction of their deposit liabilities as cash and reserves and to loan out the rest that creates the credit money. If banks were to keep 100 per cent of their deposit liabilities as reserves, then the value of the money multiplier would be equal to one. Thus, in a fractional reserves banking system, a given change in base money will lead to a multiple expansion of the money supply. The parameters that determine the money multiplier are the currency–demand deposits ratio (cd), the ratio of time to demand deposits (e), and the reserves–deposits ratio (rd). These parameters can change with changes in the interest rate. For example, if the interest rate on time deposits rises, people may economise on holding cash and more money may be kept in the form of time deposits. This will reduce the value of the currency–deposits ratio and increase the value of the ratio of time to demand deposits. As commercial banks may also reduce excess reserves, the reserves–deposits ratio can fall. The net result of all these effects of a rise in the interest rate is an increase in the value of the money multiplier. The value of the money multiplier is also affected by changes in the required reserves ratio (rr). If the government wants to reduce the money supply for a given level of monetary base, it can raise the required reserve ratio. This will raise rd and reduce the money multiplier.

However, in the short run the money multiplier can be assumed constant. Therefore, changes in the base money alone will cause the money supply to change. From the balance sheet identity (6.5), it is evident that changes in the base money or the central bank's liabilities originate on the asset side of the balance sheet. Credit to the government is an asset for the central bank. The government borrows from the central bank to finance its budget deficits. Budget deficits are also financed by borrowing from both non-bank public and commercial banks. Thus CG can be decomposed as

$$CG = PSBR - GP - GB \qquad (6.12)$$

where PSBR = public sector borrowing requirement; GP = government borrowing from the non-bank public; and GB = government borrowing from commercial banks.

Equation (6.12) shows that budget deficits financed by borrowing from the non-bank public do not affect the base money and hence the money supply. Government borrowings from commercial banks also do not affect the central bank's balance sheet.[2] However, if the government borrows from the central bank, it increases the money supply. The government generally writes cheques drawn on the central bank. The cheque recipient deposits the cheque in his/her account with the commercial bank. The bank sends the cheque to the central bank and the central bank credits the amount to the bank's account with the central bank. Thus, there will be an equivalent increase in both assets and liabilities of the central bank. As for the commercial bank, there will be excess reserves which enable it to expand credit, leading to a multiple expansion of the money supply.

Another element of the monetary base is net foreign assets. The net foreign assets change due to balance of payments outcomes under a fixed exchange rate system. When the balance of payments is in deficit, the residents of the country need more foreign currency than foreigners need local currency. This creates pressure on the domestic currency to depreciate. In order to keep the exchange rate fixed, therefore, the central bank supplies foreign currency at the fixed rate. The opposite happens when there is a balance of payments surplus.

Commercial banks borrow from the central bank whenever their reserves fall short of the legally required level. This normally happens when they make excessive loans. When the government wants to boost the economy, the central bank gives credits to commercial banks at a low rate (discount rate). It enables commercial banks to make loans to the private sector.

The link between government deficits, net foreign assets, commercial banks borrowing from the central bank and the money supply can be shown more explicitly by examining the consolidated balance sheet of the banking system. The balance sheet of commercial banks is given by

$$LP + GB + Rb = Dd + Dt + CB \qquad (6.13)$$
$$\text{(Assets)} \qquad\qquad \text{(Liabilities)}$$

where assets are loans to the non-bank public (LP), credit to government (GB), and reserves with the central bank (Rb). The liabilities are deposits (Dd + Dt) and credit from the central bank (CB).

Combining the accounting identities (6.5) and (6.13) the consolidated balance sheet of the banking system is obtained as

$$CG + NF + LP + GB = Cp + Dd + Dt \qquad (6.14)$$

Substitution of equation (6.12) in equation (6.14) yields

$$M = PSBR - GP + LP + NF \qquad (6.15)$$

Equation (6.15) shows that there are two main sources of money creation. The first is changes in the banking system's total domestic credit (PSBR − GP + LP), and the second is changes in net foreign assets (NF). This is the basic formulation used in the structural adjustment programme of the International Monetary Fund (IMF). One of the fundamental aspects of the adjustment programme is to reduce domestic credit to achieve a stock of money consistent with a target balance of payments outcome (NF). This issue is discussed in greater detail in Chapter 8.

BUDGET DEFICITS AND MONEY SUPPLY IN DEVELOPING COUNTRIES

The most common source of changes in the reserve money in developing countries is government borrowings.[3] Due to the absence of a well-developed bond market, government budget deficits are normally financed by borrowing from the central bank. Table 6.1 presents estimates of budget deficits as a percentage of GDP and the proportion of central bank's credit to the government as well as the average annual growth rates of narrow money (M1) in selected developing countries for two sample periods. It shows that a significant proportion of the central bank's credit went to the government. It also reveals that there was a close association between the proportion of credit to the government and the growth of the money supply. Therefore it supports the general hypothesis that there is a direct link between government budget deficits and the growth of money supply.

Another common feature of developing countries is a persistent large current account deficit not matched by autonomous capital inflows. Since most developing countries have a fixed or pegged exchange rate, deficits in the balance of payments have to be financed by running down the central bank's reserves of foreign currency with a negative impact on the money supply. Similarly, inflows of foreign aid and remittances from migrant workers may affect the money supply positively.[4] Of course, the central bank can offset the impact of both budget and current account deficits by changing other components of its assets through open market operations. However, the scope for open market operations is limited in developing countries due to the absence of

Table 6.1 Budget deficits and money supply in selected developing countries

Country	1963–73			1983–88		
	GBD	CBC	GM1	GBD	CBC	GM1
Ecuador	2.7	48.2	16.5	1.2	38.4	27.9
Honduras	1.3	24.2	10.4	8.0	38.5	10.7
Mexico	2.0	42.9	12.9	9.1	56.9	69.8
Nicaragua	1.2	22.8	12.0	22.9	74.3	214.4
Uruguay	2.3	44.2	16.5	3.0	46.1	27.9
Ghana	4.8	51.4	12.7	1.2	50.9	47.4
Kenya	3.8	10.8	14.8	4.2	62.4	12.0
Nigeria	2.1	41.2	13.7	4.7	77.6	11.4
Tanzania	4.6	25.4	13.4	5.9	93.3	21.9
Uganda	6.5	47.7	26.0	3.9	86.5	105.5
India	4.3	82.3	11.1	7.9	74.6	15.2
Korea	0.8	33.4	29.1	0.6	15.1	13.3
Malaysia	5.4	5.6	13.0	8.2	17.6	9.1
Singapore	0.3	–	13.1	–2.4	–	7.2
Sri Lanka	6.6	84.5	5.9	9.2	67.8	15.2

Sources: Edwards and Tabellini (1991: Tables 7A and 8); International Monetary Fund, *International Financial Statistics* (various issues)

Notes
GBD = government budget deficit as a percentage of GDP
CBC = proportion of central bank's credit to the government
GM1 = average annual growth rate of M1

secondary bond/securities market. Taylor has provided a description of these features:

> The conclusion ... is how *little* control the Central Bank ... has over the money supply. The two biggest components of its [central bank] portfolio are likely to be government debt and foreign reserves, and fluctuations in these holdings may be completely beyond its control. The Bank has to 'print' money by absorbing government obligations if the Finance Minister orders it to do so, and it has no possibility of subsequently contracting the money supply by selling in the open market. Similarly, it has little influence on the current account deficit and resulting foreign currency movements. Shifts in reserve requirements are a rather clumsy tool; if public demand for loans is not too high, rediscount [commercial banks' borrowing from the central bank] may be ineffective. The total supply of credit in the economy is determined by agents other than the Central Bank, and the money supply along with it.
>
> (Taylor, 1979: 27)

Similarly, Dornbusch (1993: 29) concludes, 'monetary policy does not play an independent role in stabilization; it is dictated by the budget and the exchange rate policy'.

There are three broad hypotheses regarding the link between budget deficits and money supply. The first, found in the literature on hyperinflation, is that the monetary authority uses money creation to finance the public sector deficit. As discussed in Chapter 2, monetary expansion is a deliberate attempt to create inflation in order to generate revenues from inflation tax for the government. This phenomenon is known as forced savings in development economics. This view is also implicit in the International Monetary Fund policy prescriptions that seek to control public sector deficits as an essential element of monetary and balance of payments stabilisation.

The second view, more prominent in the writings of the structuralist school, is that 'the authorities have imperfect control of the fiscal apparatus and that under these conditions, money creation is the only source of finance' (Dornbusch and Fischer, 1981: 330). Tanzi (1982) has identified five 'structural causes' for fiscal deficits in developing countries. They are the price-inelastic tax system, the public sector enterprise performance, increased expenditures for political exigencies or administrative weaknesses, export boom, and worsening of the terms of trade.

The price-inelastic tax system refers to a situation when the collection of tax revenues lags behind the occurrence of a tax liability during inflation.[5] This happens due to widespread use of specific *ad rem* rates, unrealistic customs valuations, and controlled prices for some taxed products. When the decline in the ratio of taxes to gross national product is not accompanied by a reduction in public expenditure, the government resorts to deficit financing through the central bank.

Many developing countries are characterised by ailing public sector enterprises. Regular bailing-out of these enterprises creates a hole in the government budget. The problem is exacerbated by the fact that governments generally control the prices of public sector goods and services to control inflation.

Governments in many developing countries also cannot resist the pressure to increase current expenditures following windfall gains from a temporary rise in export earnings. This creates budgetary problems if expenditures cannot be cut back when the export boom disappears. In fact, the roots of the debt crises of Nigeria and Mexico in the 1980s lay in the unanticipated decline in oil revenues.

The worsening of the terms of trade is the reverse of the export-boom scenario for importing countries. If the prices of essential imports rise, there will be a reduction in real income as higher import prices are passed on to consumers. This should result in a reduction in real expenditure. However, governments in developing countries are often forced to subsidise imports or reduce taxes to neutralise the inflationary impact of the import price rise.

The result of the failure to pass-through the import price increase is the fiscal disequilibrium.

The third and emerging view is the political economy explanations for the direct link between budget deficits and monetary expansion. For example, Dornbusch and Edwards (1990) refer to 'macroeconomic populism' – a policy perspective on economic management that emphasises economic growth and income redistribution. The populist governments in many developing countries undertake ambitious development programmes which are largely unfunded and are often financed by money creation. They underestimate the risks of deficit financing, inflation, external constraints and the reaction of economic agents to aggressive non-market policies. Healey and Page (1993: 284) believe that the degree of political instability in developing countries has a systematic influence on fiscal deficits and monetising them: 'The more uncertain are rulers' expectations of the duration of their power, the higher the degree of fiscal and monetary irresponsibility.' Cukierman *et al.* (1989) argue that the ruling government has a vested interest in the persistence of an inefficient tax system. The government refrains from reforming the tax system for fear that a more efficient tax system will help an incoming government formed by the opposition. Of course, the problem becomes much more acute in a society characterised by a politically more unstable and polarised system. A similar idea is shared by Tabellini and Alesina (1990), Alesina and Tabellini (1990, 1989) and Persson and Svensson (1989). They argue that political instability determines the rate of time preference for the society as a whole, and hence matters for any collective intertemporal decision. Edwards and Tabellini (1991) in their study of 21 developing countries have found strong support for the various political instability hypotheses of budget deficits.[6]

MONETARY CONTROL IN A FINANCIALLY REPRESSED ECONOMY

Most developing countries have a repressed financial sector, despite liberalisation since the late 1970s. The hallmark of financial repression is the predominance of direct and non-price indirect credit controls over indirect controls through the price mechanism wherever it is feasible. Table 6.2 presents a summary of factors that affect the money supply and the possible methods of their controls. Currency (Cp), deposits and reserves (required and excess) affect the money multiplier as they define the currency–deposit ratio (cd) and the reserves–deposits ratio (rd). The central bank's lending to the government (CG) and to commercial banks and other financial institutions (CB), commercial banks' lending to the public (LP) and net foreign assets (NF) of the banking system affect the reserve money. As the table indicates, currency, required reserves and government net borrowing from the central bank can be controlled only by direct methods. The rest can be controlled either

Table 6.2 Sources of money supply and techniques of monetary control

Factors/sources of money supply	Direct controls	Indirect controls
1 Currency (Cp)	x	
2 Deposits (Dd + Dt)	x	x
3 Required reserves of commercial banks with central bank	x	
4 Bank lending to non-bank private sector	x	x
5 Government borrowing from central bank (CG)	x	
6 Banks' borrowing from central bank (CB)	x	x
7 Non-bank private sector's borrowing from banks (LP)	x	x
8 Net foreign assets (NF)	x	x

directly or indirectly. The indirect method includes both price (interest rates) and non-price mechanisms. For example, the government can raise the required reserve ratio to reduce banks' ability to create credit indirectly. Alternatively the rediscount rate (the interest rate the central bank charges to commercial banks) can be raised to achieve the same result through the price mechanism. Finally, the government can control private sector credit directly by imposing a ceiling on bank lending.

In so far as the components of base money are concerned, changes in net foreign assets and government borrowings from the central bank cannot be truly regarded as active policy instruments for monetary control. The reason is, as mentioned earlier, that the net foreign assets outcome is the result of balance of payment objectives, and credit to the government adjusts passively to the government's budgetary position over which the central bank may not have any control.

The interest rate ceiling is one of the defining characteristics of financial repression. The maintenance of a fixed interest rate or ceiling may imply that the monetary authority is following an interest rate target by manipulating monetary aggregates. However, as discussed in the preceding section, the authority in most cases does not have much control over the money supply. Moreover, the ceiling rate is not an equilibrium rate, as is obtained under interest rate targeting. The ceiling rate is much below the interest rate that would have prevailed if the demand for money were equal to the supply of money. Thus, when an interest rate ceiling is in place, there will be an excess demand for credit. In such a situation, credit rationing becomes the main feature of monetary policy.

Credit rationing occurs both directly and indirectly. Indirect control involves moral suasion and the use of the required reserve ratio. A high reserve requirement for deposits reduces commercial banks' ability to create

Table 6.3 Reserve requirements in selected Asian countries, 1990

Country	Reserve requirement for sight deposits		Reserve requirement for time deposits		Additional required liquidity ratio		Interest paid on required reserves	
Bangladesh	10	(5)	10	(5)	25	(5)	(yes)	
India	15	(5)	15	(5)	38	(34)	yes	(yes)
Indonesia	2	(15)	2	(2.5–10)				
Korea	13[a]	(14)	13[a]	(10)			yes	(yes)
Malaysia	NA	(10)	NA	(10)	NA	(10)		
Nepal	NA	(7)	NA	(7)				
Pakistan	5	(5)	5	(5)	35	(35)		
Philippines	21	(20)	21	(20)			yes	
Sri Lanka	15	(12)	15	(5)				
Taiwan	NA	(25)	NA	(13)	NA	(7)		
Thailand	NA	(7)	NA	(7)	12	(14)[b]		

Source: Fry (1990 Tables 9 and 10)

Notes:
1980 figures in parentheses
[a] The marginal reserve requirement of 30 per cent raises the average reserve requirement to 13 per cent
[b] Liquidity ratio imposed on commercial banks that open new branches

credit. Table 6.3 presents reserve requirements in selected Asian countries. As we can see from this table, the reserve requirements have gone up in almost all countries except Indonesia and to some extent Korea, implying that reserve requirements constitute an important instrument of monetary control. The table also reveals that most countries do not pay interest on required reserves. This makes it an attractive instrument from the point of view of inflation tax or seigniorage.[7] Governments unable to borrow from the non-bank public due to the underdevelopment of capital markets require commercial banks to purchase government securities through liquidity ratios and reserve requirements. This implicitly gives the government access to low cost bank credits.

The central bank also uses its rediscount facilities whereby commercial banks borrow from the central bank to restrict credit creation. Direct credit control entails specifying the limit on commercial banks' lending to the private sector. In general, the credit ceiling is derived as a residual after the public sector financing requirements are met.[8]

However, to have both the reserve requirement and direct credit control in the armoury of a central bank involves a redundancy. Since the two operate on the assets and liabilities sides of the consolidated balance sheet of the banking system, they must always be equal. At any one time, only one of the two instruments will be binding, depending on the institutional framework in which monetary policy is conducted.

An important feature of a repressed economy is the existence of a dual financial sector – an organised and an informal sector. The informal financial market is largely outside the control of the monetary authority and thus raises the question of effectiveness of monetary or credit policy for stabilisation. Harris (1983), for example, reports increased activity in the informal sector in India when there was a credit squeeze in the formal sector. Sundaram and Pandit (1984), too, tend to believe that the presence of highly elastic supplies of funds in the informal sector offsets any contractionary formal credit policy. However, studies (Asian Development Bank, 1990; Page, 1993; Ghate, 1992) show that there are considerable interactions – both competitive and complementary in nature – between informal and formal sectors. For example, many informal financiers are found to obtain their funds from the formal sector. A study by Vongpradhip (1985) of Thailand show that the source of 48 per cent of the subscriptions in business Rotating Savings and Credit Associations (ROSCAs)[9] was the formal sector, with participants borrowing from banks to finance their subscriptions. Thus, the contraction of bank credit in 1984 was found to reduce significantly the supply of informal credit flowing to ROSCAs. This is consistent with the findings that a credit squeeze in the formal sector causes a significant rise in the informal sector interest rate. In Thailand, the 1984 credit contraction led to interest rate rises of between 50 and 100 per cent in business ROSCAs (Onchan, 1985). Similar findings are also reported in the Philippines and India.[10] Therefore, a restrictive credit policy is likely to affect informal money lending to the extent that it affects the supply of funds to the informal sector. Surveying the evidence, Ghate concludes:

> the effect of linkages was to reinforce demand forces in raising the effectiveness of monetary policy. It is likely that trade credit in particular tends to decrease or increase with formal sector credit, since a particularly large share of informal trade credit originates in the formal sector, from where it percolates down supply and distribution networks informally.
>
> (Ghate, 1992: 867)

A further feature of financial repression is exchange control. The control over capital flows enhances the effectiveness of monetary policy under the fixed exchange rate system. As mentioned earlier, under the fixed exchange rate system, there is a direct link between the changes in central bank foreign exchange reserves and the monetary base. In such a situation, 'domestic monetary policy cannot influence the total money supply, but only its composition between foreign and domestic components' (Aghevli *et al.*, 1979: 813). For example, a restrictive monetary policy through open market selling of government bonds will initially raise interest rates, inducing an inflow of foreign capital as foreigners find it more profitable to invest. The inflow of capital increases the foreign exchange reserves of the central bank and hence the monetary base. The net result is a decline of government securities and an equivalent rise in foreign reserves in the central bank's portfolio without any increase in money supply. However, evidence from Thailand, Taiwan, South Korea and ASEAN show that restrictions on capital mobility provided the monetary authority with some capacity to manipulate the money supply under a fixed exchange rate system.[11]

MONETARY CONTROL IN A FINANCIALLY LIBERALISED ECONOMY

The 1980s have witnessed an increasing number of developing countries deregulating their domestic financial sector. A major aspect of financial liberalisation is the removal of the interest rate ceiling. This means that they have to rely more and more on market-based indirect methods of controlling money supply, mainly through open-market operations and the auctioning of treasury bills. When the central bank sells outstanding government bonds in the open market to the non-bank public, it reduces money supply because people surrender currency in exchange. The non-bank public is induced to buy government bonds by lowering the bond price or raising the interest rate. The higher interest rate reduces the public's demand for credit.

However, the liberalising developing countries find the open-market operations less effective due to the absence of a well-developed capital market. Some Asian countries, for example Sri Lanka, Indonesia and the Philippines, have attempted to tackle this problem by the central bank issuing its own debt instruments, by using private money market securities for open-market operations and by taking measures to encourage the development of interbank markets (Tseng and Corker, 1991: 26). They have also brought the yields on government securities in line with market levels and refrained from forcing the central and commercial banks to absorb government securities.

The liberalisation of interest rates also requires that the mandatory reserve requirements be either relaxed or reduced. Otherwise, the high interest rates that follow liberalisation will imply a higher burden on the banking system because no interest is paid on reserves. This may encourage disintermediation as banks will be reluctant to take more deposits. In recognition of such potential problems a number of Asian countries – for example, Indonesia, Korea and Malaysia – have substantially lowered their reserve requirements. Nepal and Sri Lanka have adopted a more flexible system of averaging to meet reserve requirements and unified reserve ratios for different deposit liabilities. These measures are likely to give banks more flexibility in their portfolio management. The Philippines has adopted the more radical policy of paying interest on reserves held at the central bank (Tseng and Croker, 1991: 26).

The liberalisation of interest rates has, however, implications for the control of the money supply as variations in the interest rate may affect the money multiplier. As shown in the money multiplier model, the central bank expands or contracts bank credit automatically by expanding or contracting the monetary base, assuming that the money multiplier remains constant. One of the conditions for the successful automatic operation of the money multiplier is that demand for bank credit should be interest-elastic, a condition likely to be satisfied when credit is rationed. The removal of interest rate ceilings is likely to reduce the private sector loan-demand. In such situations, banks will have excess reserves so that the reserves–deposits ratio will rise, making the money multiplier smaller. On the other hand, as the opportunity cost of holding excess reserves rises with the increase in interest rates, banks will economise on excess reserves if the private sector demand for bank credit is relatively inelastic. This will make the money multiplier larger. Thus interest rate deregulation can potentially make the money multiplier unstable so that the transmission of changes in the money base to changes in credit expansion or contraction become less predictable. Hence the effectiveness of monetary control in a deregulated environment depends heavily on the behaviour of banks in terms of their portfolio choice between excess reserves and loans as well as the private sector's demand for bank credit.[12]

The instability of the money multiplier can also arise from households' portfolio choice between currency and deposits, as hypothesised by McKinnon (1973) and Shaw (1973). As the deposit interest rate rises people are likely to shift out of currency and other unproductive inflation hedges into bank deposits. This will reduce the currency–deposits ratio and hence raise the value of the money multiplier with the potential for increasing the supply of credit. The evidence from the Asian countries shows that interest rate liberalisation has tended to increase the money multiplier and has had a marked impact on the growth of money supply (Tseng and Corker, 1991: 27).[13]

Another aspect of financial liberalisation is the relaxation of entry restrictions for banks and financial institutions. The increased freedom of entry into the financial market can also have a dramatic impact. For example, 47 new private banks, 15 joint ventures with foreign banks and 600 new branches have been opened in Indonesia following deregulation in the 1980s (Page and Healey, 1993: 314). Furthermore, the competition in the financial sector has forced both banks and non-bank financial institutions (NBFI) to be more innovative with their products. These innovations include flexibility in withdrawing from savings deposits, automatic transfer facilities combining current and savings accounts, chequable savings accounts, automatic teller machines which allow withdrawal from either savings or current accounts. As a result, the distinction between savings and current accounts (and hence between M1 and M2) has become irrelevant for operational purposes. Time deposits have also become more liquid and are increasingly performing the transactions function of money, with the introduction of certificates of deposit which bear the characteristics of a currency note, facilities for premature withdrawal and easy borrowing against the security of time deposits. This poses a problem for the monetary authority in the use of M1, M2 and M3 as intermediate targets. While narrowly defined monetary aggregates are easier to control, their usefulness is lost as broader monetary aggregates such as M3 become more liquid. Furthermore, as the deregulated sector competes more aggressively for deposits with the unregulated sector and other financial institutions, the distinctions between banks and non-bank financial institutions become blurred. This creates additional problems for the definition of monetary aggregates and hence their control since deposits of non-bank financial institutions become part of broad money. While competing for funds, deregulated institutions accelerate the growth of monetary aggregates which are not necessarily related to changes in economic and financial conditions. If there is no significant correlation between the growth of such monetary aggregates and the growth of output then the velocity of money will fall. As we shall discuss in the next chapter, the decline in the velocity of money violates one basic requirement for the successful conduct of monetary policy.

Thus, while monetary aggregates cannot be used as reliable intermediate targets either because they become less controllable or because the relationship between their growth and economic activities weakens with financial liberalisation and innovations, there is a greater use of interest rates as an instrument of monetary policy. However, the use of interest rates as an intermediate target has a limited scope in countries which have liberalised their external sector by removing controls on capital flows. To begin with, their interest rates cannot deviate from the international rate substantially because that induces large capital inflows. This, in turn, adds to inflationary pressure and undermines monetary control. On the other hand, as the experience of Southern Cone countries (Argentina, Chile and Uruguay), the Philippines and Indonesia shows, a sharp increase in domestic interest rates may generate expectations of a large depreciation of domestic currency. This will, in turn, induce capital flight and make domestic currency vulnerable to speculative shocks. As central banks intervene to protect the domestic currency, they lose control over their money supply.

EXCHANGE RATE REGIMES AND IMPLICATIONS FOR MONETARY POLICY

Most developing countries are open economies and follow exchange rate policies that can be characterised as fixed or pegged. It has been demonstrated that under the fixed exchange rate system, changes in net foreign reserves become a major source of changes in the money supply. This implies that the scope for an independent monetary policy in these countries is limited and they cannot for long have an inflation rate different from the world rate (Aghevli *et al.*, 1979: 776). This is particularly so when the capital market is underdeveloped, restricting the central bank's ability to offset the changes in monetary base due to balance of payments deficits/surpluses through open-market operations (known as sterilisation). Hence, it raises the question whether developing countries should move towards a floating exchange rate regime.

Besides providing the monetary authority with direct control over the money supply, it is argued that floating exchange rates insulate a country from external shocks or terms of trade movements. For example, if there is a large balance of payments deficit due to an external shock such as oil price increases, money supply will decline under a fixed exchange rate system in the absence of sterilisation. This will have a contractionary impact on the domestic economy. On the other hand, under the floating exchange rate system, the exchange rate will depreciate in response to balance of payments deficits without any contractionary impact on money supply and the domestic economy.

However, a floating exchange rate regime has been found to come under speculative attacks, making the foreign exchange market more volatile. As a result, fluctuations in exchange rates have been larger than could be explained either by variations in inflation rates or by perceived structural changes among countries. The experience of Indonesia in the mid-1980s has shown that there is a greater likelihood of exchange rate volatility in developing countries if the authorities allow the exchange rate to be determined solely by market forces. As argued by Aghevli *et al.* (1979: 785), 'in the absence of a developed institutional framework – including trading mechanisms, forward markets, and the like – seasonal and random fluctuations, particularly in export earnings, can have a severe destabilizing effect on a freely floating rate'. Furthermore, due to the thinness of markets for their own currencies, the dealers in foreign exchange in developing countries must have access to world currency and capital markets for many monetary services, but the volatility of currency increases the cost of access to those markets.

The insulation property of a flexible exchange rate regime can also be questioned on three grounds. First, developing countries experience domestic supply shocks, such as crop failure, more often than external shocks. Second, sharp and continuous depreciations of domestic currency may be intolerable politically, making a floating exchange rate ineffective against external shocks. Third, if there is currency substitution, as one would expect in the absence of exchange controls, it is reasonable to believe that a rational holder of money balances will diversify his portfolio of currencies. In that case, currency substitution will make domestic money demand sensitive to changes in foreign interest and inflation rates. Consequently, the domestic economy is exposed to monetary shocks from abroad.[14]

On the other hand, by pegging to a major currency or a basket of major currencies, a fixed exchange rate system maintains stability in the foreign exchange market. It minimises the exchange rate risks and also allows holders of domestic currency access to all the services provided by the world market for the major currencies at low cost. Furthermore, under a fixed exchange rate system movements in reserves can neutralise the impact of domestic supply shocks to some extent by allowing domestic absorption to exceed domestic production in the short run. In addition, by linking monetary growth to balance of payments targets, the monetary authority can withstand political pressure for excessive monetary expansion. In fact, for many developing countries with underdeveloped capital markets, the foreign exchange market is the primary vehicle through which the central bank adjusts commercial bank reserves and the domestic money base.

The danger of a fixed exchange rate, however, is that in an inflationary situation it becomes overvalued. Overvaluation in turn creates an expectation of a devaluation. It thus becomes necessary to raise the real interest rate to stop speculation. But a high real interest rate may increase domestic debt service and is likely to worsen the budget. Quite often governments resist devaluation either for political reasons or to prevent speculation on further devaluation. This ultimately brings the economy to the brink of an outright exchange crisis.

Thus, a possible pragmatic solution is to follow a middle-of-the-road approach. It appears that small open developing countries should adopt a crawling-peg system which allows exchange rates to change at a pace that maintains external competitiveness. Singapore provides a clear example of such an approach. Its currency is pegged to an undisclosed basket of currencies. In line with the theoretical model developed by Kapur (1981) and Corden (1984), Singapore uses the exchange rate to insulate the domestic economy from foreign inflation and deflation and to stabilise the rate of inflation. In such an exchange rate regime monetary policy does not play an independent role. The issues pertaining to the choice of an exchange rate regime and monetary policy are again taken up in Chapter 8.

MONETARY POLICY IN SELECTED DEVELOPING COUNTRIES

This account of the conduct and design of monetary policy in developing countries draws on Chowdhury and Islam (1993), Killick and Mwega (1993), Lane *et al.* (1993), Leeahtam, *et al.* (1991), Sowa (1993), Treadgold (1990), and Tseng and Corker (1991).

Kenya

Killick and Mwega (1993) have studied various aspects of monetary policy in Kenya during the period 1967–88. According to them, the government has not seriously attempted to define and execute an independent monetary policy. They also observe that monetary policy has been driven by developments in the balance of payments. The only time Kenya has seriously attempted to control domestic credit was when there were balance of payments difficulties and the IMF programme was in place. For example, in December 1987 the government imposed ceilings on commercial bank lendings to the private sector and parastatals to increase by no more than 0.8 per cent per month. However, the effectiveness of such ceilings can be doubted on the grounds that NBFI credits can substitute bank credits. Moreover, the IMF itself has been relaxed about various creative accounting techniques to manipulate figures in order to bring them within the IMF performance criteria.

The money multiplier in Kenya has been found to be negatively related to the changes in the monetary base. This suggests that discretionary interventions by the central bank to control money supply by variations in the monetary base are likely to be partially offset by the changes in the money multiplier. However, more importantly, the Central Bank of Kenya (CBK) has been found to have very little control over the monetary base. It has virtually no control over the planned level of public sector borrowing requirements. This means that CBK takes the government's domestic financing requirements as given and must work out 'the best ways of raising the necessary loans and of reconciling the government's financing needs with those of parastatal bodies and of private sector to remain within the overall [domestic] credit ceilings' (Killick and Mwega, 1993: 61). This task of the CBK has been reflected in its experiment to sell Treasury bonds in 1986 in order to provide a non-inflationary source of financing the government deficit and at the same time to mop up the excess liquidity due to the coffee boom. However, the exercise was not wholly successful as the non-bank public was generally reluctant to invest in these bonds due to the absence of any established secondary market, making them illiquid, and a tax on interest.

Besides the issue of attractiveness of Treasury bonds, the effectiveness of such tasks of the CBK depends crucially on obtaining reliable estimates of the government's financing requirements. Unfortunately, the budgetary outcomes have not been very predictable. Estimates show that the deficit was subject to extremely large deviations from budget intentions, with a coefficient of variation ranging from 259 per cent to 114 per cent for two sub-periods. This indicates that the CBK has no firm basis to work out the credit limit for the rest of the economy. The expansion of credit to the public sector has always been more rapid than the growth of total credit, and the main source of changes in money supply in Kenya has been found to be the Treasury's claim on the central bank to finance government deficits.

Killick and Mwega's findings also lend support to the monetary theory of balance of payments, that the expansion of domestic credit, especially to the government, has been the main source of balance of payments problems. These findings are also consistent with earlier work by King (1979), and Grubel and Ryan (1979).

Ghana

The money supply in Ghana during the 1970s and early 1980s increased at an annual rate of over 40 per cent, primarily due to large budget deficits financed by borrowing from the Bank of Ghana (BG) and credit to the public institutions such as the Ghana Cocoa Marketing Board and the Ghana Supply Commission. Since the IMF's Economic Recovery Programme in 1983, the money supply growth rate has declined to over 20 per cent per annum. This decline was achieved mainly by fiscal discipline which has brought the budget into surplus since 1985. The dominant source of changes in the money supply in recent times has been the inflow of funds from foreign multinationals, and foreign aid and loans.

The Bank of Ghana attempts to control money supply and credit according to its 'Monetary and Credit Plan' for each year. The BG uses interest rates, reserve requirements, sectoral credit ceilings and mandatory lending ratios to control money supply. The banks are penalised for exceeding the overall credit limits. For example, in February 1989 six banks which violated their credit limits were barred from sponsoring clients to the foreign-exchange auctions for two weeks. The strict enforcement of penalties seems to have made the overall credit ceiling an effective instrument (Sowa, 1993: 103). High inflation has, however, made interest rates ineffective as a tool for monetary control.

Sowa has found that both currency–deposits and reserves–deposits ratios 'exert significant influences on the supply of money' (1993: 97). While the currency ratio is outside the direct control of the BG, the reserve ratio could not serve as an effective instrument for monetary control as banks had excess reserves. Thus, the BG's ability to control the money supply depends on its control over the monetary base. As indicated earlier, the BG has not much control over the monetary base, which is influenced by developments in government budget and balance of payments.

Bangladesh

Like most developing countries with a repressed and underdeveloped financial sector, monetary policy in Bangladesh is restricted mainly to the use of direct or selective controls. The Bangladesh Bank (BB) also uses rediscount facilities to regulate bank credits. The rediscount rate was increased from 5 to 8 per cent in 1974 and to 11 per cent in 1985. However, the upward adjustments of rediscount rates did not discourage commercial banks' borrowing from the BB as these were accompanied by increases in commercial bank lending rates. The liberalisation of the financial sector since the late 1970s has seen the privatisation of commercial banks and the growth of private banks. This has been accompanied by the broadening of the securities market, which has allowed the BB to conduct limited open market operations.

Hossain and Chowdhury's (1994) study shows that the monetary expansion in Bangladesh originates from both domestic and foreign sources. While credit to the public sector was the most dominant factor in the 1970s, domestic bank credit to the private sector has been the single most important source of money supply during the 1980s. Ghafur and Chowdhury (1988) have also pointed out that since 1978 the refinancing programme of the Bangladesh Bank contributed more to the expansion of the monetary base than the government fiscal operations. This reflects the shift in the industrial policy towards increasing liberalisation and privatisation. It also shows that monetary policy in Bangladesh is primarily driven by development objectives rather than stabilisation goals.

Although Bangladesh has a pegged exchange rate system, through controls on capital account it can have independence in setting monetary targets. For example, one major source of foreign capital inflows, workers' remittances, is not included in official reserves of the banking system and neither the Bangladesh Bank nor any commercial banks which maintain foreign exchange accounts of expatriates can create money against deposits maintained in those accounts. However, remittances are used to finance imports under the wage earners' scheme. Hence, inflows of foreign remittances, aid and loans determine the extent of official reserves that are required to finance the balance of payments deficits. This means that the unpredictability of remittances and foreign aid can still have an unforeseen impact on money supply growth.

Sri Lanka

With the liberalisation of the economy since 1977, monetary policy has moved away from the use of conventional instruments such as bank rates and reserve ratios towards market-oriented measures. For example, the primary market for Treasury bills is being used increasingly to achieve broad monetary policy objectives. Since December 1986 arrangements have been made to conduct weekly auctions for Treasury bills. The Central Bank of Sri Lanka buys only the residuals and this has enabled sharp reductions in its holdings of Treasury bills to as low as 40 per cent of total outstanding stock by the mid-1980s from about 90 per cent a few years earlier. Open-market operations in central bank securities and Treasury bills during 1986–7 contributed to a substantial deceleration in the growth of reserve money. But the growth of reserve money accelerated in 1988 due to a sharp increase in the government's financing requirements. Faced with falling foreign reserves and rising inflation, the Central Bank intensified the sales of Treasury bills to the non-bank public in 1989 in order to mop up excess liquidity (Tseng and Corker, 1991: 31).

For the successful implementation of the open-market operations steps have been taken to improve the capital market. Money brokers have been allowed to operate so as to lower the intermediation costs and 'new features were added to the market in response to the emerging demand and supply conditions' (Leeahtam, *et al.*, 1991: 83). For example, rediscount rates have been reduced and required reserve ratios unified at a lower average level of 10 per cent. The banking sector was also deregulated by allowing in foreign banks. The greater competition in the banking sector resulted in innovations in deposit-taking and bank operations. The monetary aggregates have been redefined in 1980 for policy purposes to be in line with developments in the banking system.

Malaysia

Malaysia floated its currency in 1973 and removed all restrictions on capital flows. Although the net foreign assets of the central bank were subject to large year-to-year fluctuations due to the volatility of exports and the capital market, the Bank Negara was able to maintain a stable growth of reserve money by neutralising movements in net domestic assets (Tseng and Corker, 1991: 30). Until 1987 the Bank Negara actively used foreign exchange swaps and the recycling of government deposits (that is, the movement between the central bank and commercial banks) together with adjustments in statutory reserves as instruments of monetary policy. However since then '[o]pen market operations have increasingly replaced the foreign exchange swap arrangements, although reserve and liquidity ratios and credit allocation rules continued to be used as monetary instruments particularly during 1989–90' (Leeahtam, *et al*, 1991: 77). The required reserve ratio has been raised from 3.5 per cent prior to May 1989 to 6.5 per cent by January 1990 in order to mop up the excess liquidity caused by the export boom and large capital inflows. However, this statutory reserve ratio is far less than it was in the mid-1970s. During 1975–6 the statutory reserves and liquidity ratios were approximately 20 per cent.

The financial sector in Malaysia has been liberalised considerably since 1978. The interest rate is almost fully liberalised with the floating of the base lending rate in February 1991, although the sectoral allocation of bank loans is still guided by the industrial prioritisation policy.

The Philippines

Since financial liberalisation and the deregulation of interest rates during the early 1980s, open-market operations have been the main instrument of monetary policy in the Philippines. However, the Central Bank of the Philippines took a pioneering step during the mid-1970s in redressing the problem of a thin capital market by issuing its own liabilities in which to conduct open-market operations. As a result, open-market operations were used increasingly as an instrument of monetary control, although direct allocation of credit to priority sectors remained in place until the early 1980s. During the early

1980s the Philippines went through extreme political uncertainty and macro-economic instability which had significant impacts on monetary growth and external debt, culminating in a foreign exchange crisis in October 1983. However, large net sales of central bank bills during 1984–5 were able to offset a significant expansion of the Central Bank's other assets, notably government securities, and there was a substantial deceleration in the growth of reserve money. Open-market operations in central bank securities were replaced towards the end of 1986 by weekly auctions of Treasury bills. The proceeds were deposited at the Central Bank in special sterilised accounts and these operations limited the expansionary effects of continued increases in the Central Bank's unclassified assets,[15] of emergency lending to two commercial banks, and of increases in foreign reserves during 1987–8 (Tseng and Corker, 1991: 31).

Indonesia

Money supply was largely endogenous in Indonesia until the mid-1960s, driven by rising government expenditures. However, since the stabilisation programme of 1966–8, the government is committed to a balanced budget and there is legislation in place against the monetisation of government debt. The long-term objectives of monetary policy since the failed coup have been a satisfactory rate of economic growth with moderate rates of inflation, a sustainable balance of payments and adequate foreign exchange reserves (Lane et al., 1993: 137–8).

Ceilings on bank credit were the major monetary policy instrument during the 1970s and early 1980s. The overall domestic credit targets were set as a residual, taking the government budget and balance of payments outcomes as given. The overall monetary growth target took account of target GDP growth and a tolerable inflation rate. Like most other developing countries, reserve requirements and interest rate ceilings (for state-owned banks) were also used as monetary policy tools. For example, commercial banks were required to keep 30 per cent of their liabilities as reserves in 1977. However, reserve requirements were largely redundant as the credit ceiling was a binding constraint on bank lending.

Indonesia responded to the first oil price shock with an expansionary credit policy which resulted in the rise of the credit growth rate from 33 per cent in 1972 to 65 per cent in 1973. This had an inflationary impact as the rate of inflation soared from a modest 6.7 per cent in 1972 to 40.6 per cent in 1974. High inflation prompted the authority to curtail credit expansion. During 1976–8 the expansion of commercial bank assets (credit and other items) was less than 5 per cent over target. Money supply grew at a slower rate than expected as banks did not have the incentive to raise deposits because their lending was constrained by credit ceilings. In contrast to the response to the first oil price shock, domestic credit grew much more slowly during the second oil price shock. The growth rate of domestic credit rose from 5 per cent in 1978 to only 9 per cent in 1979. As a result, inflation remained in check. It rose from 8.2 per cent in 1978 to 12.2 per cent in 1981.

Unrestricted capital movements coupled with erratic adjustments of the exchange rate attracted speculative attacks on Indonesian currency in 1984. The fear of sharp devaluation resulted in a heavy outflow of foreign exchange reserves from Bank Indonesia and a sharp rise in the overnight inter-bank rate to a peak of 90 per cent per annum from an average of 22 per cent per annum in the previous month. Bank Indonesia realised that the activity in the inter-bank market was contributing to the speculation against the rupiah, so it responded by reducing the ceiling on interbank borrowing from 15 per cent to 7.5 per cent of total deposits. Bank Indonesia also supplied emergency credits for up to six months to banks with liquidity shortages. Later in 1985, it introduced a new money-market instrument, called *Surat Berarga Pasar Uang* (SBPU), to be used to supply reserves. Bank Indonesia also used foreign-exchange swap facilities[16] aimed at encouraging the repatriation of working balances held abroad in order to increase its own reserves, at least temporarily. However, these measures failed to stabilise the money market completely and speculative pressures continued, especially after the devaluation of the rupiah in 1986 by 31 per cent. This resulted in a loss of US$1.7 billion of Bank Indonesia's foreign reserves in December 1986 and an outflow of US$1.1 billion in May–June 1987.

The government finally took direct and drastic action in late June 1987. The four large state-owned enterprises were asked to transfer part of their deposits at the state-owned banks into a new monetary instrument issued by Bank Indonesia to reduce the state-owned banks' excess liquidity. The commercial banks' excess liquidity was also reduced essentially by requiring them to buy back their SBPUs from Bank Indonesia. These measures wiped out overnight the equivalent of all the available legal reserves, and the only ways in which banks could meet their reserve requirements was by selling foreign exchange to Bank Indonesia or by borrowing through the discount window. However, the rise of the discount rate from 20 per cent to 30 per cent acted as a disincentive for banks to use the discount facility. These measures had dramatic effects, with large inflows of foreign exchange.

The government introduced a series of financial reform measures after 1983. For example, credit ceilings and most interest rate controls on the state-owned banks were removed in June 1983. This necessitated the need for market-oriented instruments of monetary control. Following the experience of the Philippines, Bank Indonesia introduced its own debt certificates to be used in open-market operations in 1984. According to Balino and Sundararajan (1986: 192), these new instruments 'in general proved adequate for day-to-day monetary management'.

147

South Korea

South Korea was the only East Asian newly industrialising country (NIC) to give priority to growth over price stability until the late 1970s. This is quite evident from the fact that South Korea experienced double-digit inflation (nearly 17 per cent) in the 1960s and 1970s while the inflation rate in other NICs was well below 10 per cent during the same period. As Park (1983: 323) has pointed out, 'All groups including business in Korea ... have seldom been willing to put up with the possible setbacks to growth that price stability may require.'

Thus, monetary policy was largely accommodating in response to developments in the real sector of the economy, such as the export-led growth strategy, the grain support programme and the promotion of heavy and chemical industries. As Fry (1985: 300) has noted, 'loans for export activities have been heavily subsidized through an automatic rediscount mechanism. A rapid increase in exports and, hence, export credit has caused a rapid expansion of high-powered money in the form of increased export rediscount.' Accordingly, the money supply growth rate was high (well above 20 per cent on average) during the 1970s.

However, in the aftermath of the second oil price shock, Korea switched its macroeconomic objective to price stability. As Cole and Park (1983: 214) have observed, '[r]ecently ... inflation has become the most important issue in Korea, and there is some indication that both the government and the general public would be willing to trade 1 or 2 per cent growth for greater stability of prices'. Thus, money supply growth rate fell from nearly 25 per cent in 1978 to 4.6 per cent in 1981. In general, the central bank was able to control monetary growth in the first half of the 1980s despite the rise in the money multiplier due to reductions in reserve requirements and increases in interest rates associated with financial liberalisation chiefly by using indirect monetary policy instruments. Even the extension of credit to banks to forestall a financial crisis in 1983–5 did not eventuate in an acceleration of monetary growth because the central bank succeeded in offsetting operations (Tseng and Corker, 1991: 29). Through its control over the banking sector and capital flows Korea has been able to control money supply even when it targeted exchange rates. However, it appears that such controls have weakened with the growth of the external sector and the liberalisation of the economy. Thus, in the latter half of the 1980s, more direct measures, such as a reduction in preferential discounting for export industries, the raising of reserve requirements, the reintroduction of marginal reserve requirements and direct controls on credits, were used to supplement open-market operations such as the sales of monetary stabilisation bonds (MSB) to offset the impact of external payments surpluses. The rediscount rates on most bank loans were also raised during this period.

Taiwan

In contrast to South Korea, Taiwan always had a firm anti-inflationary attitude and was willing to slow down economic growth if there was any sign of overheating. The inflation rate, therefore, was below 5 per cent during the 1960s and 1980s; it reached a two-digit level only during the 1970s, due mainly to the two oil price shocks.

Taiwan pursued an 'active monetary policy both to sterilise the effects of the large overall balance of payments surpluses on the supply of money and to counteract monetary disruptions generated domestically' (Fry, 1985: 310). Like Korea, Taiwan was able to control the money supply, despite following a pegged exchange rate system, through its control over the capital account of the balance of payments. However, at times a rapid build-up of foreign reserves weakened the control over monetary aggregates. In order to cope with such situations, Taiwan revalued its exchange rate and raised reserve requirements. The central bank also issued large volumes of central bank certificates in order to absorb the huge increases in bank reserves arising from trade surpluses in the 1980s. This operation has been successful in reducing the excess reserves of deposit money banks to about only 2 per cent of total reserves since 1986. Again in the late 1980s, the central bank engaged in selective credit controls, adopted higher required reserve ratios and rolled over the central bank-issued bills to tighten excessive money growth when there was a build-up of inflationary pressure. These measures resulted in the rise of interest rates, lessened the growth of bank deposits and credit and hence reduced money supply.

Hong Kong

Hong Kong's macroeconomic adjustments are dictated by the balance of payments situation. Its primary objective is to keep Hong Kong competitive in the international market by controlling inflation. However, the Hong Kong government has so far refused to equip itself with traditional instruments of monetary control. It does not have a central bank, no mandatory cash-reserve requirement, no discount facility and the government does not engage in open-market operations. Until 1972 Hong followed a fixed exchange rate pegged to sterling, a currency board system under which two private banks were entitled to issue bank notes subject to the matching purchase (using foreign exchange) of Exchange Fund certificates of indebtedness; and correspondingly they were required to withdraw notes from circulation, equivalent to the amount of certificates of indebtedness they surrendered to the Fund. Money supply adjusted automatically to maintain equilibrium in the balance of payments.

The link between money supply and balance of payments was broken during Hong Kong's nine-year (1974–83) experiment with floating exchange rates. As Treadgold (1990: 23) has pointed out, during this period Hong Kong provided the purest example of an endogenous money supply linked to domestic economic activities. In 1972, the two note-issuing banks were permitted to acquire certificates of indebtedness simply by crediting the account of the Exchange Fund held at these banks with Hong Kong dollars instead of foreign exchange. This severed the link between net foreign exchange receipts and new issues of notes. Moreover, 'the fact that the currency issue could be increased on demand by the note-issuing banks . . . meant that the currency base was not subject to any direct policy influence' (Treadgold, 1990: 24). Thus, attempts to control money supply through moral suasion, influence on interest-fixing bank cartel and sterilisation of fiscal surpluses were all found to be ineffective. Commenting on money supply during this period, Ho (1983: 351) has noted that 'the money supply seems to be determined mainly by the behavioural parameters of banks rather than by the actions of the monetary authority' (quoted in Treadgold, 1990: 24).

Hong Kong reverted to a fixed exchange rate system pegged to the US dollar in 1983, thus securing a nominal anchor for its currency. This was done in recognition of the fact that in a regime without a central bank, the market could not be relied upon to determine both domestic interest rates and the exchange rate without risking monetary instability (Leeahtam et al., 1991: 68).

Singapore

Singapore has the least inflationary economy among the four East Asian NICs. This has been achieved primarily by using an exchange rate policy. The policy of targeting the exchange rate, however, means that the money supply becomes linked with developments in the balance of payments. Thus, to quote Goh (1982), the former Chairman of the Monetary Authority of Singapore (MAS), 'monetary policy – that is control of money supply – has no place in Singapore . . . Nobody in the Monetary Authority in Singapore (MAS) bothers if M1, M2 or M3 is going up or down.'

This, however, does not mean that the MAS has no influence on money supply at all. The MAS has both internal and external means for varying the size and growth rate of the money supply. Its huge foreign assets can be liquidated and proceeds remitted to Singapore to enhance the volume of local currency in circulation. It can also use its control over the banking sector to put pressure on the commercial banks to repatriate their foreign assets. In addition, the MAS can sterilise a portion of the net inflow of private funds by requiring that it be deposited by the banks at the MAS, as it did in 1972–3 to counteract an anticipated inflationary net inflow of short-term capital. It also imposed credit ceilings on bank lending in 1973 in response to inflationary pressure. Furthermore, the Singapore government can shift its deposits from commercial banks to the MAS and vice versa, and thereby affect money supply.

SUMMARY AND CONCLUSION

The money supply in developing countries is found to be partly endogenous. The endogeneity arises from the link between the monetary base and the government budget deficit and balance of payments developments, as these countries find it difficult to finance budget deficits by borrowing from the non-bank private sector, and they follow a fixed or pegged exchange rate system. Experience shows that monetary policy in developing countries has been passive and accommodating to developments in the real sector. Among the instruments of monetary control, credit ceilings and reserve requirements loom large, although only one of them is effective at any point in time. These instruments are used predominantly to achieve developmental goals rather than price stability, except in a few cases. The lack of a well-developed capital market makes it difficult for any effective open-market operations. The prospect for using discretionary monetary policy to fine-tune the economy in developing countries is poor due to institutional constraints on the flexibility of specific monetary instruments, an absence of well developed information systems giving rise to relatively long 'problem recognition' lags, and a lack of full internal economic integration (Aghevli et al., 1979). The recent liberalisation of the financial sector in developing countries has not improved the situation as the money multiplier has become unstable in response to interest rate changes, and financial innovations have rendered traditional measures of monetary aggregates inappropriate.

However, the experience of the East Asian NICs, especially of Taiwan, shows that it is possible to use monetary policy to control inflation. It is also evident from the experience of Taiwan and Indonesia that the effectiveness of monetary policy can be enhanced significantly if the government is committed to a balanced budget and the central bank is prevented from monetising the government debt. From the low inflation experience of Singapore, it appears that a crawling peg is a pragmatic exchange rate regime for a small open economy. In addition to being an effective anti-inflationary tool, such an exchange rate regime can impose monetary discipline by linking the monetary development to the balance of payments.

NOTES

1 For a more general model of money supply process, see Papademos and Modigliani (1990).
2 This is true if commercial banks do not immediately replenish their reserves by borrowing from the central bank and make credit to the public sector by recalling private sector loans. If, on the other hand, commercial banks borrow from the central bank to adjust their balance sheet for increased holdings of government

securities then it will affect the base money and hence money supply.

3 Summarising the findings of six case studies involving three Asian and three African countries, Page and Healey (1993: 306) note that, with the exception of Indonesia and to some extent Côte d'Ivoire, monetary base was the major factor in variations in money supply: 'Credit to the public sector was the major source of highpowered money.' Also see Aghevli and Khan (1978).

4 In most cases foreign aid and loans do not directly increase the level of foreign exchange reserves as they have counterpart imports. Foreign remittances are also used to finance imports and they constitute a transfer of the ownership of money from importers to the recipients of foreign currency remittances.

5 Known as collection lag. It refer to lags between the time a tax liability occurs and the time the government actually receives the corresponding payments.

6 The central idea of Cukierman et al. (1989) is as follows. An inefficient tax system acts as a constraint on the revenue-collecting capacities of the government. This constraint may be welcomed by those who disagree with the goals pursued by the present government. In particular, a government may deliberately refrain from reforming a tax system, since a more efficient tax apparatus will be used in the future for expenditure and distributive programmes by a government of a different political persuasion. Alesina and Tabellini (1989) consider an economy with two groups – the 'workers' and the 'capitalists' – who have their own political parties that alternate in office. Each party, when in office, attempts to redistribute income in favour of its constituency. With political uncertainty about the identity of future governments, it is optimal for the current government to issue debt as it does not have to bear the future costs of servicing the debt. On the other hand, it can transfer the income through borrowing to its own constituency.

7 For example, if the required reserve ratio is lr then a bank holds \$lrX reserves for deposits of \$X and loans out \$(X − lrX). If the loan rate is b, the bank will earn \$$b$ (X − lrX). Assuming that there is no transactions cost, the bank will pay a deposit rate d of \$$d$ (X − lrX) spread over \$X in deposits. Thus, there will be a wedge between the loan rate b and deposit rate d, given by $(b − d)$ = $b$lr which is the amount of seigniorage. The relationship between deposit and loan rates can be written as:

$$d = b(1 - 1\text{r}) \tag{1}$$

If there is an inflation of p per cent, the loan rate will rise to $b + p$. Therefore, from (1) the deposit rate is

$$d^* = (b + p)(1 - 1\text{r}) \tag{2}$$

Thus, the real deposit rate is

$$d^{**} = d^* - p = b(1 - 1\text{r}) - p\text{lr} \tag{3}$$

Equation (3) shows that inflation creates a further wedge between deposit and loan rates. The amount of inflation tax is $p$lr.

8 This may have an important crowding-out effect on private investment. If public sector investment is less productive, this will have adverse impacts on economic growth.

9 ROSCAs are self-help saving and lending schemes often found in developing countries. They normally do not have any direct linkage with financial institutions and rely on the mobilisation of savings within the informal sector to provide the capital for loans.

10 See Archarya and Madhur (1983), Chandavarkar (1985) for findings on India. For the Philippines study, see Agabin et al., (1989).

11 See Treadgold (1990) for an excellent survey of literature on Asia-Pacific countries

12 Papademos and Modigliani (1990: 441) have developed explicit models of bank behaviour and conclude that 'an analysis of the process of money creation and of the effectiveness of monetary controls in a deregulated environment must place greater emphasis on the behaviour of banks and on their role in the money supply mechanism'.

13 This debate is largely irrelevant where banks continue to behave as in the pre-liberalisation era and do not adjust their interest rate in response to market rates. For example, Cole and Slade (1992: 136) report that in Indonesia after interest rate controls were abolished in 1983 banks simply continued to behave as before. Fry (1993: 37) reports similar situations in Malaysia, Thailand, Turkey and India. Both Arndt (1982: 425) and Drake (1980: 225) have also pointed out that despite the complete abolition of government control on bank interest rates, banks can collectively act as a cartel and refrain from raising deposit rates.

14 Currency substitution also affects the stability of money demand function. For details see Chapter 7.

15 The increases in net other items were associated with losses on the Central Bank's forward cover and foreign exchange swaps and net interest payments on the Central Bank's domestic and foreign liabilities.

16 A swap transaction is a simultaneous purchase and sale for two different value dates. It usually occurs between a commercial bank and a customer who wishes to borrow offshore and convert into domestic currency. The swap transaction covers exchange rate risk.

7

DEMAND FOR MONEY
AND THE RELIABILITY OF
MONETARY POLICY

Money affects output (real and/or nominal) to the extent that it is being spent. If, for example, people hold the increased money supply as cash, then it will not have any impact on expenditure and output. Therefore the monetary authority should be able to predict how much additional supply of money people will hold as cash balances and how much they will spend. Thus the demand for money and its stability hold a critical place in the discussion about the effectiveness of monetary policy. However, the existence of a stable money demand function is only a necessary condition for the reliability of monetary policy. It forms a part of the 'transmission mechanism' that links changes in the money supply to ultimate target variables. The other part of the transmission mechanism involves the way any disequilibrium in the money market impacts on aggregate demand. If people adjust by spending excess cash balances directly on goods and services, then there would be an immediate impact of monetary expansion on aggregate demand. However, if the monetary imbalance works its way through its impact on interest rates via the bond market, it becomes a lengthy and uncertain process.

Economists of all persuasions have expressed doubt about the certainty of the transmission mechanism for one reason or other. For example, according to Friedman (1973: 39):

> monetary policy is a poor instrument . . . thanks to the length and the variability of the lag in the effect of monetary policy, and the limitations of our knowledge about the factors responsible for such lags and about other short-term effects of monetary policy . . .

Keynes (1936) was also sceptical about the effectiveness of monetary policy as he believed that money does not affect spending directly; rather, it works its way through various intermediate channels which can be long and fraught with uncertainty. Despite sharing the scepticism about the reliability of monetary policy, a great deal of controversy centres around the sources of uncertainty in the transmission mechanism. Therefore, it is useful to begin this chapter with a discussion of the transmission mechanism of monetary expansion.

154

THE TRANSMISSION MECHANISM

The followers of the classical school steeped in the quantity theory of money believe that people get rid of any excess money supply by buying goods and services, so that an increase in the money supply in excess of desired demand for it translates directly into increased expenditure. On the other hand, Keynesians hold the view that any excess money supply affects expenditure via the bond market. As people buy bonds, the interest rate falls (bond prices rise), which in turn induces investment spending. Thus, according to the Keynesian school, the relationship between the money supply and spending is indirect.

Schematically, the classical transmission mechanism for monetary policy can be shown as:

$$\Delta M \rightarrow \Delta E \rightarrow \Delta Y \approx \Delta P + \Delta y \approx \Delta y \ (\text{i.e. } \Delta P \approx 0 \text{ in the short run})$$

$$\Delta M \rightarrow \Delta E \rightarrow \Delta Y \approx \Delta P + \Delta y \approx \Delta P \ (\text{i.e. } \Delta y \approx 0 \text{ in the long run})$$

where ΔM = growth rate of the nominal money supply, ΔE = growth rate of nominal spending, ΔY = growth rate of nominal income, ΔP = growth rate of the price level, and Δy = growth rate of real income.

The above relationship between the money supply and output (income) follows from the quantity theory of money expressed as an equation of exchange:

$$MV = Py \tag{7.1}$$

Assuming that the velocity of money (V) is constant, equation (7.1) can be expressed in growth rate form as:

$$\Delta M \approx \Delta P + \Delta y$$

If in the short run prices are fixed or sticky, implying a horizontal aggregate supply curve, then changes in the money supply will change real output. However, in the long run, real output is fixed at a full employment level and the aggregate supply curve is vertical, so that changes in the money supply translate into proportionate changes in the price level.

One crucial factor in the above classical transmission mechanism is the assumption of constancy of the velocity of money. If there is an opposite and equal movement in velocity with changes in the money supply, then the impact of money supply changes will not be transmitted to either the price level or real output. They will be absorbed fully by changes in the velocity. Therefore, both the direction and extent of the velocity's movement have profound implications for the reliability and effectiveness of monetary policy. If the velocity of money remains constant, then *nominal* output will be proportional to the stock of money regardless of the slope of the aggregate supply curve so that monetary policy can be used to target nominal income.

As is well known, the equation of exchange (7.1) can be rewritten as

$$M = \theta Py \quad (\theta = 1/V) \tag{7.1a}$$

Equation (7.1a) represents an equation for the demand for money. Therefore, the constancy of velocity implies that the demand for money is stable.

It is argued that the velocity of money depends mainly on the payments system and expenditure habits.[1] While the payments system depends largely on financial and monetary institutions which do not change in the short run, expenditure habits are influenced by real income, the rate of inflation and/or the interest rate. A rise in the interest rate lowers the demand for real money balances. As the opportunity cost of holding cash increases with the rise in the interest rate, the money holders make their money do more work and turn it over more often, resulting in an increase in the velocity. Similarly, as money loses its value in a situation of accelerating inflation, people economise on cash holdings, causing the velocity to rise. It is believed that transactions need increases with an increase in real income so that people demand more cash balances. Therefore the way in which changes in real income affect the velocity of money depends on the income-elasticity of the demand for money. If the demand for money increases proportionately with an increase in real income (that is, income-elasticity equals one), then the velocity of money will not change. On the other hand, if the income-elasticity of demand for money is less than one, then an increase in real income will increase the velocity. In most developing countries, the income-elasticity of the demand for money has been found to be greater than one. One reason for it may be the process of monetisation of subsistence economic activities (Aghevli et al., 1979; Khan, 1980). A greater than unity income-elasticity of the demand for money may also be the result of the lack of alternative financial assets which wealthholders can hold in their portfolios (Adekunle, 1968). It implies that the demand for money does not entirely originate from transaction needs, and that money also serves as an alternative asset.

The idea that money is an alternative financial asset constitutes a hallmark of Keynes's monetary theory. According to him, money is demanded for both transactions and speculative purposes.[2] Keynes's liquidity preference theory suggests that people hold cash in order to take advantage of fluctuations in bond prices. For example, when bond prices are low (interest rates are high), people buy bonds and hold less cash balances and vice versa. Therefore, it follows that when money supply increases, people get rid of excess cash by buying bonds and thereby drive the bond prices up (i.e. interest rates down). The lower interest rate induces more investment and hence higher output. Schematically,

$$\Delta M \rightarrow \Delta r \rightarrow \Delta I \rightarrow \Delta Y \approx \Delta P + \Delta y$$

where r is the real interest rate and I is investment.

Thus, in the Keynesian model, the money supply affects real output via the interest rate and investment. It makes the impact of monetary policy uncertain. In this scheme the reliability of monetary policy depends on the impact of excess money supply on the interest rate, changes in investment in response to changes in the interest rate and the value of the expenditure multiplier. If the demand for money is such that people keep the entire excess money supply as cash balances, then there will be no impact on the interest rate and output will remain unchanged.[3] Thus, it is important to know the demand for money in order to predict any change in the interest rate as a result of changes in the money supply.

The interest rate or the cost of fund is only one, but an important, factor that influences investment decisions. If other factors, such as future profitability, dominate investment decisions, then changes in the interest rate may not have any significant impact on investment spending. Again, changes in investment will not result in large changes in output if the expenditure multiplier is small. A small expenditure multiplier can result from a high marginal propensity to save, a high marginal propensity to import, and a high tax rate.

In most developing countries, other than high-performing Asian economies, the savings rates are small and the tax systems are ineffective. As a result the value of the expenditure multiplier will be large, although the openness of an economy will dampen the multiplier effect. However, in a financially repressed economy where the bond market is almost absent and the interest rates are controlled, the Keynesian transmission mechanism has little relevance. As Khan notes:

> In such economies, the relatively thin markets for financial securities make the substitution between money and goods, or real assets, quantitatively more important. Added to this general absence of adequate financial assets is the problem created by the authorities who maintain controls, or ceilings, over the interest rates .., Since changes are made fairly infrequently, the interest rate series display very little variation over time, and thus make it exceedingly difficult to empirically detect any systematic relationship between money and interest rates.
>
> (Khan, 1980: 253–4)

Consistent with the above hypothesis, the interest-elasticity of the demand for money in developing countries is often found to be not significantly different from zero (Aghevli, 1977; Aghevli et al., 1979). Furthermore, in financially repressed economies, investment is constrained by the availability of credits. Consequently, any discretionary change in the money supply (credit) may have a significant direct impact on investment and output (Blejer and Khan, 1984; Montiel, 1986; Wijnbergen, 1982, 1985).

Thus, it can be argued that the transmission mechanism in developing countries is closer to the classical description and hence that changes in the money supply are likely to affect expenditure directly. The rationale for such a claim also rests on the fact that most financially repressed developing economies are liquidity constrained. In such a situation, any increase in the money supply will create a large real balance effect and the excess cash balances will find its way to expenditure. Schematically,

$$\Delta M \rightarrow \Delta ERMS \rightarrow \Delta RE \approx \Delta Y \approx \Delta P + \Delta y$$

where ERMS is the excess real money supply and RE is real expenditure.

The idea that an excess real money supply affects real expenditure is a major feature of the monetary approach to inflation and the balance of payments theory (Paris, 1961; Swoboda, 1976; Aghevli and Sassanpour, 1982; Hossain 1989). In this theory, the adjustment process to monetary disequilibrium implicitly assumes an aggregate private expenditure function which depends not only on the level of real disposable income but also on a variable which measures the extent of disequilibrium in the real money market. Economic agents are assumed to spend more or less than their real disposable income depending on whether they are running down or accumulating money balances. Therefore, an excess money supply positively affects the level of private expenditure, and excess demand for money balances results in a reduced level of private expenditure.

In sum, a well-defined and stable demand for money function is a necessary condition for discretionary changes in the money supply to have predictable effects on ultimate target variables, such as inflation, output, employment and the balance of payments (Aghevli et al., 1979: 788). The sufficient condition involves the way money market imbalances impact aggregate demand via either the interest rate effect on investment and/or the liquidity (real balance) effect on expenditure. This, in turn, depends on the structure of financial system. Specifically, it is influenced by the maturity and depth of financial markets and the flexibility of the interest rate. In a financially repressed economy, where interest rates are administratively fixed and credit rationing is the principal element of monetary policy, it is likely that the availability of credit will have a direct and immediate impact on expenditure (both consumption and investment) and output.

MONETARY POLICY IN A REPRESSED ECONOMY

such [financially repressed developing] countries seldom have financial markets and banking institutions sufficiently developed and sufficiently sophisticated to permit what has to be called fine tuning of monetary policy . . .

Friedman (1973: 39–40)

Montiel (1991) developed an elaborate model to examine the impact of monetary policy on aggregate demand in a financially repressed economy.

Table 7.1 The effect of monetary policy on aggregate demand in a financially repressed economy

Monetary policy instrument	Interest rate effect	Wealth effect	Fiscal effect	Total effect
Bank credit	+	+	+	+
Required reserve ratio	−	−	+	?
Administered interest rate	?	+	+	?

Specifically, he examined the impact of four monetary policy instruments: the level of administered bank interest rates, the required reserve ratio, the amount of credit extended by the central bank to the commercial banks, and the intervention of the monetary authorities in the parallel foreign exchange market. He showed that any change in each of the above monetary instruments has three kinds of effects: the interest rate effect, the household wealth effect, and the government fiscal effect. The wealth effect originates from the fact that financial repression entails an implicit system of taxes and subsidies on households as creditors and debtors of the banking system. The present value of these taxes and subsidies changes when changes in the monetary policy instruments affect the effective degree of financial repression, both by changing the rate at which financial repression taxes household portfolios of a given composition and by altering the composition of portfolios in ways that affect the base to which the financial repression tax applies. For example, when the interest rate is not allowed to adjust with inflation, holders of money lose purchasing power just as when they pay taxes. At the same time, if households hold more nominal money in order to maintain the real value of their money holdings, then it represents an increase in the tax base. Therefore, an increase in the administered interest rate reduces the degree of repression and increases the net wealth of households.

The fiscal effect arises from the fact that the central bank's profit is a source of revenue for the government. Changes in monetary policy instruments affect the net profit of the central bank. For example, if the administered interest rate is raised, the central bank's profit and hence the government's seigniorage income rise as the central bank does not pay interest on deposit reserves of commercial banks.

Table 7.1 presents a summary of the effects on aggregate demand of changes in the four monetary policy instruments. The role of bank credit as a demand management instrument is obvious and unambiguous. Within the Montiel model, an increase in bank credit lowers the demand for loans in the curb market (informal financial market). It lowers the curb market rate. As the interest rate in the curb market falls, the degree of financial repression decreases and increases the level of private wealth. A rise in the level of bank credit may then increase aggregate demand for at least three reasons. First, the fall in the interest rate increases investment spending. Second, the wealth effect increases consumption spending. Third, the supply of bank credit to commercial banks increases the profit level of the central bank, which is transferred to the government for spending on domestic goods and services. However, although the net effect of bank credit on aggregate demand is unambiguous, such an increase in demand will be inflationary if bank credits do not have a supply effect. But there are a number of reasons to believe that an increase in bank credit is likely to raise output in developing countries (Hossain, 1989). To begin with, developing countries suffer from the problem of under-utilisation of their capital stocks. An increase in demand will raise their capacity utilisation. Second, as there are many worthwhile projects, an increase in credit is likely to increase investment and hence the productive capacity of the economy. Third, as pointed out by Fry (1981, 1983, 1985), in financially repressed economies the supply-constrained volume of real bank credit limits real working capital funds and hence output. Thus, an increased credit availability will raise working capital and smooth the production process, at least in the short run.

The effect on aggregate demand and output of any rise in the administered interest rate is ambiguous. Adherents of the McKinnon–Shaw hypothesis maintain that raising interest rates on deposits is likely to increase output in the short run. It happens because the rise in the interest rate may induce an increase in savings, which in turn increases the supply of loanable funds and facilitates private investment. For example, according to Kapur, in pursuing an anti-inflationary monetary policy in a financially repressed economy,

> the monetary authorities should initially raise the average nominal deposit rate paid on money holdings, thereby reducing the excess supply of money by raising the demand for real balances. Concomitant with this increase in real money balances there will . . . occur an immediate increase in the flow of real bank credit and hence in real output.
>
> (Kapur, 1976: 778–9)

On the other hand, the neo-structuralists cite the importance of informal credit markets in providing firms with working capital to purchase their variable inputs (labour, intermediate imports, and so on). Thus the cost of credit forms an important element of the variable cost of production and changes in the interest rate can cause a shift in aggregate supply for real output.[4] They also emphasise the possibility that increases in bank interest rates would draw funds from the informal market causing the marginal cost of funds to rise, which in turn would have a contractionary effect on both demand and output. Van Wijnbergen (1982, 1985) cited evidence from South Korea to substantiate this claim. Based on the evidence from the Philippines, Burkner (1982) also argued that, with all asset-holdings unchanged, changes in the informal financial sector and commercial bank deposit holdings must exactly offset each other. The neo-structuralists then go on to claim that such a phenomenon will reduce the overall supply of credit. It happens because banks are required to keep reserves while the informal sector is not, so that the amount of new bank credit created is going to be less than the decline in informal credit. This, however, presupposes that the demand for credit is relatively interest-inelastic. Kapur (1992), on the other hand, argues that the total productive credit may not necessarily decline. He derives his results by considering the motive of the government which receives a 'windfall' seigniorage gain as the monetary base increases with the rise in reserves as a result of higher deposit takings. The government can channel this newly created monetary base to development banks or to commercial banks themselves.[5]

The impact of an increase in the required reserve ratio on aggregate demand is also ambiguous. The direct interest rate effect is negative. Since an increase in the required reserve ratio raises the degree of financial repression, it lowers the level of aggregate demand through the wealth effect. On the other hand, an increase in the required reserve ratio may raise the government revenue from the increased profits of the central bank.

In sum, although the availability of credit is likely to have a direct impact on aggregate demand, there is a considerable ambiguity and lack of consensus about the impact of other monetary policy instruments in a repressed economy.

THE DEMAND FOR MONEY

The existence of a well-defined and stable money demand function is an essential condition for the reliable transmission of the impact of changes in the money supply to aggregate expenditure. In the theoretical literature at least three broadly defined groups of money demand models are dominant. They are single equation demand theory models, portfolio theory models, and inventory theory models. The Chicago School-based demand theory models derive the money demand function in the same way as for the demand for any other durable good. Friedman's (ed., 1956) restatement of the quantity theory of money provided the intellectual inspiration for this model. The portfolio theory models are associated with the Yale School view of the demand for money. The original insight of this theory is attributed to Keynes and has been further developed by Tobin (1958). In these models the demand for money is viewed in the context of a portfolio choice problem with emphasis on risk and expected returns from various financial assets. The inventory theoretic approach to transactions demand for money was developed by Baumol (1952) and Tobin (1956) and later extended by Feige and Pearce (1977). It focuses on the need to hold money in order to smooth the difference between income and expenditure flows, and it explicitly specifies a transactions cost function, where the cost function includes inventory holding costs as well as brokerage costs.

161

As mentioned earlier, the absence of a well-developed capital market, and the resultant lack of various kinds of financial assets of domestic and foreign origin in developing countries, makes the portfolio approach less appropriate. It is often suggested that in developing countries the demand for money originates from the transactions motive. Therefore, it follows that the Baumol–Tobin transactions demand theory should be more appropriate for such economies. However, the inventory theoretic approach is too rigid in its specification[6] and one faces serious practical difficulties in finding necessary data series on brokerage costs and other forms of transactions costs. Moreover, the fact that money is used primarily for transactions purposes does not necessarily imply that a more general theory of the demand for money is inappropriate in developing countries. As Laidler (1985) pointed out, theories of the demand for money based on an application of the general theory of demand are not logically incompatible with the notion that the demand for money arises from its usefulness in making transactions, or with the proposition that it is an excellent hedge against the risks inherent in holding other assets. In a world of certainty, the two reasons for holding wealth are to straighten out the consumption stream and to earn interest. However, in a world of uncertainty which characterises most developing countries, an important motive for holding wealth is the availability of a reserve for emergencies (Friedman, 1957). Of the various forms of wealth, money has always been an attractive asset to wealthholders because of its versatility (Friedman and Schwartz, 1963: 67). Thus the Chicago-based demand theory models à la Friedman are widely used for empirical studies of the demand for money in both developed and developing countries.

Perhaps no other economic theory has received as much empirical attention as the demand for money both in developed and developing countries. In order to review the empirical evidence on money demand behaviour in developing countries, it is necessary to examine the kind of money demand function which is often used for empirical works.

Specification of a long-run money demand function

A typical long-run money demand function[7] for a developing country is specified in the following semi-logarithmic form:[8]

$$\ln m_t^d = \alpha_0 + \alpha_1 \ln y_t^p + \alpha_2 \pi_t^e + \alpha_3 i_t \tag{7.2}$$

where m^d is the desired demand for real money balances (defined as nominal demand for money deflated by the actual or expected price level); y^p is real permanent income, π^e is the expected rate of inflation, i is the nominal interest rate; ln is natural logarithmic operator; subscript t represents time, and αs are structural parameters. The expected signs of the parameters are $\alpha_1 > 0$, $\alpha_2 < 0$ and $\alpha_3 < 0$.

There is considerable controversy over the appropriate definition of money as it affects the interest-elasticity of the demand for money. For example, Friedman's use of the broad money stock variable (Friedman, 1966; Friedman and Schwartz, 1963) has come under criticism. His empirical findings suggest that the interest-elasticity of the demand for money is either statistically insignificant or very low. Many believe that the use of a broad definition of money and the lower interest-elasticity of the demand for money are correlated. In response, Friedman (1959, 1968) and Meltzer (1963) suggested that the appropriate definition of money should be an empirical matter and if the broad money is empirically found to have a more stable relationship with other economic variables than the narrow money, then broad money should be used in empirical analysis.

The use of permanent rather than measured income in the money demand function has also generated a debate. In developed countries, permanent income is usually found to be an appropriate scale variable (Brunner and Meltzer, 1963; Laidler, 1966, 1971, 1985). However, in developing countries, which of the two measures of income is superior is yet to be determined empirically. Adekunle (1968), Diz (1970), Mammen (1970), Fan and Liu (1970) and Khan (1980) found that permanent and measured income-elasticities of the demand for money are more or less close to each other. On the other hand, Fry (1978), Mangla (1979) and Trivedi (1980, 1983) found permanent income a better scale variable.

While in developed countries the nominal interest rate is considered an appropriate proxy for the opportunity cost of holding money, the same does not hold for developing countries (Laidler, 1985; Dornbusch and Fischer, 1990). Because of the fact that in most developing countries the nominal interest rate is institutionally determined and is normally kept below the market clearing rate, it does not capture fully the opportunity cost of holding money. Furthermore, the institutional nominal interest rates are not often adjusted for changes in inflation and consequently the real interest rate becomes negative. In fact, in the absence of a broad range of financial assets, asset substitution in developing countries usually takes place between money and real assets (durable consumer goods, gold and jewellery) as inflation hedges and not between money and other financial assets. Thus the expected rate of inflation, rather than the nominal interest rate, can be regarded as a better proxy for the opportunity cost of holding money in developing countries.[9] However, its coefficient can be used as an indirect measure of the interest-elasticity of demand for money (Aghevli et al., 1979).

Specification of a short run money demand function

Unlike the long-run money demand function where the desired demand for real money balances equals the actual real money stock, the two may not be equal in the short run. Thus the specification of a short-run money demand function depends on channels through which actual real money balances adjust to the desired level. The most widely used form of adjustment function suggests that when there is a discrepancy between desired and actual real money balances, actual real money balances do not move towards the desired level instantaneously; rather, the movement involves a series of partial adjustments over time because of both pecuniary and non-pecuniary portfolio adjustment costs. This partial adjustment function was originally used by Chow (1966). It was derived from the general value theory on the assumption that individuals adjust their actual real money balances to the desired level along the same lines as they would bring stocks of consumer durables to their desired levels. According to Chow, actual changes in real money balances spring from two sources: first, a fraction of the discrepancy between the desired and actual real money balances is eliminated through changes in actual real money balances; and second, a fraction of saving[10] out of transitory income is held in monetary form and hence changes actual real money balances. Assuming that changes in real money balances arising from savings out of the transitory component of income are white noise, the Chow real money balance adjustment function can be specified as

$$\ln m_t - \ln m_{t-1} = \gamma(\ln m_t^d - \ln m_{t-1}) + u_t \qquad (7.3)$$

where m is actual real money balances, γ is the coefficient of elasticity of adjustment whose value is expected to lie between zero and unity, and u is the disturbance term which allows for random influences in the adjustment process.

Substitution of equation (7.2) into equation (7.3), and rearrangement of terms, yields the following:

$$\ln m_t = \gamma\alpha_0 + \gamma\alpha_1 \ln y_t^p + \gamma\alpha_2 \pi^e + \gamma\alpha_3 i_t + (1 - \gamma) \ln m_{t-1} + u_t \qquad (7.4)$$

The above is a typical short-run money demand model in which the short run or impact effects are measured by the composite coefficients $\gamma\alpha$s. The corresponding long-run coefficients are obtained by dividing each of the composite coefficients by the estimate of γ yielded by the coefficient on the lagged dependent variable.

The empirical evidence

It is almost impossible to survey the vast literature involving empirical estimation of the demand for money. However, at the risk of over-simplification it can be said that most studies find that the demand for real money balances in developing countries is a stable function of real income and the actual or expected rate of inflation (Treadgold, 1990). The findings with regard to the interest rate are mixed – in most cases it is found insignificant. The lack of significance of the interest rate can possibly be attributed to the infrequency

Table 7.2 Long-run income elasticities of real money demand

Country	Period of study	Narrow money	Broad money
Indonesia	1968 II–1976 IV	1.63	1.85
Malaysia	1970 I–1978 I	1.23	1.65
Philippines	1957 II–1977 IV	0.85	1.54
Singapore	1966 II–1976 IV	1.34	1.33
Sri Lanka	1957 II–1976 IV	1.08	1.48
Thailand	1957 III–1977 IV	0.68	1.49

Source: Aghevli et al. (1979: Table 3)

of changes in the administered rate. This section briefly reviews some major studies on the money demand function in Asian countries.

One of the earlier works in this area was by Fan and Liu (1970). They used annual data for Japan, Formosa (Taiwan), South Korea, India, Pakistan, Burma, Sri Lanka, the Philippines and Thailand covering the period of 1953–68. For Japan, Korea, the Philippines, Thailand and Burma the call money rate, and for others the government bond yield were used for the interest rate variable. Fan and Liu did not use permanent income as they believed that 'the concept of "permanent income" loses its meaningfulness' in unstable economies. They found the income variable significant with an expected positive sign. The estimated value of income-elasticity was found within a range from 0.79 (Thailand) to 2.55 (Burma). However, the interest rate variable came out with mixed signs and was not significant.

Aghevli et al. (1979) estimated a short-run money demand function of the form (7.4) using quarterly data for Indonesia, Malaysia, the Philippines, Singapore, Sri Lanka and Thailand. As the interest rates in those countries were administratively fixed during the period of the study, they used the expected rate of inflation as a measure of the opportunity cost of holding money. They also used actual rather than permanent real income. Aghevli et al. found that the demand for real money balances was a stable function of real income, the inflation rate and the lagged real balances for both narrow and broad money. Only in the case of Singapore was the income coefficient found to be insignificant at the 5 per cent level. The effect of inflation on broad money holdings was found 'somewhat stronger than was observed in the narrow money equations' (Aghevli et al., 1979: 793). As is seen from Table 7.2, the findings generally support the hypothesis that the long-run response of broad money holdings to real income changes is greater than the corresponding response of real narrow money. It also shows that the income-elasticity is greater than one for broad money as well as for narrow money (except in the Philippines and Thailand). As mentioned earlier, the greater than unity income-elasticity of demand for money may be a result of the monetisation of economic activities, limited opportunities to economise on cash balances, and the paucity of other financial assets in which to hold savings.

Khan's (1980) study of 11 countries including seven Latin American and four Asian countries (India, Malaysia, the Philippines and Thailand) for the period starting from the first quarter of 1962 to the fourth quarter of 1976 lends support to the standard partial adjustment money demand function of the type (7.4). However, an extended model incorporating a further adjustment mechanism relating to unexpected changes in the nominal money supply was found to fit the data even better. His estimated coefficients are similar to those of Aghevli et al. (1979). In particular the long-run income-elasticity of the demand for broad money was found to be greater than unity. The results also indicate that the elasticity of demand for money with respect to the expected rate of inflation is 'positively related, to some degree, to the level of inflation' (Khan, 1980: 271). It implies that in countries where the inflation rates are high, money holders may respond more to a given change in the expected rate of inflation because of a greater awareness of the costs of holding money.

Tseng and Corker's (1991) study is to some extent different from earlier works. To begin with, they used the interest rates rather than expected inflation in the money demand function. Second, to capture the sluggish adjustment of money demand towards desired equilibrium holdings, they specified an error-correction model which is regarded as more general than the partial adjustment model.

Table 7.3 presents Tseng and Corker's estimation results. As can be seen, the estimated long-run income-elasticities of demand for narrow money vary substantially. It ranges from as low as 0.67 for the Philippines to as high as 1.75 for Nepal. Except for Singapore, Malaysia, Myanmar and Nepal, the long-run income-elasticities do not reflect their stages of financial development in the sense of monetisation of the economy. For example, an income-elasticity less than one for Singapore is consistent with its advanced financial system. Similarly, a greater than unity income-elasticity for Nepal can be explained in terms of its underdeveloped financial system. With the exception of Korea, the long-run income-elasticities of broad money were found to exceed unity. Tseng and Corker (1991: 18) maintained that the large income-elasticities of demand for broad money did not necessarily reflect monetisation – a phenomenon usually associated with narrow money. Rather, it might be due to the growth of wealth in excess of that of real income in high-saving Asian countries. In fact, there has been a rapid growth of savings in the form of time deposits following financial liberalisation in Asian countries. But this explanation is at odds with high income-elasticities of broad money demand in Nepal and Myanmar.

In the narrow money demand function the deposit rates of interest were found to be significant with a negative coefficient in most countries. On

Table 7.3 Long-run relationship between money, income and the interest rate

Country	Income elasticity		Interest rate elasticity	
	Narrow	Broad	Narrow	Broad
Indonesia			−0.66	−2.05
Korea	0.79	1.00	−0.84	−0.78
Malaysia	1.11	1.63	−	
Myanmar	1.27	1.43	−	−
Nepal	1.75	2.60	−	−
Philippines	0.67	1.47	−1.16	−
Singapore	0.86	1.37	−1.17	−2.13
Sri Lanka	0.92	1.22	−1.60	0.46
Thailand	0.85	1.72	−1.53	−2.46

Source: Tseng and Corker (1991: Table I)

Note − Not significant

the other hand, the inflation rate did not fare well as a measure of the opportunity cost of holding narrow money.

For Indonesia, Korea, Malaysia, the Philippines and Thailand the broad money demand was found to be negatively related to an opportunity cost variable measured by the difference between returns on alternative assets and the average interest rate paid on broad money holdings. It means that the demand for broad money is affected by relative asset returns as opposed to the general level of interest rates.

FINANCIAL LIBERALISATION AND THE DEMAND FOR MONEY

Interest in the stability of the demand for money was rekindled in the 1980s following financial liberalisation and financial innovations in many developing countries. Financial liberalisation reforms can affect the stability of the money demand function in a number of ways. First, with liberalisation, the interest rate is likely to become a significant variable in the demand for money function. Second, any reform measure that promotes financial market development may create financial assets with attractive yields, which may lead to portfolio shifts away from monetary assets. It will cause a shift in the intercept term of the money demand function. Third, the observed relationships among money, income, prices and interest rates may alter following the relaxation of direct controls over bank credits, interest rates and exchange rates, and the shift from direct to indirect monetary policy instruments (Jonson and Rankin, 1986; Tseng and Corker, 1991). Any promotion of competition among financial institutions may also lower financial transactions costs and thereby cause money demand to respond differently than before to interest rate changes. Furthermore, financial deregulation may lead to unpredictability of money demand by changing the speed of adjustment at which actual money balances move towards the desired level. In short, financial deregulation may cause a once only or a gradual shift in the level of money holdings and alter the sensitivity of money demand to changes in income and interest rates. However, the similarity of long-run income-elasticities found in Aghevli *et al.* (1979) with Tseng and Corker's estimates as reported in Tables 7.2 and 7.3 intuitively indicates a stable long-run money demand function in these countries. Incidentally these values are not much different from those of Fan and Liu (1970).

Tseng and Corker (1991) provide a comprehensive and systematic study of the stability of the money demand function since financial deregulation in Asian countries. They used a two-stage estimation procedure to investigate the stability of the money demand function. At the first stage, they applied the cointegration method[11] to test for a cointegral relationship between money, income and the interest rate. The significance of cointegration is that two or more non-stationary variables may combine to form a stationary variable and the existence of a cointegral or long-run relationship between a group of economic variables can be tested.[12] A rejection of cointegration in the money demand function would imply that money, income and the interest rate are not stably related during the period under investigation.

Their cointegration tests suggest that at least one monetary aggregate in most sample countries has a stable long-run relationship with income and the interest rate. For example, in the cases of Indonesia, Nepal, Malaysia and Singapore, the long-run relationship for the narrow money demand function remained stable during the sample period. However, the test results for Nepal are not conclusive. And, despite unsatisfactory statistical tests, they argue that there might have been a shift in the long-run narrow money demand function in Indonesia following financial liberalisation in 1983. Similarly, the introduction of financial liberalisation reforms in the Philippines in the early 1980s and the demonetisation of currency in Myanmar in 1987 might have caused an intercept term shift in the long-run demand for narrow money function.

Although the introduction of financial liberalisation reforms in the late 1970s and early 1980s appears to have shifted the long-run demand relationship for narrow money, a weak support for a cointegral relationship was found for broad money for Korea and Sri Lanka. The estimated long-run relationship for broad money was also found to be stable for Indonesia and the Philippines. However, it was not so for Singapore, Nepal and Thailand.

Following the test for a cointegral relationship, Tseng and Corker also estimated an error-correction model of money demand for all sample countries and then tested for its stability across different subperiods. The error-correction model was found to be stable for only four countries – Indonesia, Malaysia (for both narrow and broad money), Korea and Sri Lanka (only for broad money). It implies that financial liberalisation in most of these countries has caused instability in the short-run money demand function.

Hossain (1993, 1994) has applied the methods of both cointegration and error correction for examining the stability of the money demand function in Bangladesh and Pakistan. His results indicate that the long-run money demand function in these countries has remained largely stable following financial reforms.

CURRENCY SUBSTITUTION AND THE DEMAND FOR MONEY

Currency substitution describes a situation where domestic economic agents use foreign currencies as a medium of exchange, unit of account and store of value. Currency substitution, often referred to as 'dollarisation', is predominantly a Latin American phenomenon. It is, to a lesser extent, also found in some Asian and other developing countries.[13]

Table 7.4 reports the extent of currency substitution in selected Latin American countries in the early 1990s. It shows that the phenomenon is significantly high in Bolivia, followed by Peru and Argentina. Note that currency substitution as a store of value has a long history in Latin America. However, currency substitution for transactions is a relatively recent phenomenon caused by hyperinflation. Another new development in currency substitution is the use of dollar deposits in domestic banks.[14]

One major problem with currency substitution is that as people hold foreign currencies in increasing amounts, the domestic government loses substantial amounts of seigniorage to the governments of countries whose currencies substitute the domestic currency. It is also claimed that currency substitution raises inflation to a higher level than would otherwise be the

Table 7.4 Percentage share of foreign currency in monetary aggregates, Latin America, mid-1991

Country	Narrow money	Broad money	Quasi-money
Argentina	11	48	65
Bolivia	29	79	98
Chile	na	15	20
Mexico	9	11	12
Paraguay	na	30	50
Peru	na	60	79

Source: Clements and Schwartz (1993: Figures 1–6)

Notes na = not available
Quasi-money is defined as the sum of domestic and foreign currency denominated time deposits. Broad money includes quasi-money, domestic currency in circulation, and domestic and foreign currency denominated chequing accounts.

case. It, however, presupposes that the causality between currency substitution and inflation runs from the former to the latter and ignores the possibility of a reverse causation.

From the monetary policy point of view, the important aspect of currency substitution is that it introduces instability in the demand for domestic money function (McKinnon, 1981, 1982). Edwards has summarised the problem of currency substitution for macroeconomic management:

> How is macromanagement affected with the existence of currency substitution? Two things are involved here: (a) money-demand instability. It is clear that the demand for money is much more unstable once we have currency substitution, in particular the one that allows domestic banks to issue foreign-currency denominated deposits, and (b) the effectiveness of exchange-rate policy under currency substitution – in particular the issue of devaluation.
>
> (Edwards, 1993: 3)

Furthermore, when wealthholders respond to changes in the relative opportunity costs of holding foreign money balances, foreign monetary disturbances have the potential to destabilise the domestic economy through changes in the demand for domestic money. In other words, currency substitution makes the insulation property of the flexible exchange rate system weaker. To illustrate, if the monetary authority of country A increases its domestic money supply, the inflation rate in A will rise and money holders will expect A's currency to depreciate. With a flexible exchange rate system, A's monetary authority does not intervene in the foreign exchange market.[15] The expected depreciation of A's currency will then increase the opportunity cost of holding it relative to country B's currency. This will result in a decline in the demand for A's currency and an increase in the demand for B's currency in both countries. If B follows the policy of maintaining a targeted monetary growth, it will mean a higher interest rate in B than would otherwise have been the case without currency substitution. On the other hand, if B follows the policy of pegging the domestic interest rate, it will have to increase the money supply. Thus, if there is currency substitution, the policy action taken by country A leads to a similar action by country B even in a world of flexible exchange rates. In other words, the monetary authority cannot have an independent monetary policy which the flexible exchange rate system is supposed to provide.

SUMMARY AND CONCLUSION

In view of the importance of money demand and its stability in the design and conduct of monetary policy, this chapter has provided a review of relevant issues. It has been found that the income-elasticity of the demand for narrow money in most developing countries is around one. In cases where it exceeds unity, it reflects a lower degree of monetisation of the economy and a lack of alternative financial assets. It also implies that the demand for money does not necessarily arise from transaction needs. In most developing countries with high inflation, the rate of inflation has been found to represent a better proxy for the opportunity cost of holding money than the interest rate.

In financially repressed economies, the absence of a well-developed capital market makes open-market operations, an important tool of discretionary monetary policy, almost ineffective. In such economies, the transmission mechanism through which changes in the money supply work has been found to be close to the classical description rather than being Keynsian in nature. It implies that changes in the money supply are likely to have a direct and immediate impact on aggregate spending and hence the price level. However, there is a considerable debate about the net effect of variations in the administered interest rate on aggregate demand in a financially repressed economy.

The long-run demand for money in developing countries has been found to be mostly stable even after financial liberalisation. However, it is the short-run money demand function which displayed some instability after financial liberalisation. It was especially so in countries where opening the capital account in the balance of payments increased currency substitution. The instability in the short-run money demand function implies that it would be difficult to use discretionary monetary policy reliably for short-run macroeconomic management. On the other hand, the existence of a stable long-run demand for money function and the fact that in the long-run money supply affects the price level, not real output, suggest that monetary policy should have a long-run-target of controlling inflation.

NOTES

1 According to Friedman (ed., 1956) velocity is a predictable function of a small number of variables like expected average long-run real income or permanent income and the expected rates of returns on money and other financial and real assets. Since in a developed competitive financial system the expected returns on bonds and equity relative to money remains fairly constant with the rise in the interest rate, Friedman argues that the demand for money and velocity is practically insensitive to the interest rate.

2 The precautionary motive for demand for money is subsumed in the transactions demand for the sake of simplicity.

3 This is the situation known as liquidity trap. It can happen when the interest rate is too low and people expect it to rise in the near future.

4 The impact of changes in interest rates on production through changes in working capital costs is known as the Cavallo effect. See D. Cavallo, ('Stagnationary Effects of Monetarist Stabilization Policies', unpublished PhD Thesis, Harvard University, 1977). Lim (1987), Manasan (1988) and Montes (1987) have found support for so-called Cavallo effect in the Philippines.

5 This debate is largely irrelevant where banks continue to behave as in the pre-liberalisation era and do not adjust their interest rate in response to market rates. For example, Cole and Slade (1992: 136) report that in Indonesia after interest rate controls were abolished in 1983 banks simply continued to behave as before. Fry (1993: 37) reports similar situations in Malaysia, Thailand, Turkey and India. Both Arndt (1982: 425) and Drake (1980: 225) have also pointed out that despite the complete abolition of government control on bank interest rates, banks can collectively act as a cartel and refrain from raising deposit rates.

6 The well known Baumol–Tobin formulation has a very rigid form which suggests that the income-elasticity of the demand for money is 0.5 while the interest elasticity is –0.5. But as mentioned earlier, empirical evidence overwhelmingly suggests that the income-elasticity of the demand for money is significantly greater than one in developing countries while the interest-elasticity is not significantly different from zero (Aghevli et al., 1979).

7 The demand for money is conventionally expressed in real terms, this being a factor distinguishing the money demand function from the money supply function. The money supply function is usually expressed in nominal terms. Friedman (1959) argues that the nominal stock of money is determined in the first instance by the monetary authorities and wealthholders cannot alter this amount directly. But the wealthholders can make the real amount of money anything that in aggregate they want to. An assumption implicit in the demand for real money balances is that the price elasticity of the demand for nominal money balances is unity or that there is no money illusion.

8 There is no clear-cut theoretical guideline for the appropriate functional form of the demand for money function. But a log-linear form is widely used and has been found to perform better.

9 The argument in favour of using the nominal interest rate has some merits. This is because with money narrowly defined so as to exclude interest-bearing assets, the expected real return from holding narrow money will simply be equal to minus the expected rate of inflation ($-\pi^e$), whilst the expected real return from holding interest-bearing substitute assets will equal the nominal rate of interest minus the expected rate of inflation ($i - \pi^e$). It follows that the appropriate measure of the relative return from holding narrow money compared with other financial assets is simply measured by the nominal interest rate, as $\{-\pi^e - (i - \pi^e)\} = -i$. Tanzi (1985) suggested that in an aggregate money demand function, both the nominal interest rate and the expected rate of inflation should be used jointly and their roles in the money demand function should be tested empirically. However, this approach may not work if there is a close association between the nominal interest rate and the expected rate of inflation, which follows from the Fisher equation. On the other hand, if the nominal interest rate is institutionally fixed, there should not be any problem in using the nominal interest rate and the expected inflation rate simultaneously.

10 Saving is defined as measured income less consumption expenditure where consumption is a fixed proportion of permanent income.

11 Cointegration is closely related to the concept of equilibrium in economic analysis. The following description by Engle and Granger (1987: 251–252) makes the concept clear:

> An individual economic variable, viewed as a time series, can wander extensively and yet some pairs of series may be expected to move so that they do not drift too far apart. Typically economic theory will propose forces which tend to keep such series together. Examples might be short and long term interest rates . . . household income and expenditures . . . A similar

idea arises from considering equilibrium relationships, where equilibrium is a stationary point characterized by forces which tend to push the economy back toward equilibrium whenever it moves away.

12. The validity of most time series econometric techniques is dependent on the assumption of stationarity. However, most macroeconomic series are non-stationary; i.e., they are auto-correlated with time trends. Thus, any regression of one non-stationary variable on another such variable may give a statistically spurious relationship due to their common time trend while in fact there is no relationship between them.

13 For example, the Singapore dollar is used as a medium of exchange in some neighbouring countries, especially in Brunei. However, currency substitution does not appear to have created any serious problem (Treadgold, 1990: 17).

14 See Liviatan (ed., 1993) for discussions on currency substitution in Latin America.

15 Under a fixed exchange rate system, the monetary authority intervenes to maintain the prevailing rate and hence cannot have an independent monetary policy.

8

MONEY, CREDIT, BALANCE OF PAYMENTS AND INFLATION

The review of empirical literature on money, inflation and economic growth in Chapter 3 revealed that although the relationship between inflation and economic growth is weak and complex, high and unstable inflation rates can retard economic growth. It also revealed that there is an almost linear relationship between the growth of money and the rate of inflation. Chapter 5 examined the role of monetary policy in stabilisation. It was demonstrated that the demand management role of monetary policy is limited in developing countries and that an active monetary policy after a negative supply shock may create sustained inflation. Therefore the primary role of monetary policy in developing countries is to maintain price stability for economic growth.

However, how to conduct monetary policy to achieve price stability is an old question. Monetary targeting is one approach. As mentioned in Chapter 6, two fundamental assumptions behind monetary targeting are, first, that there exists a stable money demand function, and second, that the monetary authority has control over the money supply.

In Chapter 7 the question of stability of the money demand function was examined for developing countries. It was found that despite financial reform and structural change, the long-run money demand function in most developing countries remained stable. Therefore the first prerequisite for reliably conducting monetary policy by monetary targeting is satisfied.

However, it is not so for the second prerequisite. As we mentioned in Chapter 6, after the generalised floating of major currencies in the early 1970s most developing countries chose not to float their currencies freely and opted for pegged exchange rate arrangements of one kind or another by fixing their currencies to a single hard currency or a basket of hard currencies (Aghevli *et al.*, 1991). It created a number of issues relating to the conduct of monetary policy. First, the goal of monetary policy changed from price stabilisation to the stability of the balance of payments, which changed the intermediate target of monetary policy from the growth rate of the money supply to the growth rate of central bank credit. Second, domestic inflation remained pegged to world inflation. These problems have led to a debate on whether the developing countries should adopt a flexible exchange rate system so that they have a choice of inflation. Apparently the scope for a choice of inflation remains an attractive proposition; it could be both good and bad for a developing country. It is good because, if the country wishes, it can in principle choose 'a tailor-made' inflation rate. It is bad because when the country lacks fiscal-monetary discipline, it may create an excessive and non-optimal rate of inflation (Argy, 1992). For a developing country, the floating exchange rate system (and monetary policy independence) may therefore be a 'curse' in disguise.[1]

The broad implications of exchange rate policies on the conduct of monetary policy were discussed in Chapter 6; this chapter focuses on specific issues with the aid of stylised models. In particular, it develops the relationships among money, credit, balance of payments and inflation under both fixed and flexible exchange rate systems.

CENTRAL BANK CREDIT AND THE BALANCE OF PAYMENTS

In the monetary literature on the balance of payments there is an emphasis on the relationship between central bank credit and the balance of payments. It is the essence of the monetary approach to the balance of payments theory. Polak (1957) and others at the IMF originated it in the 1950s, while Mundell (1968, 1971), Johnson (1972) and others developed it in the 1960s and 1970s. In a historical context the monetary approach is 'the intellectual grandchild of the price-specie-flow theory' originally advanced by David Hume in the eighteenth century.[2]

In its purest form the monetary approach suggests that the balance of payments and the exchange rate are monetary phenomena in which the demand for and supply of money play a critical role. While it is acknowledged that real variables affect the balance of payments and the exchange rate, they operate through monetary channels (Mussa, 1978). The focus of the monetary approach is the balance of payments as a whole so that any disequilibrium in the balance of payments is equivalent to changes in foreign exchange reserves. Recall that in the money supply identity foreign exchange reserves are one component of the monetary base.

At the analytical level the monetary approach incorporates the adjustment process in the money market. It suggests that the money market is stable in the sense that, if there is a disequilibrium in the money market, it initiates an adjustment process which results in the attainment of equilibrium in the long run through the external sector. Under the fixed exchange rate system, and when all goods are traded freely and there is perfect capital mobility, any disequilibrium in the money market adjusts through changes in foreign exchange reserves. Under the flexible exchange rate system, any disequilibrium in the money market adjusts through changes in the exchange rate because the balance of payments remains in equilibrium. Under an adjustable pegged exchange rate system, any disequilibrium in the money market adjusts through changes in both foreign exchange reserves and the exchange rate in which the monetary authority determines to what extent the pressure on the exchange rate would be relieved by allowing the exchange rate to change and to what extent it would be absorbed through changes in foreign exchange reserves.

The credit growth rule and the balance of payments

The monetary approach suggests that under the fixed exchange rate system the money supply is endogenous in the sense that, although the monetary authority can control the central bank credit, it cannot control the money supply. Importantly, any change in the domestic component of the money base (central bank credit) is expected to be offset by an equal but opposite change in foreign exchange reserves. It indicates that, given a stable money demand function, a credit growth rule can be devised to conduct monetary policy with the objective of achieving equilibrium in the balance of payments. Following Rivera-Batiz and Rivera-Batiz (1985), a credit growth rule is derived below.

The basic model of the monetary approach to the balance of payments theory is specified as follows:

$$\hat{M}^d = \hat{M}^s \qquad (8.1)$$

(the money market equilibrium condition)

$$\hat{M}^d = \hat{P} + \hat{m}^d \qquad (8.2)$$

(the nominal money demand growth equation)

$$\hat{m}^d = \eta_y \hat{y} + \eta_i \hat{i} \qquad (8.3)$$

(the real money demand growth equation)

$$\hat{M}^s = m\hat{m} + BOPn/H - (Cr/H)\,\hat{Cr} \qquad (8.4)$$

(the money supply growth equation)
where $\hat{M}^d$ is the growth rate of the demand for nominal money, $\hat{m}^d$ is the growth rate of the demand for real money balances, $\hat{y}$ is the growth rate of real income (or output), $\hat{i}$ is the growth rate of the interest rate, η_y is the income elasticity of demand for real money balances, η_i is the interest elasticity of demand for real money balances, and $\hat{M}^s$ is the growth rate of the money supply, $\hat{P}$ is the growth rate of the price level, BOPn is the money account of the balance of payments (which in a simplified model is equal to changes in foreign exchange reserves of the central bank), $m\hat{m}$ is the growth rate of the money multiplier, $\hat{Cr}$ is the growth rate of central bank credit, and H is the high-powered or base money.

After a series of substitutions and rearrangements the following expression for the balance of payments is obtained:

$$BOPn/H = \hat{P} + \eta_y \hat{y} + \eta_i \hat{i} - m\hat{m} - (Cr/H)\,\hat{Cr} \tag{8.5}$$

It shows the effects of growth in monetary and real variables on the balance of payments. For example, a rise in economic growth improves the balance of payments position, while a rise in the growth rate of central bank credit deteriorates it.

By setting $BOPn/H = 0$ the following expression for the credit growth rate is derived:

$$\hat{Cr}_0 = H/Cr\,(\hat{P} + \eta_y \hat{y} + \eta_i \hat{i} - m\hat{m}) \tag{8.6}$$

The credit growth rate in equation (8.6) is consistent with balance of payments equilibrium. It indicates that when the actual growth rate of central bank credit exceeds the critical rate $\hat{Cr}_0$ there would be deficit in the balance of payments. Such a credit growth rule can, in principle, maintain the balance of payments equilibrium. However, the credit growth rule is dependent on a restrictive assumption that the determinants (the growth rate of real output, the inflation rate and the interest rate) of the growth of the demand for nominal money, as specified in equations (8.2) and (8.3), are exogenously determined. This restrictive assumption, of course, has several implications. For example, an exogenous growth rate for real output implies a (neo)classical aggregate supply function; an exogenous inflation rate implies that all output is tradable, that the economy is a price-taker in international markets for goods and services, and that the exchange rate is fixed; and an exogenous interest rate (assuming no financial repression) implies that the economy is a price-taker in international capital markets and there are no restrictions on the movement of capital between the economy and the rest of the world.

BALANCE OF PAYMENTS DEFICITS AND IMF CONDITIONALITY

The IMF is the major international financial institution which provides accommodating finance to developing countries for temporary balance of payments deficits. In cases where such deficits tend to persist, any finance from the IMF requires the borrowing countries to undertake corrective policy measures. The IMF regards sustained balance of payments deficits as a consequence of excess demand in the economy caused by expansionary fiscal and monetary policies. Therefore the provision of finance[3] by the IMF for balance of payments deficits is conditional on the borrowing countries adopting restrictive monetary and fiscal policies.

Credit ceilings are the primary component of the IMF stabilisation programme. Relying on the relationship between central bank credit and the balance of payments as in equation (8.6), the IMF argues that any reduction in central bank credit would reduce both inflation and trade deficits by lowering excess demand in the economy. The IMF estimates the size of trade deficit that a borrowing country can afford and then suggests the limit on bank credit that is consistent with the balance of payments target. The implicit rationale of the limit on bank credit is that it will put pressure on the government to impose fiscal discipline and on the central bank not to expand credit to the government if it runs persistent budget deficits. As was shown in Chapter 6, credit to the public sector is the main source of monetary growth in developing countries.

The IMF's ceiling on bank credit is accompanied by a sub-ceiling on credit to the non-financial public sector. It is designed to serve two purposes. First, it monitors the overall credit ceiling because any violation of such a ceiling is likely to originate from credit expansion to the public sector. Second, it ensures that the availability of credit to the private sector is not curtailed by the ceiling on overall credit. At the analytical level the target credit expansion to the private sector is estimated from the demand for credit relationship. It is postulated that the growth of credit to the private sector should keep pace with the growth of nominal output. It indicates that given the target level of credit to the private sector, the level of credit to the non-financial public sector is residually determined once the ceiling on overall credit is known. It also indicates that if the non-financial public sector runs greater deficits than it can finance by borrowing from the banking system, it has to lower the deficit by either raising revenues or lowering expenditures (Khan *et al.*, 1990).

The IMF credit ceiling approach to the amelioration of trade deficits has been subject to criticisms. Nevertheless, it remains popular and useful in policy-making. As Dornbusch and Fischer point out:

> The use of domestic credit ceilings is a crude policy to improve the balance of payments. But the simplicity of the conceptual framework, and the apparent definiteness of the policy recommendations to which it leads, frequently makes it the best policy tool available, particularly if dramatic action is needed and the credibility of the government's policies need to be restored . . . It is correct in arguing that monetary or domestic credit restraint will improve the balance of payments. But this mechanism is not painless, since the tight money policy produced by slow domestic credit growth typically produces a recession.
>
> (Dornbusch and Fischer, 1990: 766)

Experience of developing countries with IMF stabilisation programmes

Since the early 1970s most developing countries have frequently taken loans from the IMF for financing trade deficits. Such loans have been made available under the condition that the borrowing countries adopt stabilisation programmes. The introduction of IMF stabilisation programmes in the 1970s and 1980s has generated a passionate debate over their effects on growth, income distribution and poverty in developing countries. The major criticisms of these programmes have come from the new structuralist economists working in and about Latin American economies, who suggest that the application of stabilisation measures to developing economies retards economic growth and increases poverty and income inequality.

The structuralist argument is that inflation is inevitable in a developing country which attempts to raise economic growth in the presence of structural bottlenecks or constraints. In particular, the agricultural, foreign trade and fiscal sectors are considered to suffer from institutional rigidities which one way or another inhibit expansion and cause inflation. The lower growth of agricultural productivity due to a feudal land tenure system is responsible for rising relative food prices and ultimately for the rise in general price levels. In the foreign trade sector, it is suggested that the growth of imports exceeds the growth of exports because at the early stage of development the developing countries need to import capital goods to develop an industrial base. Such a deficit needs to be financed rather than eliminated because any premature attempt to reduce trade deficits by curtailing essential imports of capital goods is likely to halt the development process itself. Once the domestic industries begin to produce capital goods, structural trade deficits will automatically come down. Moreover the policies suggested by the IMF are inappropriate to mitigate the structural disequilibrium in the balance of payments. For example, the government's devaluation of the exchange rate of the domestic currency may accelerate the rate of inflation instead of improving the balance of payments. Therefore the structuralist view on inflation and balance of payments problems contrasts with the IMF view that such problems in developing countries are caused by expansionary fiscal and monetary policies. The structuralists see the IMF stabilisation measures 'as a recession-inducing growth-wrecking agent' (Pastor, 1987: 251).

Marxist economists working within the dependency paradigm pioneered by Frank (1967) and others strongly criticise the IMF for its alleged role in draining off economic surplus from the Third World (periphery) to the First World (core). Payer (1974) argues that the short-run stabilisation policies recommended by the IMF in the typical stand-by arrangement have a negative effect on growth since they open up the economy and effectively destroy the basis that may have been carefully laid for autonomous development along the lines of import-substituting industrialisation. The Fund's general encouragement of export production is believed to reinforce dependency by locking Third World economies into the vagaries of markets in the core. Moreover, it is argued that the IMF leads peripheral economies into a debt trap. An arrangement with the IMF can open the door to new official and private sources of credit, and this allows Third World countries to survive balance of payments crises through either increasing indebtedness or auctioning their domestic assets to foreign investors. In the process the nations become 'aid junkies'.

Empirical evidence on the effects of IMF adjustment programmes in developing countries is inconclusive. Two major IMF studies (Donavan, 1982; Reichmann and Stillson, 1978) found that these programmes in non-oil developing countries in the 1960s and 1970s improved their current account position and that they did not have any systematic negative effect on growth. In contrast, Pastor (1987: 249) found that 'IMF programs are associated with insignificant changes in the current account, significant improvement in the overall balance of payments, increases in inflation, mixed effects on growth, and a strong and consistent pattern of reduction in labor share of income'. A number of other review studies have also reached the conclusion that the IMF stabilisation programmes did not have the desired economic effects in developing countries. For example, Killick writes:

> The general outcome of the evidence surveyed so far is to throw doubt on the ability of Fund programmes to bring countries to BOP [balance of payments] viability, to promote liberalization and to reduce inflation. If (as we probably should) we confine ourselves to the statistically significant effects of Fund programmes, then they appear to make little difference to anything.
>
> (Killick, 1984: 250)

Despite the lack of evidence that the IMF adjustment programmes are effective in reducing both inflation and balance of payments deficits without sacrificing growth and increasing poverty, the IMF remains a powerful institution to put pressure on borrowing developing countries to undertake structural adjustment measures. Besides monetary restraint and credit ceilings, IMF conditionality now includes reduction of budget deficits, devaluation of the exchange rate, liberalisation of foreign trade, and the removal of controls over prices and capital flows. The primary objective of all these measures is to create an efficient market economy by lowering intervention by the government in economic activities. However, as was mentioned in Chapter 4, financial liberalisation reform created problems for many reforming countries. On the other hand, mild repression was argued to be growth-promoting. To the extent that structural reform measures are undertaken under pressure from the IMF, there remains scope for criticisms of IMF intervention in economic policies in developing countries when such policies have an adverse affect on growth, income distribution and poverty.

BUDGET DEFICITS, FOREIGN RESERVES AND EXCHANGE RATE REGIMES

The early version of the monetary approach emphasised that monetary disequilibrium is the source of imbalance in the balance of payments. It has now been broadened to incorporate budget deficits as a source of monetary expansion. As budget deficits are the major source of growth of the money supply in developing countries, it is plausible that inflation and the balance of payments deficits in developing countries originate from the fiscal sector. This is the view of the IMF. To reduce these problems, the IMF therefore suggests lowering budget deficits. There is another related matter of concern: a country which runs persistent budget deficits may not be able to maintain a fixed exchange rate system because persistent budget deficits can create balance of payments crises and force the country to adopt a flexible exchange rate system and to experience high inflation. Sachs and Larrain (1993) examined the experiences of Latin American countries in the 1970s and 1980s and substantiated the above contention.

A model of balance of payments crises

Under the fixed exchange rate system any budget deficit that is financed by borrowing from the central bank depletes foreign exchange reserves; if the budget deficit persists, the country eventually runs out of reserves. When foreign exchange reserves fall to a critically low level, the fixed exchange rate regime collapses after a speculative attack in which residents, fearing devaluation and inflation, attempt to convert domestic money into foreign currency or financial assets. Such a phenomenon, experienced by Latin American countries in the late 1970s and early 1980s, is called a balance of payments crisis (Agenor *et al.*, 1992; Krugman, 1979; Sachs and Larrain, 1993). Krugman (1979) shows that the speculative attack on the domestic currency takes place before the central bank would have run out of reserves in the absence of speculation.

The basic model of balance of payments crises is presented below:[4]

$$LM_t - LP_t = \epsilon\, Ly_t - \zeta\, i_t \tag{8.7}$$

$$LM_t = \xi\, LCr_t + (1 - \xi)\, LR_t \tag{8.8}$$

$$d\,LCr_t = \mu \tag{8.9}$$

$$LP_t = Lner_t \tag{8.10}$$

$$i_t = i_t^* + E_t\, d\,Lner_t \tag{8.11}$$

where LM is the log of nominal money, LP is the log of price level, Ly is the log of real income, LCr is the log of domestic credit which grows at the rate of μ, LR is the log of domestic currency value of foreign reserves held by the central bank, Lner is the log of the nominal exchange rate, i^* is the foreign interest rate, i is the domestic interest rate, d is a time derivative, and E is the expectational parameter conditional on information available at time t.

Equation (8.7) defines the demand for real money as a positive function of real income and a negative function of the domestic interest rate. Equation (8.8) is a log-linear approximation of the identity linking the money stock to domestic credit and foreign exchange reserves. Equation (8.9) shows that domestic credit grows at the rate of μ. Equations (8.10) and (8.11) define the purchasing power parity (the foreign price level is normalised to one) and uncovered interest parity.

Under the fixed exchange rate system and perfect capital mobility, the central bank accommodates any change in domestic public demand for foreign currency assets by buying and selling of foreign currencies. Assume that i^* is constant. Substitute equation (8.11) into equation (8.7). As under perfect foresight $E_t d\text{Lner}_t = d\text{Lner}_t$, and assuming that domestic money and foreign bonds are two assets available to domestic residents, equations (8.7) and (8.10) show that a high rate of domestic inflation (or devaluation) leads to a substitution of foreign currency assets. When the demand for money does not grow (that is, assume that $d\text{Ly} = 0$), the relationship between the growth rate of domestic credit and the loss of foreign exchange reserves is given by

$$d\text{LR} = -\mu/\theta \quad \text{(where } \theta = 1 - \zeta/\zeta) \tag{8.12}$$

The fixed exchange rate collapses when the prevailing exchange rate Lner_0 equals the shadow floating rate Lner, defined as the exchange rate that would prevail if LR = 0 and the exchange rate were allowed to float freely. The following relation shows the time of collapse of the fixed exchange rate regime:

$$t_c = \theta \, \text{LR}_0/\mu - \zeta \tag{8.13}$$

where LR_0 is the initial stock of reserves.

It shows that the higher the initial stock of reserves, or the lower the rate of credit growth, the longer the period before the collapse occurs. When there is no speculation, the collapse would occur when reserves run down to zero.

The semi-interest-elasticity of demand (ζ) for real money determines the size of the downward shift in money demand and reserves when the fixed exchange rate regime collapses and the nominal interest rate jumps to reflect the expected depreciation of the domestic currency. The larger ζ is, the earlier the crisis. The stock of reserves just before the attack is given by

$$\text{LR}_c = \mu\zeta/\theta \tag{8.14}$$

The top panel of Figure 8.1 shows the behaviour of reserves, domestic credit and the money supply before and after changes in exchange rate regimes. The bottom panel shows the behaviour of the exchange rate and the price

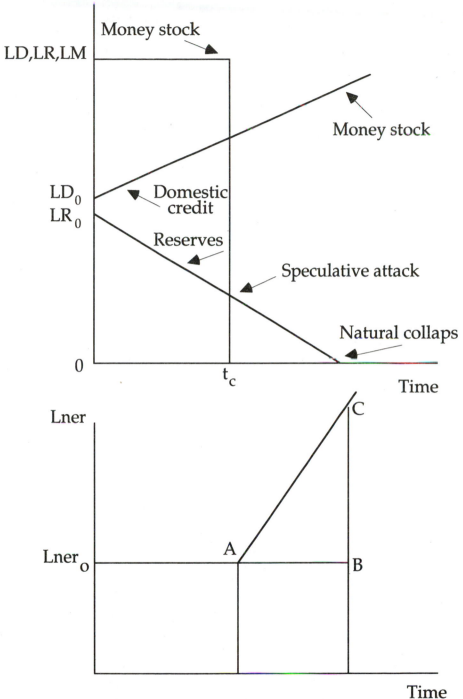

Figure 8.1 A balance of payments crisis model

level. Prior to the collapse at t_c, the money stock is constant, but its composition varies. Domestic credit increases at the rate of μ and reserves decline at the rate of μ/θ. When the speculative attack occurs, both reserves and the money stock fall by $\mu\zeta/\theta$. As reserves are exhausted by the attack, the money stock becomes equal to domestic credit in the post-collapse regime. Until the collapse the exchange rate remains at Lner$_o$. When there is no speculative attack, the path of the exchange rate would be through AB followed by a discrete exchange rate jump BC.

Implications of the balance of payments crisis

The main implication of the balance of payments crisis model is that a fixed exchange rate system is viable only if the fiscal and monetary authorities are able to maintain fiscal-monetary discipline. Balance of payments crises are the equilibrium outcome of maximising behaviour by rational agents faced with inconsistent monetary and exchange rate policies rather than the result of exogenous shocks. Although measures such as foreign borrowing and capital controls may temporarily enhance the viability of a fixed exchange rate regime, they may not be able to prevent the ultimate collapse of the regime unless there are fundamental fiscal policy changes.

In general, the viability of a fixed exchange rate regime depends on the growth rate of credit and is also affected by the consistency and sustainability of macroeconomic policies. The credibility of a fixed exchange rate regime is important to avoid balance of payments crises. When rational agents perceive that the authorities' commitment and ability to maintain a fixed exchange rate regime is weak, speculative attacks may occur. Such an attack may take place when the competitiveness of a high inflation country is eroded by adherence to the nominal exchange rate parity. It can reduce the degree of confidence in the existing exchange rate regime and raise expectations about devaluation of the currency. Speculative attacks may therefore be self-fulfilling.

Another implication of the balance of payments crises model is that under a fixed exchange rate system, a country can avoid inflation from budget deficits as long as foreign exchange reserves are available. Once foreign reserves run out, the authorities cannot defend the fixed exchange rate from speculative attacks. Therefore, budget deficits would cause inflation after the collapse of the fixed exchange rate system.

CENTRAL BANK CREDIT, INFLATION AND EXCHANGE RATE REGIMES

Given the relationship between money growth and inflation and between domestic credit and money supply, we can derive a relationship between the growth of domestic credit and inflation. However, in an open economy such a relationship depends on the exchange rate system. For example, under a fixed exchange rate system, any expansion of bank credit would create balance of payments deficits which in turn would lower the money supply and put downward pressure on inflation.

As indicated earlier, despite the generalised floating of major currencies since the early 1970s, most developing countries have been operating under adjustable fixed exchange rate arrangements. As these countries have also experienced current account deficit problems, they have been subjected to credit rules of one form or another under IMF conditionality. Therefore, a credit growth rule-based monetary policy obscured the relationship between credit growth and inflation.

This section develops an inflation model in which there is a link between the growth rate of credit and inflation in a fixed (or an adjustable) fixed exchange rate system.

A traded–non-traded goods model of inflation under a fixed exchange rate

Assume that the goods transacted in an open economy can be divided into traded and non-traded goods. The domestic prices of transacted goods (P_t) can then be defined as the weighted average of the prices of traded (PT_t) and non-traded goods (PNT_t). The price level identity can be specified in the following logarithmic form:

$$\ln P_t = \phi \ln PT_t + (1 - \phi) \ln PNT_t \tag{8.15}$$

where ϕ is the share of traded goods in total expenditure. For simplicity, assume that ϕ is constant.[5]

For a small open economy the prices of tradable goods in foreign currency are exogenously determined in the international market. From the purchasing power parity proposition, it can be expressed as:

$$\ln PT_t = \ln ner_t + \ln PT_t^f \tag{8.16}$$

where ner is the exchange rate of domestic currency per unit of foreign currency, and PT_f are the prices of tradable goods in foreign currency.

Equation (8.16) suggests that the prices of tradable goods in domestic currency may change because of changes in both the exchange rate of domestic currency and the prices of tradable goods in foreign currency. When the exchange rate is fixed, changes in PT are exogenously determined in a small economy. In contrast, when there is a flexible exchange rate system, changes in PT would depend on changes in the exchange rate even though changes in PT^f are exogenously determined.

The prices of non-tradable goods are determined by domestic demand for and supply of them, implying that equilibrium prices are established to clear the non-tradable goods market. Assume that the prices of non-tradable goods change in response to a discrepancy between the log of actual real money balances at the beginning of a period ($\ln m_{t-1}$) and the log of real money balances that individuals desire to hold at the end of a period ($\ln m_t^d$), such that

$$\ln \text{PNT}_t - \ln \text{PNT}_{t-1} = \gamma (\ln m_{t-1} - \ln m_t^d) + u_t \qquad (8.17)$$

where m = M/P (M is the nominal money supply and P is the price level), γ is the coefficient of adjustment whose value is expected to lie between zero and unity, and u is a random error term. Equation (8.17) shows that only a proportion (γ) of the logarithmic difference between the desired and actual real money balances is eliminated within the period t–1 and t.

Take the first-order logarithmic difference of equations (8.15) and (8.16) as follows:

$$\ln (P_t / P_{t-1}) = \phi \ln (\text{PT}_t / \text{PT}_{t-1}) + (1 - \phi) \ln (\text{PNT}_t / \text{PNT}_{t-1}) \qquad (8.18)$$

$$\ln (\text{PT}_t / \text{PT}_{t-1}) = \ln (\text{ner}_t / \text{ner}_{t-1}) + \ln (\text{PT}_t^f / \text{PT}_{t-1}^f) \qquad (8.19)$$

Substitution of equations (8.17) and (8.19) into equation (8.18), and rearrangement of terms, yields the following equation:

$$\ln (P_t / P_{t-1}) = \phi (\ln (\text{ner}_t / \text{ner}_{t-1}) + \ln (\text{PT}_t^f / \text{PT}_{t-1}^f) +$$
$$(1 - \phi) \gamma (\ln m_{t-1} - \ln m_t^d) + (1 - \phi) u_t \qquad (8.20)$$

Specify the desired demand for real money balances as follows:

$$\ln m_t^d = \beta_0 + \beta_1 \ln y_t - \beta_2 \ln i_t - \beta_3 \ln \pi^e \qquad (8.21)$$

where y is real income, π^e is expected inflation, i is the nominal interest rate and βs are structural parameters. As expected, inflation is unobservable, one period forward actual inflation is assumed to approximate it (i.e., $\pi_t^e = \pi_{t+1}$). Substitution of equation (8.21) into equation (8.20) and the use of $\pi_t^e = \pi_{t+1}$ would yield

$$\ln (P_t / P_{t+1}) = - (1-\phi) \gamma \beta_0 + \phi (\ln \text{ner}_t / \text{ner}_{t-1}) + \ln (\text{PT}_t^f / \text{PT}_{t-1}^f)$$
$$+ (1-\phi) \gamma \ln m_{t-1} - (1-\phi) \gamma \beta_1 \ln y_t + (1-\phi) \gamma \beta_2 \ln i_t$$
$$+ (1-\phi) \gamma \beta_3 \ln \pi_{t+1} + (1-\phi) u_t \qquad (8.22)$$

Equation (8.22) is an estimable regression model of inflation for a developing country. It shows that domestic inflation is linked with the rate of devaluation of the domestic currency, changes in the prices of tradable goods in foreign currency, real income, the interest rate, expected inflation and one-period-lagged real money supply.

Under a fixed exchange rate system the growth rate of central bank credit is a monetary policy variable. Equation (8.22) shows the effect of credit growth on inflation. For example, an expansion of central bank credit, if not accompanied by an increase in money demand, will increase the size of excess money supply for two reasons. First, it will increase the money supply at a given level of foreign exchange reserves. Second, it will lower the demand for money if an increase in credit growth raises expected inflation. An increase in excess money supply leads to an excess demand for goods and services. Given that the prices of traded goods are determined internationally, excess demand for goods and services will increase the prices of non-traded goods and through them the general price level. However, as any increase in domestic expenditure falls partly on traded goods, there will be trade deficits which will lower foreign exchange reserves and the money supply. Any reduction in money supply will put downward pressure on the price level, suggesting that even though the expansion of bank credit may increase domestic inflation above world inflation, such an inflation will converge to world inflation in the long run.

Money growth and inflation under a flexible exchange rate system

The argument that the main objective of monetary policy should be price stability rather than lowering unemployment and/or promoting economic growth is based on the assumption that there is a one-to-one relationship between money supply growth and inflation in the long run. It has been shown above that under a fixed exchange rate system there is no clear cut relation between money growth and inflation. However, under a flexible exchange rate system, there is an unambiguous relationship between money supply growth and inflation.

A model is developed below to show that inflation in the long run converges to the money supply growth rate.

Assume that the money demand function takes the following form:

$$m^d = y^{\epsilon 1}\, e^{-\epsilon 2 i} \tag{8.23}$$

where m^d is the demand for real money balances, y is real income, i is the nominal interest rate, $\epsilon 1$ is the income elasticity of demand for money, and $\epsilon 2$ is the semi-interest-elasticity of demand for money.

Assume that the government runs budget deficits and finances them by creating money, such that

$$\hat{M} = P\,(\text{def}) \tag{8.24}$$

where P is the price level, def is the real budget deficit, M is the stock of money supply, and $\hat{M}$ is dM/dt.

Following Krugman (1979), assume that the government adjusts its expenditures so as to keep the budget deficit a constant fraction of the money supply, such that

$$\hat{M} = P\,(\text{def}) = \lambda_0 M \tag{8.25}$$

187

Equilibrium in the money market requires that the demand for and supply of real money are equal, such that

$$m^d = m^s = M/P \qquad (8.26)$$

where m^s is the real money supply.

The flow equilibrium in the money market requires that a change in the demand for real money is associated with an equal change in the supply of real money, such that

$$dm^d/dt = dm^s/dt = dm/dt \qquad (8.27)$$

By using the notations: $\hat{M} = dM/dt$ and $(dP/dt)(1/P) = \pi$, dm/dt can be written as

$$dm/dt = \hat{M}/P - m\pi \qquad (8.28)$$

Since $\hat{M}/P = \lambda_0 m$, equation (8.28) can be written as

$$dm/dt = (\lambda_0 - \pi) \qquad (8.29)$$

It shows that the growth rate of real money balances $(dm/dt)(1/m)$ is inversely linked with the rate of inflation and that in the steady state $(dm/dt = 0)$, $\lambda_0 = \pi$.

Adjustment of disequilibrium in the money market

There can be disequilibrium in the money market because of any policy-induced (or exogenous) shocks that affect the demand for or supply of real money. Monetarists assume that monetary disequilibrium originates from the supply side of money. Assume that the money market is in equilibrium, but the monetary authority decides to raise the money growth rate from λ_0 to λ_1.

Although neither the money nor the goods market adjusts instantaneously, the adjustment of the money market is quicker than that of the goods market. There are many interpretations of slow adjustment in each of the money and goods markets, but none of them is satisfactory.

For analytical simplicity, assume that any disequilibrium in the money market adjusts through the partial adjustment mechanism, such that

$$(dm/dt)\,(1/m) = \gamma\,(\ln m^d - \ln m) \qquad (8.30)$$

where γ is the coefficient of adjustment which takes a value between zero and unity.

Since $(dm/dt)(1/m) = \gamma - \pi$, equation (8.30) can be written as:

$$\pi = \lambda - \gamma\,(\ln m^d - \ln m) \qquad (8.31)$$

It describes the dynamic behaviour of inflation when there is disequilibrium in the money market. It shows that π will exceed λ if there is an excess supply of money (or excess demand for goods and services). From an equilibrium situation when the growth rate of the money supply is increased from λ_0 to λ_1, it will create an excess money supply or an excess demand for goods and accelerate inflation.

Intertemporal equilibrium inflation in developing economies

Most developing economies are considered inflation-prone. As the aim of monetary policy is essentially to maintain price stability, the question is whether monetary targeting can stabilise inflation. It is shown below that a fixed money supply growth rule can ensure an intertemporal stability in inflation. However, it presupposes that the country follows a flexible exchange rate system.

For analytical simplicity, the demand for money is specified here as a function of expected inflation alone. (This is the case of a highly inflationary economy where real income can be considered constant.) As discussed in Chapter 7, expected inflation in such an economy acts as a better proxy for the opportunity cost of holding money because the interest rates are not market-determined.

Assuming that actual inflation approximates expected inflation, the money demand function is specified as

$$\ln m^d = \epsilon \pi \tag{8.32}$$

Substitute equation (8.32) in the money market adjustment function (8.30) and write it in the following form:

$$\pi = \lambda - \gamma \epsilon \pi - \gamma \ln m \tag{8.33}$$

Take the time derivatives of equation (8.33). After simplification it will take the following form (it is assumed that $d\lambda/dt = 0$):

$$d\pi/dt + z\pi = z\lambda \tag{8.34}$$

where $z = (\gamma/1-\gamma\epsilon)$

This is a non-homogeneous linear differential equation. The solution of this equation is given by

$$\pi(t) = [\pi(0) - \lambda] e^{-zt} + \lambda \tag{8.35}$$

It gives a dynamically stable inflation, provided that z is positive. Given that γ and ϵ are positive, z will be positive if $\gamma\epsilon < 1$. That is, the e^{-zt} term in the complementary function of the solution tends to zero as t tends to infinity. It implies that when the inflation rate deviates from equilibrium inflation to the rate of λ, it moves towards it as time passes. It is shown in the following phase diagram.

Given that the differential equation (8.34) is of the form $dy/dt = f(y)$, it is possible to plot $d\pi/dt$ against π (Figure 8.2). The slope of the phase line

189

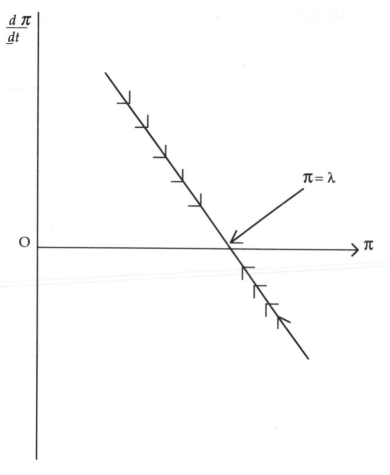

Figure 8.2 A phase diagram of inflation

is given by z which implies that the phase line slopes downward. That is, $\pi(t)$ converges to equilibrium because starting from a non-equilibrium position, the convergence of $\pi(t)$ hinges on the prospect that e^{-zt} tends to zero as t tends to infinity. This is clearly the case. Therefore, it is possible to say that inflation in the long run would converge to the rate of money supply growth. However, if z is negative (i.e. $\gamma\epsilon > 1$), inflation will diverge from equilibrium. Such a situation arises when the demand for real money balances falls more than proportionately to a rise in the rate of inflation.

CHOICE OF EXCHANGE RATE REGIMES FOR DEVELOPING COUNTRIES

Although most developing countries opted for a fixed exchange rate system of one form or other after the generalised floating of the exchange rates in the 1970s, a significant number of developing countries have moved away from the fixed exchange rate system. Over time, they adopted the flexible exchange rate system for at least three reasons.[6] First, when inflation in many developing countries accelerated in the 1980s, they allowed their currencies to depreciate to restore external competitiveness. Second, the switch from pegging to a flexible exchange rate arrangement was to minimise the adverse effect of the fluctuations of the exchange rates of major currencies. Third, the move was politically convenient for developing countries to devalue their currencies. As Aghevli *et al.* aptly put it:

> given the political stigma attached to devaluation under a pegged regime, an increasing number of countries have found it expedient to adopt a more flexible arrangement for adjusting the exchange rate on the basis of an undisclosed basket of currencies. Such an arrangement enables the authorities to take advantage of the fluctuations in major currencies to camouflage an effective depreciation of their exchange rate, thus avoiding the political repercussions of an announced devaluation.
>
> (Aghevli *et al.*, 1991: 3)

The growing adoption of the freely floating exchange rate arrangement by developing countries has drawn some criticism because it has been associated with high inflation.[7] It gives prominence to the view that the depreciation of the exchange rate causes inflation, although it is often difficult to detect the direction of causality between them.[8] Nevertheless, some IMF Executive Board members have been arguing for fixed exchange rate arrangements for developing countries as they believe that such an arrangement would impose fiscal-monetary discipline and act as nominal anchors (Edwards, 1993). By discouraging recourse to inflationary finance, the fixed exchange rate system is also believed to achieve price stability. Recall that the fixed exchange rate system is incompatible with sustained budget deficits financed by money creation. Another prominent argument for the fixed exchange rate system is that it is credible and time consistent and hence is able to keep inflation low. As Edwards puts it:

> Much of the recent enthusiasm for fixed nominal exchange rates is intellectually rooted on the modern credibility and time consistency literature. According to this approach governments that have the discretion to alter the nominal exchange rate will tend to abuse their power, introducing an inflationary bias into the economy. The reason for this is that under a set of plausible conditions, such as the existence of labor market rigidities that preclude the economy from reaching

full employment, it will be optimal for the government to 'surprise' the private sector through unexpected devaluations. By engineering these unexpected devaluations, the government expects to induce a reduction in real wages and, thus, an increase in employment and a boost in output. Naturally, in equilibrium the public will be aware of this incentive faced by the authorities, and will react to it by anticipating the devaluation surprises and hence rendering them ineffective. As a consequence of this strategic interaction between the government and the private sector, the economy will reach a high inflation plateau.

(Edwards, 1993: 17)

The above discussion reveals that the merit of adopting a fixed exchange rate system in developing countries is that the authorities in those countries tempt to misuse the discretion to change the exchange rates under an adjustable fixed exchange rate system. In the literature this issue is discussed within the perspective of the political economy of inflation. Persson and Tabellini (1990) find that there is a close relationship between the degree of political instability and polarisation and the reliance on inflation tax: countries which are politically unstable have a higher proclivity towards inflation. Edwards and Tabellini (1991) have devised an index to measure the degree of political instability and found that Asian nations tend to have a lower degree of political instability compared with that observed in Latin American countries. Therefore, Asian countries have a lower temptation to misuse their exchange rate discretion, and the benefits associated with fixed exchange rates would be smaller in those countries compared with Latin American countries. As Singapore shows, such countries may be better off by adopting a system of crawling-peg or adjustable fixed rate. In contrast, if a country is characterised by political instability and shows a lack of fiscal-monetary discipline, a fixed exchange rate offers a better choice as it will remove the discretion from the monetary authority and impose fiscal discipline. This has led many Latin American observers to recommend a currency board.

A currency board is an independent organisation with exclusive authority to create base money. This is done entirely by buying and selling foreign exchange at a fixed rate. The currency board must keep the exchange rate convertible and must back the base money by at least 100 per cent in foreign exchange reserves. Therefore, under the currency board system, the money supply is determined by the balance of payments and is also influenced by the money multiplier. While such a system imposes monetary discipline by removing discretion from the monetary authority and thereby establishes price stability, there is a clear trade-off. As pointed out by Drake (1969, 1980), the currency board system will have a contractionary bias since the money supply cannot expand in step with growing domestic production. However, this problem does not arise if prices are flexible downwards, there is perfect international mobility of capital, and/or there is a secular growth of external reserves through a trade surplus and/or net capital inflow. Any tendency towards contraction will push up interest rates and reduce prices, thereby generating a balance of payments surplus which induces money supply growth.

SUMMARY AND CONCLUSION

This chapter has developed the relationships among bank credit, money, balance of payments, prices and the exchange rates. It is found that under a fixed exchange rate system, there is a relationship between central bank credit and the balance of payments. In fact a credit growth rule can be devised to maintain the balance of payments in equilibrium. Such a credit growth rule is commonly used by the IMF for stabilisation programmes in developing countries.

As inflation is a major problem in developing countries, the fixed exchange rate system is considered appropriate in those countries in the belief that it would act as a nominal anchor. The fixed exchange rate system can also impose monetary-fiscal discipline. Under a fixed exchange rate system any fiscal deficit financed by borrowing from the central bank may deplete foreign exchange reserves and, if fiscal deficits persist, the country may eventually run out of reserves. Consequently the pegged or fixed exchange rate regime may collapse after a speculative attack as residents fearing devaluation and inflation attempt to convert their money for foreign currency or financial assets.

NOTES

1 Aghevli *et al.* (1979) argue that in practice there is no clear-cut gain in choosing either the fixed or flexible exchange rate system in terms of its disciplinary role:

> [while] a fixed exchange rate regime could bring a desirable element of discipline by providing additional leverage for economic policymakers to use in resisting political pressures for rapid monetary expansion . . ., [i]t should be recognized that even under a floating system, monetary authorities would not have the freedom to expand the money supply indiscriminately unless they were willing to accept the political consequences of a continual depreciation of the currency.
>
> (Aghevli *et al.*, 1979: 786)

2 See Frenkel and Johnson (1976, 1978) for collections of papers on different aspects of the monetary approach to balance of payments theory and the exchange rates. And for a critical review of this approach, see Kreinin and Officer (1978).
3 When countries access their IMF tranches, the finance is not technically in the form of loans. It involves the purchase of foreign currency with domestic currency.
4 This section draws on materials from Agenor *et al.* (1992).
5 Let QT and QN be real outputs in the traded and non-traded goods sectors. By definition, total output $Q = QT + QN$. ϕ can be expressed as $PTQT/Q$ and $(1-\phi) = PNQN/Q$. The assumption that ϕ is constant implies that the rates

of inflation in the two sectors are equal. If this assumption is violated, say, for example, $\Delta PN\delta > \Delta PT\delta$, ϕ will fall. For details, see Prachowny (1975).

6 The number of developing countries under the pegged exchange rate arrangement has declined from 86 per cent in 1976 to 66 per cent in 1989 (Aghevli *et al.*, 1991).

7 Aghevli *et al.* (1991: 13) report that 'the inflation performance of the countries that have operated under a fixed exchange rate regime has been, on the whole, superior to that of the group operating under more flexible arrangements'.

8 Exchange rate changes do not impart a permanent effect on the inflation rate, but cause temporary changes. Once the exchange rate of the currency stops appreciating or depreciating, its direct effect on domestic inflation tends towards zero. Hafer (1989) argues that the depreciation of the exchange rate and the acceleration of inflation may be the manifestation of the same thing, namely, the rise in the growth rate of the money supply.

9

FINANCIAL STABILITY, MONETARY DISCIPLINE AND INSTITUTIONS

Money's short- and long-run roles in economic stabilisation and growth have produced one of the most passionate debates in economic literature. Economists of the Keynesian persuasion believe that the fundamental problem of economic growth is the lack of adequate accumulation of capital. It arises from various market failures which are responsible for both low savings and underinvestment. According to them, a policy of interest rate ceilings below the equilibrium rate and monetary expansion can promote capital formation. While the former encourages investment by keeping the cost of investible funds low, monetary expansion creates forced savings through inflation, which redistributes income from households with a low propensity to save to those with a high propensity to save. Inflation also induces portfolio shifts towards real investment as returns on financial assets decline with inflation.

On the other hand, the neoclassical orthodoxy holds the view that the low level of savings is the fundamental cause of underdevelopment. Therefore, raising the savings rate is a prerequisite for higher investment and economic growth. This is particularly so in developing countries where investment depends on personal finance. According to this view, administratively controlled low interest rates coupled with high inflation are an impediment to growth as they discourage savings and lower the efficiency of investment. Furthermore, the concomitant policy of arbitrary credit allocation induces government failures as it generates rent-seeking activities. What follows from this theoretical proposition is financial liberalisation reform. The reform is expected to promote growth by raising savings and both the quantity and quality of investment.

While the forced-savings view dominated the policy making in developing countries in the 1950s and 1960s, the financial liberalisation paradigm has been the catch-phrase of the 1970s and 1980s. However, none of the views stood up to empirical evidence. High and rapidly rising inflation is found to impede economic growth. Similarly, only countries with large financial repressions and arbitrary rules for credit allocation are found to have dismal growth performance. Out of the empirical evidence a consensus has emerged that mild inflation and repression may promote economic growth.

Monetarists and Keynesians debated the issue of whether monetary policy should be used in stabilising short-term fluctuations in output and employment. Although Keynes was not enthusiastic about the efficacy of monetary policy because of the possibility of uncertainties in the long process through which money supply affects output, Keynesians believe that monetary policy has a role in stabilisation. On the other hand, monetarists hold the view that monetary policy should be used only to stabilise the price level. If it is assigned to do more than that, monetary policy itself can become a source of instability. A consensus is now emerging that while money can affect output in the short run, it should be used primarily to stabilise the price level and/or the exchange rate.

The debate about the short-run stabilisation role of monetary policy did not receive much attention in developing countries where the predominant concern has been money's long-term role in economic growth. It is now increasingly realised that the dichotomy between the short-run and long-run roles of monetary policy is artificial. The experience of high-performing East Asian economies shows that monetary policy, by providing a stable macro-economic environment characterised by low inflation and realistic exchange rates, can contribute significantly to long-term growth of per capita real income.

If the emerging consensus is that mild inflation and financial repression can be conducive to growth and that monetary policy should be used to achieve price stability, then how is the danger of excesses by an over-zealous government to be prevented? In other words, if the policy of inflationary finance and financial repression is to some degree an optimal response to market failures, what can minimise the possibility of government failures? The fact that many developing countries experienced growth-inhibiting large financial repressions in the sense of negative real interest rates and high and unstable inflation rates is clear evidence that, just as markets can fail, governments can fail, too. However, as the financial crises of many liberalising countries show, the wholesale *laissez-faire* approach is not the appropriate response to government failures (Killick, 1990; Stiglitz, 1990). Rather, what is required is to find an appropriate institutional framework which can induce responsible government behaviour and restrain abuses of macroeconomic policies. Therefore, the challenge is to design institutional arrangements that would simultaneously minimise both financial market failures and government failures.

INSTITUTIONAL ARRANGEMENTS FOR THE FINANCIAL MARKET

Market failures are endemic in financial markets. These failures manifest themselves in underinvestment in socially desirable sectors, moral hazards in both lender and borrower behaviour, uncompetitive behaviour of the banking sector, and so on. How can a government minimise these failures without necessarily engendering its own failures? Once it is recognised that the main source of government failures is the complexity and arbitrariness of regulations, it is not difficult to devise regulatory principles that can prevent government failures while at the same time minimise financial market failures.

One simple and less-costly way to reduce arbitrariness is to remove discretion from the regulator by adopting an indirect control mechanism (Stiglitz, 1994). This entails incentives and restraints. Governments can reduce moral hazards by restricting risky actions by financial institutions. Since financial scandals are often found to be associated with loans to 'insiders', restrictions on such loans can reduce the possibility of fraud and embezzlement of funds. Similarly, some restraints on the cross-ownership of financial institutions and business enterprises can mitigate the problem of fraudulent or unsecured loans. The financial institutions will also have the incentive not to take too risky an action if they stand to lose more in the event of failure. Restrictions and incentives are the same principles that the insurance industry applies to minimise moral hazards. The dependence on indirect mechanisms reduces the burden of checking and reviewing a whole range of activities. It also resolves the problem that arises from the inability to measure many performance variables properly. In fact the measurement problem may itself contribute to arbitrariness. Furthermore, indirect control mechanisms are also appropriate for developing countries which do not have large endowments of administrative capabilities to handle complex regulatory concepts and procedures. As Levy and Spiller (1994: 217) point out, '[a] country's institutional endowment strongly affects whether it can put in place a regulatory system with the capacity to credibly restrain arbitrary administrative action'.

Where an indirect mechanism is not possible, direct intervention can only be prescribed under established guidelines. However, such guidelines must be simple and easily monitored. Otherwise, there is a danger of either wrongly penalising some or not taking actions against offenders. Tightening of the rules increases the probability of one type of error while reducing the other. Therefore, the costs and benefits of the two types of error must be weighed in devising the appropriate rules for intervention. A corollary of this principle is that when a policy of selective credit is needed to direct funds to some 'priority' sectors, it must be done against a simple and directly measurable traget. The experience of the East Asian NIEs reveals that export is a better criterion than employment or output, which are often used in inward-looking countries. This perhaps explains why directed credit policy and financial repression did not produce the desired high economic growth in countries following an import-substituting industrialisation policy as they did in the case of outward-oriented high-performing Asian economies.

One important issue involving the regulatory mechanism is who monitors the monitors. Apart from the possibility of being corrupt, all monitoring is fallible. One possible solution lies in the institution of peer monitoring. While each monitoring agency monitors the financial institutions, they also monitor each other. This, however, may generate the wasteful duplication of services, and the costs of duplication must be weighed against the benefits of reducing corruption and monitoring fallibility.

While the above should guide the principle of prudential regulation, the fundamental objective of government intervention should be the provision of consumer protection, ensuring the stability and solvency of the financial system, improving allocative efficiency, and enhancing competition in the financial market.

INSTITUTIONAL FRAMEWORK AND MONETARY POLICY CREDIBILITY

The credibility of government policy in general depends on government's commitment to carry out its policy announcements. It is linked to policy-makers' actual and perceived objective functions.[1] The issue becomes complex when policy-makers have the incentive to conceal their true stance on policy and are motivated by personal, political and other factors. Once again the solution lies in simple rules.

First, as revealed in both theoretical and empirical reviews, monetary policy should be assigned the sole role of price stability. This single objective monetary policy has the advantage of being easy to monitor. The monetary authority can be made accountable and it cannot hide its failures behind other objectives. This simple rule has the added advantage of being credible. In contrast, when monetary policy is given the role of achieving multiple objectives, such as inflation control and unemployment reduction, it creates dynamic inconsistency and credibility problems because the private sector knows that at some stage in the future the government must create surprise inflation to reduce unemployment.

The second simple rule is the removal of the discretionary power of the monetary authority to vary money supply. One way to do so is to follow a simple money supply growth rule tied to the natural growth of the economy. For example, if the long-run growth rate of the economy is g_y per cent and the income-elasticity of the demand for money is unity, then money supply should not grow at a rate greater than g_y per cent to facilitate the extra transaction needs created by additional output. If the money supply grows at the same rate as the growth rate of real output and if the velocity of money is constant, then from the quantity theory it follows that the inflation rate will be zero. However, g_y per cent or a constant money supply growth rule implies that the monetary authority has control over the monetary base and it can choose an inflation rate. It also assumes that the money multiplier is stable, or at least predictable.

What institutional arrangements will ensure the implementation of these simple rules for the enhancement of monetary policy credibility and monetary stability? To begin with if the government resorts to deficit budgets financed through borrowing from the central bank, the monetary authority will lose control over the monetary base and hence it cannot credibly apply the simple money supply growth rule. As a matter of fact, in most developing countries government deficits financed by borrowing from the central bank have been found to be a major source of monetary expansion and unsustainable inflation. Recent research and the experience of some high-performing Asian countries has shown that if the central bank is made independent[2] from other parts of the government and granted a mandate for maintaining price stability, then a government can strengthen its commitment to price stability. Thus, central bank independence can provide a necessary institutional limit on the unsustainable monetary creation that results from persistent budget deficits. The empirical evidence gathered by Cukierman *et al.* (1992) does indeed show that central bank independence contributes to low inflation.

However, it must be emphasised that central bank independence by itself cannot ensure monetary policy credibility; this depends ultimately on the credibility of the government policy as a whole (Swinburne and Castello-Branco, 1991).[3] For example, if the budgetary process is not reformed, and the government budget deficits persist, eventually the central bank will have to cave in.

Thus, given the imperfect constraints on their inefficient governments that the political systems in developing countries have, constitutional safeguards may well be necessary on fiscal, debt and money-creation capacities (Brenan and Buchanan, 1980; Islam, 1995). In the extreme cases it may involve having legislation, to make all unfunded government spending programmes constitutionally illegal. This arrangement is referred to as a 'fiscal constitution'. In fact, it is not difficult to find the existence of such a fiscal constitution in reality. Indonesia, for example, is often cited as a case where a fiscal constitution has apparently been followed (Pangestu, 1991; Woo and Nasution, 1989). Other countries where some sort of fiscal constitution exist are Thailand and Taiwan.

In sum, a fiscal constitution and central bank independence must go hand in hand in order to reduce policy uncertainty and variablity. The twin institutions of fiscal constitution and central bank independence lay the foundations of good governance.

Of course, such institutional arrangements could lead to debilitating inflexibility, especially in developing countries which are prone to both internal and external supply shocks.[4] But, as discussions in Chapter 5 showed, discretionary monetary policy in response to supply shocks can make the situation even worse in the long run. Furthermore the evidence shows that the growth dividend of macroeconomic stability far outweigh the costs of inflexibility.

OPENNESS AND MONETARY AND FINANCIAL STABILITY

The openness of an economy can serve as a further institutional constraint on macroeconomic mismanagement and financial instability. One factor is that policy mistakes cannot continue for long or go far in an open economy. The reaction of the financial market will be swift to enforce fiscal and monetary discipline. Large and persistent budget deficits can fuel the expectations of accelerating inflation and create balance of payments and exchange rate crises that lead to an eventual sharp devaluation of the domestic currency. The fear of large depreciations of currency may cause massive capital flights, exacerbating the exchange rate crises.

Countries which are characterised by high inflation and large budget deficits should consider following a fixed exchange rate system. They can achieve monetary discipline by pegging the currency to a stable currency or a basket of currencies. This acts as a nominal anchor and can be used to persuade political leaders to restrain their propensity to deficit financing and macroeconomic populism. This, however, means that the constant money supply growth rule cannot be applied rigidly because the movements in foreign reserves will affect the monetary base.

However, the question of the degree of commitment to a fixed exchange rate system remains an issue. We can find a continuum that starts with adjustable peg, and goes through stronger commitments such as are found in Singapore or Hong Kong. The institutional arrangement of a currency board can impose a strict commitment to a fixed exchange rate system. The currency board implements full convertibility and is managed by an authority which is independent of the central bank. It signals a strong commitment to the exchange rate policy that cannot be easily reversed.

As we mentioned in Chapter 8, the currency board system however can have a contractionary effect in the absence of a continuous surplus in the balance of payments commensurate with the expansion of the domestic economy. It underpins the importance of the growth of the traded goods sector and of outward-oriented economic policies. The costs and benefits of a strong commitment in the form of a currency board, of course, involve a trade-off between credibility and flexibility. For a country with a long inflationary history, it may be argued that the currency board will yield positive net gains.

SUMMARY AND CONCLUSION

The principles for the institutional framework for government action in the field of monetary and financial policies which can safeguard against government failures can be set out in a number of guidelines:

(a) While the government should primarily follow market-based and private-sector-driven initiatives for the mobilisation of savings and the allocation of investible funds to growth-promoting activities, it has a role in financial markets as an insurer. It cannot abandon its responsibility as a prudential regulator to ensure the solvency and stability of the financial system.

(b) Governments should intervene in financial markets only in cases of clearly established market failures, such as underinvestment in the financial infrastructure. Even in such situations, attempts must be made to implement workable and incentive-compatible policies.

(c) The government should maintain macroeconomic stability through appropriate institutional arrangements such as a fiscal constitution and a monetary constitution in the form of central bank independence.

(d) Commitment to the free international exchange of goods and services and free international capital movements can provide added safeguards against fiscal and monetary indiscipline.

(e) In the context of an open economy, the institution of a fixed exchange rate system or a currency board may enhance policy credibility and monetary stability.

NOTES

1 Policy-makers are classified as Type I and Type II. Type I policy-makers are strongly anti-inflationary in their preferences and do not seek to create surprise inflation. Type II policy-makers expose themselves as anti-inflationary but are tempted to create surprise inflation. The problem for the private sector is to distinguish between a Type I and a Type II policy-maker (Blackburn and Christensen, 1989).

2 Many authors prefer to use a different expression to refer to central bank independence. Hetzel (1990) uses 'central bank autonomy' or 'autonomy with discretion' in order to avoid the risk of implying a lack of constraints. Similarly, Fair (1979) uses 'independence within government' rather that 'independent from government'.

3 However, as Friedman (1962) pointed out, central bank independence can be abused by inefficient officials who may have their own agenda and are motivated by factors which are different from those in an altruistic social welfare function.

4 See Swinbourne and Castello-Branco (1991) for a critical analysis of the issue of central bank independence.

BIBLIOGRAPHY

Abel, A.B. (1990) 'Consumption and Investment', in Friedman, B. and Hahn, F.H. (eds), *Handbook of Monetary Economics*, Amsterdam: North-Holland.

Acharya, S. and Madhur, S. (1985) 'Informal Credit Markets and Black Money: Do They Frustrate Monetary Policy?', *Economic and Political Weekly*, 18 (41).

Adekunle, J. (1968) 'The Demand for Money: Evidence from Developed and Less Developed Economies', *IMF Staff Papers*, 15(2): 220–266.

Adelman, I. and Morris, C.T. (1973) *Economic Growth and Social Equity in Developing Countries*, Stanford, Cal.: Stanford University Press.

Agabin, M. *et al.* (1989) 'Integrative Reports on the Informal Credit Markets in the Philippines', Working Paper Series no. 88–12, Quezon City: Philippine Institute of Development Studies.

Agenor, P., Bhandari, J. and Flood, R. (1992) 'Speculative Attacks and Models of Balance of Payments Crises', *IMF Staff Papers*, 39(2): 357–394.

Aghevli, B. (1977) 'Inflationary Finance and Growth', *Journal of Political Economy*, 85: 1295–1307.

Aghevli, B. and Khan, M. (1978) 'Government Budget Deficits and Inflationary Process in Developing Countries', *IMF Staff Papers*, 25: 383–416.

Aghevli, B. and Khan, M. (1980) 'Credit Policy and the Balance of Payments in Developing Countries', in Coates, W. and Khatkhate, D., *Money and Monetary Policy in Less Developed Countries: A Survey of Issues and Evidence*, Oxford: Pergamon Press, 685–711.

Aghevli, B., Khan, M. and Montiel, P. (1991) *Exchange Rate Policy in Developing Countries: Some Analytical Issues*, IMF Occasional Paper no. 78, Washington, D.C.: International Monetary Fund.

Aghevli, B., Khan, M., Narvekar, P. and Short, B. (1979) 'Monetary Policy in Selected Asian Countries', *IMF Staff Papers*, 26: 775–824.

Aghevli, B. and Sassanpour, C. (1982), 'Prices, Output and the Trade Balance in Iran', *World Development*, 10: 791–800.

Ahmed, I. (1981) 'Wage Determination in Bangladesh Agriculture', *Oxford Economic Papers*, 33(2): 298–322.

Ahmed, L. (1986) 'Stabilization Policies in Developing Countries', *World Bank Research Observer*, 1(1): 79–110.

Ahmed, S. (1984) 'Inflation in Bangladesh: Causes and Consequences', unpublished PhD dissertation, Department of Economics, Boston University.

Alesina, A. and Summers, L. (1993) 'Central Bank Independence and Macroeconomic Performance', *Journal of Money, Credit, and Banking*, 25: 151–162.

Alesina, A. and Tabellini, G. (1989) 'External Debt, Capital Flights and Political Risk', *Journal of International Economics*, 104: 325–345.

Alesina, A. and Tabellini, G. (1990) 'A Political Theory of Fiscal Deficits and Government Debt', *Review of Economic Studies*, 57: 403–414.

Amin, A.T.M.N. (1982) 'An Analysis of Labour Force and Industrial Organization of the Informal Sector in Dacca', unpublished PhD dissertation, Department of Economics, University of Manitoba.

Amsden, A. (1989) *Asia's Next Giant: South Korea and Late Industrialization*, New York: Oxford University Press.

Amsden, A. (1991) 'Diffusion of Development: the Late Industrializing Model and Greater Asia', *American Economic Review* (Papers and Proceedings), 81(2): 282–286.

Amsden, A. and Euh, Y. (1993) 'South Korea's 1980s Financial Reforms: Good-bye Financial Repression (Maybe), Hello Institutional Restraints', *World Development*, 21(3): 379–390.

Argy, V. (1970) 'Structural Inflation in Developing Countries', *Oxford Economic Papers*, 22: 73–85.

Argy, V. (1992) *Australian Macroeconomic Policy in a Changing World Environment*, Sydney: Allen & Unwin.

Arndt. H. (1982) 'Two Kinds of Credit Rationing', *BNL Quarterly Review*, December.

Arndt, H. (1983) 'Financial Development in Asia', *Asian Development Review*, 1(1): 86–100.

Arrow, K.J. (1962) 'The Economic Implications of Learning by Doing', *Review of Economic Studies*, 29 (June): 155–173.

Artis, M. and Lewis, M. (1990) 'Money Demand and Supply', in Bandyopadhyay, T. and Ghatak, S. (eds), *Current Issues in Monetary Economics*, New York: Harvester Wheatsheaf.

Asian Development Bank (1990) *Asian Development Outlook 1990*, Manila: Asian Development Bank.

Asilis, C.M. and Milesi-Ferretti, G.M. (1994) 'On the Political Sustainability of Economic Reform', Paper on Policy Analysis and Assessment PPAA/94/3, Washington, D.C.: International Monetary Fund.

Athukorala, P. (1992) 'Liberalization of the Domestic Financial Market: Theoretical Issues with Evidence from Sri Lanka', Discussion Paper 16/92, School of Economics, La Trobe University, Australia.

Baer, W. (1967) 'The Inflation Controversy in Latin America: a Survey', *Latin American Research Review*, February: 3–25.

Baer, W. and Kertenetzky, I. (eds) (1964) *Inflation and Growth in Latin America*, Homewood, III: Irwin.

Bailey, M.J. (1956) 'The Welfare Cost of Inflationary Finance', *Journal of Political Economy*, 64: 93–110.

Balino, T.J.T. (1987) *Argentine Banking Crisis of 1980*, Working Paper 87–77, Washington, D.C.: International Monetary Fund.

Balino, T.J.T. and Sundararajan, V. (1986), 'Financial Reform in Indonesia: Causes, Consequences, and Prospects', in Cheng, H. (ed.), *Financial Policy Reform in Pacific Basin Countries*, Lexington, Mass.: Lexington Books.

Bandyopadhyay, T. and Ghatak, S. (1990) 'Monetary Growth Models: the Role of Money Demand Functions', in Bandyopadhyay, T. and Ghatak, S. (eds), *Current Issues in Monetary Economics*, New York: Harvester Wheatsheaf.

Bardhan, K. (1977) 'Rural Employment, Wages and Labour Markets in India: A Survey of Research, Part I, Part II, and Part III', *Economic and Political Weekly* 12(26):A34–48, 12(27): 1062–1074, 12(28): 1108–1118.

Bardhan, P. (1979) 'Wages and Unemployment in a Poor Agrarian Economy: a Theoretical and Empirical Analysis', *Journal of Political Economy*, 87(3): 479–500.

Barro, R.J. (1979) 'Money and Output in Mexico, Colombia and Brazil', in Behrman, J. and Hanson, J. (eds), *Short-term Macroeconomic Policy in Latin America*, Cambridge, Mass.: Harvard University Press.

Barro, R.J. (1981) 'Rational Expectations and the Role of Monetary Policy,' in Lucas, R. and Sargent, T. (eds), *Rational Expectations and Econometric Practice*, London: Allen & Unwin.

Barro, R.J. (1991) 'Economic Growth in a Cross Section of Countries', *Quarterly Journal of Economics*, 106: 407–433.

Baumol, W. (1952) 'The Transactions Demand for Cash: an Inventory Theoretic Approach', *Quarterly Journal of Economics*, 66: 545–556.

Bhagwati, J. (1978) *Foreign Trade Regimes and Economic Development: Anatomy and Consequences of Exchange Control Regimes*, New York: National Bureau of Economic Research.

Bhalla, S. (1981) 'The Transmission of Inflation into Developing Countries', in Cline, W. *et al.* (eds), *World Inflation and the Developing Countries*, Washington, D.C.: Brookings Institution.

Bhatia, R. (1960–1) 'Inflation, Deflation and Economic Development', *IMF Staff Papers*, 8: 101–114.

Blackburn, K. and Christensen, M. (1989) 'Monetary Policy and Policy Credibility', *Journal of Economic Literature*, 27: 1–45.

Blanchard, O.J. (1990) 'Why Does Money Affect Output? A Survey' in Friedman, B.M. and Hahn, F.H. (eds), *Handbook of Monetary Economics*, vol. 2, Amsterdam: North-Holland.

Blanchard, O.J. and Fischer, S. (1989) *Lectures on Macroeconomics*, Cambridge, Mass.: MIT Press.

Blanchard, O.J. and Summers, L.H. (1986) 'Hysteresis and the European Unemployment Problem', in Fischer, S. (eds), *NBER Macroeconomics Annual*, Cambridge, Mass.: MIT Press.

Blejer, M. and Khan, M. (1984) 'Government Policy and Private Investment in Developing Countries', *IMF Staff Papers*, 31: 379–403.

Bomhoff, E. (1983) *Monetary Uncertainty*, Amsterdam: North-Holland.

Bottomley, A. (1965) 'Keynesian Monetary Theory and the Developing Countries', *Indian Economic Journal*, 12: 1–32.

Branson, W.H. (1989) *Macroeconomic Theory and Policy*, New York: Harper & Row.

Brenan, G. and Buchanan, J.M. (1980) *The Power to Tax: Analytical Foundations of a Fiscal Constitution*, Cambridge: Cambridge University Press.

Brunner, K. and Meltzer, A. (1963) 'Predicting Velocity: Implications for Theory and Policy', *Journal of Finance*, 18: 319–354.

Brunner, K. and Meltzer, A. (1968) 'Liquidity Traps for Money, Bank Credit and Interest Rates', *Journal of Political Economy*, 76(1): 1–37.

Bruno, M. (1979) 'Stabilization and Stagflation in a Semi-industrialised Economy', in Dornbusch, R. and Frenkel, J.A. (eds), *International Economic Policy, Theory and Evidence*, Baltimore, Md.: Johns Hopkins University Press.

Bruno, M. (1991) 'High Inflation and the Nominal Anchors of an Open Economy', Princeton Essays in International Finance no. 183, Princeton, N.J.: Princeton University.

Bruno, M. and Fischer, S. (1990) 'Seigniorage, Operating Rules, and the High Inflation Trap', *Quarterly Journal of Economics*, (May): 353–374.

Bruno, M. and Sachs, J. (1985) *Economics of Worldwide Stagflation*, Oxford: Blackwell.

Buchanan, J. and Wagner, R. (1977) *Democracy and Deficit*, New York: Academic Press.

Buchanan, J., Rowley, C. and Tollison, R. (1987) *Deficits*, Oxford: Blackwell.

Buckle, R. and Stemp, P. (1991) 'Reserve Bank Autonomy and the Credibility of Monetary Policy: a Game Theoretic Approach', *New Zealand Economic Papers*, 25(1): 51–85.

Burkner, H.P. (1982), 'The Portfolio Behaviour of Individual Investors in Developing Countries: an Analysis of the Philippines Case', *Oxford Bulletin of Economics and Statistics*, 44: 127–144

Burton, D. and Gilman, M. (1991) 'Exchange Rate Policy and the IMF', *Finance and Development*, 28: 18–21.

Cabalu, H. (1993) 'Philippine Development Experience: a Case of "What Not to Do" ', paper presented at the Second International Conference of the International Institute of Development Studies, University of Western Australia, 13–15 December 1993.

Cagan, P. (1956) 'The Monetary Dynamics of Hyperinflation', in Friedman, M. (ed.), *Studies in the Quantity Theory of Money*, Chicago, Ill.: University of Chicago Press.

Calomiris, C.W. and Himmelberg, C.P. (1994) 'Directed Credit Programs for Agriculture and Industry: Arguments from Theory and Fact', Proceedings of the World Bank Annual Conference on Development Economics 1993, Washington, D.C.: World Bank, 113–154.

Calvo, G. *et al.* (1993) 'Capital Inflows and Real Exchange Rate Appreciation in Latin America', *IMF Staff Papers*, 40(1): 108–151.

Campbell, J. Y. and Mankiw, N.G. (1987) 'Are Output Fluctuations Transitory?', *Quarterly Journal of Economics*, 102(4): 857–880.

Campos, R. (1967) *Reflections on Latin American Development*, Austin, Tx.: Texas University Press.

Canavese, A. (1982) 'The Structuralist Explanation in Theory of Inflation', *World Development*, 10: 523–530.

Cardoso, E. (1981) 'Food Supply and Inflation', *Journal of Development Economics*, 8: 269–284.

Cavallo, D. (1977) 'Stagflationary Effects of Monetarist Stabilization Policies', unpublished PhD thesis, Harvard University.

Chadha, B. and Teja, R. (1989) 'Macroeconomics and Famine', *Working Paper WP/89/25*, Washington, D.C.: International Monetary Fund.

Chandavarkar, A. (1985) 'The Informal Financial Sector in Developing Countries: Analysis, Evidence and Implications', paper presented to SEACEN Seminar in Jakarta, Indonesia. Also in *Finance and Development*, 22: 24–27.

Chandavarkar, A. (1992) 'Of Finance and Development', *World Development*, 20: 133–142.

Chick, V. (1973) *The Theory of Monetary Policy*, London: Gray-Mills.

Cho, T.J. (1989) 'Finance and Development: the Korean Approach', *Oxford Review of Economic Policy*, 5(4): 88–102.

Cho, Y.J. (1990), 'McKinnon–Shaw versus the Neostructuralists on Financial Liberalization: a Conceptual Note', *World Development*, 18(3): 477–480.

Cho, Y.J. and Khatkhate, D. (1989) 'Lessons of Financial Liberalization in Asia: a Comparative Study', Discussion Paper no. 50, Washington, D.C.: World Bank.

Chow, G. (1966) 'On the Long-run and Short-run Demand for Money', *Journal of Political Economy*, 74(2): 111–131.

Chowdhury, A. and Islam, I (1993) *The Newly Industrialising Economies of East Asia*, New York: Routledge.

Claassen, E. and Salin, P. (eds), (1976) *Recent Issues in International Monetary Economics*, Amsterdam: North-Holland.

Clayton, G., Gilbert, J. and Sedgwick, R. (eds), (1977) *Monetary Theory and Monetary Policy in the 1970s*, Oxford: Oxford University Press.

Clements, B. and Schwartz, G. (1993) 'Currency Substitution: the Recent Experience of Bolivia', *World Development*, 21(11): 1883–1893.

Coates, W. and Khatkhate, D. (1980) *Money and Monetary Policy in Less Developed Countries: A Survey of Issues and Evidence*, Oxford: Pergamon Press.

Coates, W. and Khatkhate, D. (1984) 'Monetary Policy in Less Developing Countries: Main Issues', *Developing Economies*, Dec.: 329–348.

Cohen, D. (1985) 'Inflation, Wealth, and Interest Rates in an Intertemporal Optimizing Model', *Journal of Monetary Economics*, 16: 73–85.

Cole, D. (1988) 'Financial Development in Asia', *Asian Pacific Economic Literature*, 2(2): 26–47.

Cole, D. and Park, Y.C. (1983) *Financial Development in Korea, 1945–1978*, Cambridge, Mass.: Harvard University Press.

Cole, D. and Patrick, H. (1986) 'Financial Development in the Pacific Basin Market Economies', in Tan, A. and Kapur, B.K. (eds), *Pacific Growth and Financial Independence*, Sydney: Allen & Unwin.

Cole, D. and Slade, B. (1992) 'Indonesian Financial Development: a Different Sequencing?', in Vittas, D. (ed.), *Financial Regulation: Changing the Rules of the Game*, EDI Series in Economic Development, Washington, D.C.: World Bank.

Collier, P. and Mayer, C. (1989) 'The Assessment: Financial Liberalization, Financial Systems, and Economic Growth', *Oxford Review of Economic Policy*, 5(4): 1–12.

Corbo, V. (1985) 'Reforms and Macroeconomic Adjustments in Chile During 1974–84', *World Development*, 13(8): 893–916.

Corbo, V. (1988) 'Problems, Development Theory, and Strategies of Latin America', in Ranis, G. and Schultz, T.P. (eds), *The State of Development Economics*, New York: Blackwell.

Corbo, V. and de Melo, J. (1985) 'Liberalization with Stabilization in the Southern Cone: Overview and Summary', *World Development*, 13(8): 863–866.

Corbo, V. and de Melo, J. (1987) 'Lessons from Southern Cone Policy Reforms', *World Bank Research Observer*, 2: 111–142.

Corden, W.M. (1984) 'Macroeconomic Targets and Instruments for a Small Open Economy', *Singapore Economic Review*, 24: 27–37.

Corden, W.M. (1987) 'The Relevance for Developing Countries of Recent Developments in Macroeconomic Theory', *World Bank Research Observer*, 2(1): 171–188.

Corden, W.M. (1988) 'Macroeconomic Adjustment in Developing Countries', *Working Paper WP/88/13*, Washington, D.C.: International Monetary Fund.

Crockett, A. and Nsouli, S. (1977) 'Exchange Rate Policies for Developing Countries', *Journal of Development Studies*, 13: 125–143.

Cukierman, A., Edwards, S. and Tabellini, G. (1989) 'Seigniorage and Political instability', NBER Working Paper no. 31999, Cambridge, Mass.: NBER.

Cukierman, A., Webb, S.B. and Neyapti, B. (1992) 'Measuring the Independence of Central Banks and its Effects on Policy Outcomes', *World Bank Economic Review*, 6(1): 353–398.

Cuddington, J. (1986) *Capital Flight: Estimates, Issues and Explanations*, Princeton Studies in International Finance no. 58, Princeton, NJ: Princeton University.

Danthine, J.P. (1992) 'Superneutrality', in Eatwell, J. *et al.* (eds), *The New Palgrave Dictionary of Money and Finance*, London: Macmillan.

Diaz-Alejandro, C. (1985) 'Good-bye Financial Repression, Hello Financial Crash', *Journal of Development Economics*, 19: 1–24

Diz, A. (1970), 'Money and Prices in Argentina 1935–62', in Meiselman, D. (ed.), *Varieties of Monetary Experience*, Chicago, Ill.: Chicago University Press.

Domar, E. (1946) 'Capital Expansion, Rate of Growth, and Employment', *Econometrica*, 137–147.

Domar, E. (1947) 'Expansion and Employment', *American Economic Review*, 37(1): 34–55.

Donavan, D.J. (1982) 'Macroeconomic Performance and Adjustment under Fund-supported Programs: The Experience of the Seventies', *IMF Staff Papers*, 29: 171–203.

Dooley, M.P. and Mathieson, D.J. (1987) 'Financial Liberalization and Stability in Developing Countries', Working Paper WP/87/19, Washington, D.C.: International Monetary Fund.

Dornbusch, R. (1980) *Open Economy Macroeconomics*, New York: Basic Books.

Dornbusch, R. (1983) 'Exchange Rate Economics: Where Do We Stand?', in Bhandari, J.S. and Putnam, B.H. (eds), *Economic Interdependence and Flexible Exchange Rates*, Cambridge, Mass.: MIT Press.

Dornbusch, R. (1984) *External Debt, Budget Deficits and Disequilibrium Exchange Rates*, NBER Working Paper no. 4, Cambridge, Mass.: NBER.

Dornbusch, R. (1988a) *Exchange Rates and Inflation*, Cambridge, Mass.: MIT Press.

Dornbusch, R. (1988b) 'Lessons from the German Inflation Experience of the 1920s', in *Exchange Rates and Inflation*, Cambridge, Mass.: MIT Press.

Dornbusch, R. (1991) 'Policies to Move from Stabilization to Growth', in Proceedings of the World Bank Annual Conference on Development Economics, Washington, D.C.: World Bank.

Dornbusch, R. (1993) *Stabilization, Debt, and Reform: Policy Analysis for Developing Countries*, New York: Harvester Wheatsheaf.

Dornbusch, R. and Edwards, S. (1990) 'The Macroeconomics of Populism in Latin America', *Journal of Development Economics*, 32: 247–277.

Dornbusch, R. and Fischer, S. (1981) 'Budget Deficits and Inflation', in Flanders, J. and Razin, A. (eds), *Development in an Inflationary World*, New York: Academic Press.

Dornbusch, R. and Fischer, S. (1990) *Macroeconomics*, New York: McGraw-Hill.

Dornbusch, R. and Frenkel, J.A. (1973) 'Inflation and Growth: Alternative Approaches', *Journal of Money, Credit, and Banking*, 5: 141–156.

Dornbusch, R. and Giovannini, A. (1990) 'Monetary Policy in the Open Economy', in Friedman, B.M. and Hahn, F.H. (eds), *Handbook of Monetary Economics*, vol. 2, Amsterdam: North-Holland

Dornbusch, R. and Park, Y.C. (1987) 'Korean Growth Policy', *Brookings Papers on Economic Activity*, 2: 389–444.

Dornbusch, R. and Reynoso, A. (1989) 'Financial Factors in Economic Development', *American Economic Review (Papers and Proceedings)*, 79(2): 204–209.

Dorrance, G. (1966) 'Inflation and Growth: the Statistical Evidence', *IMF Staff Papers*, 13: 82–102.

Drake, P.J. (1969) *Financial Development in Malaysia and Singapore*, Canberra: Australian National University Press.

Drake, P.J. (1980) *Money, Finance and Development*, Oxford: Martin Robertson.

Easterly, W. *et al.* (1992) 'Money Demand and Seigniorage-Maximizing Inflation', Policy Research Working Paper Series WPS1049, Washington, D.C.: World Bank.

Edel, M. (1969) *Food Supply and Inflation in Latin America*, New York: Praeger.

Edwards, S. (1983) 'The Short-run Relationship between Growth and Inflation in Latin America: Comment', *American Economic Review*, 73(3): 477–482.

Edwards, S. (1984) 'The Order of Liberalization of the External Sector in Developing Countries', *Essays in International Finance no. 156*, Princeton, N.J.: Princeton University.

Edwards, S. (1993) 'Exchange Rates as Nominal Anchors', *Review of World Economics*, 129(1): 1–32.

Edwards, S. (1994) 'The Political Economy of Inflation and Stabilization in Developing Countries', *Economic Development and Cultural Change*, 235–266.

Edwards, S. and Edwards, A.C. (1987) *Monetarism and Liberalization: The Chilean Experiment*, Cambridge, Mass.: Ballinger.

Edwards, S. and Tabellini, G. (1991) 'Explaining Fiscal Policies and Inflation in Developing Countries', *Journal of International Money and Finance*, 10: 16–48.

El-Erian, M. (1988) 'Currency Substitution in Egypt and the Yemen Arab Republic', *IMF Staff Papers*, 35: 85–103.

Engle, R. and Granger, C. (1987) 'Cointegration and Error Correction: Representation, Estimation and Testing', *Econometrica*, 55: 251–276.

Engle, R. and Granger, C. (eds) (1991) *Long-run Economic Relationships*, Oxford: Oxford University Press.

Fair, D. (1979) 'The Independence of Central Banks', *Banker*, October.

Fama, E. (1982) 'Inflation, Output, and Money', *Journal of Business*, 55: 201–231.

Fan, L.S. and Liu, Z.R. (1970), 'Demand for Money in Asian Countries: Empirical Evidence', *Indian Economic Journal*, 18(4–5): 475–81

Faruqi, S. (ed.), (1993) *Financial Sector Reforms in Asian and Latin American Countries: Lessons of Comparative Experience*, Washington, D.C.: Economic Development Institute of the World Bank.

Feige, E. and Pearce, D. (1977) 'The Substitutability of Money and Near Monies: A Survey of the Time Series Evidence', *Journal of Economic Literature*, 15(2): 439–469.

Fernandez, R. (1985) 'The Expectations Management Approach to Stabilization in Argentina During 1976–82', *World Development*, 13(8): 871–892.

Findlay, R. (1984) 'Growth and Development in Trade Models', in Jones, R. and Kennen, P. (eds), *Handbook of International Economics*, vol. 1, Amsterdam: North-Holland, 185–236.

Fischer, B. (1989) 'Savings Mobilization in Developing Countries: Bottlenecks and Reform Proposals', *Savings and Development*, 13(2): 117–131

Fischer, S. (1979a) 'Capital Accumulation on the Transition Path in a Monetary Optimizing Model', *Econometrica*, 47: 1433–1439.

Fischer, S. (1979b) 'Anticipations and the Nonneutrality of Money', *Journal of Political Economy*, 87(2): 225–252.

Fischer, S. (1990) 'Rules versus Discretion in Monetary Policy', in Friedman, B. and Hahn, F. (eds), *Handbook of Monetary Economics*, vol. 2, Amsterdam: Elsevier.

Fisher, I. (1928) *The Money Illusion*, New York: Adelphi.

Fisher, I. (1930) *The Theory of Interest*, New York: Macmillan.

Frank, A.G. (1967) *Capitalism and Development in Latin America: Historical Studies of Chile and Brazil*, New York: Monthly Review Press.

Frenkel, J. (1977) 'The Forward Exchange Rate, Expectations, and the Demand for Money: the German Hyperinflation', *American Economic Review*, 67(4): 653–670.

Frenkel, J. (1983) 'Panel Discussion on Southern Cone', *IMF Staff Papers*, 30(1): 164–173.

Frenkel, J.A. (1991) 'The Cost of Capital in Japan: a Survey', *Pacific Basin Working Paper*, San Francisco: Federal Reserve Bank of San Francisco.

Frenkel, J. and Goldstein, M. (1991) 'Monetary Policy in an Emerging European Economic and Monetary Union', *IMF Staff Papers*, 38: 356–373.

Frenkel, J. and Johnson, H. (eds) (1976) *The Monetary Approach to the Balance of Payments*, Toronto: University of Toronto Press.

Frenkel, J. and Johnson, H. (eds) (1978) *The Economics of Exchange Rates*, London: Addison-Wesley.

Frey, B. and Schneider, F. (1981) 'Central Bank Behavior: a Positive Empirical Analysis', *Journal of Monetary Economics*, 7(3): 291–315.

Friedman, M. (1953) 'The Case for Flexible Exchange Rates', in *Essays in Positive Economics*, Chicago, Ill.: Chicago University Press.

Friedman, M. (1957) *A Theory of Consumption Function*, New York: National Bureau of Economic Research.

Friedman, M. (1959) 'The Demand for Money – Some Theoretical and Empirical Results', *Journal of Political Economy*, 67: 327–351.

Friedman, M. (1962) 'Should There be an Independent Monetary Authority?', in Yeager, L.B. (ed.), *In Search of a Monetary Constitution*, Cambridge, Mass.: Harvard University Press.

Friedman, M. (1966) 'Interest Rates and the Demand for Money', *Journal of Law and Economics*, 9: 71–85.

Friedman, M. (1968) 'The Role of Monetary Policy', *American Economic Review*, 58(1): 1–17.

Friedman, M. (1969) *The Optimum Quantity of Money*, Chicago, Ill.: Aldine.

Friedman, M. (1971) 'Government Revenue from Inflation', *Journal of Political Economy*, 79: 846–856.

Friedman, M. (1971) 'A Monetary Theory of Nominal Income', *Journal of Political Economy*, 79: 323–337.

Friedman, M. (1973) *Money and Economic Development*, Toronto: Lexington Books.

Friedman, M. (1992) 'Quantity Theory of Money', in Eatwell, J. *et al.* (eds), *The New Palgrave Dictionary of Money and Finance* vol. 3, London: Macmillan.

Friedman, M. (ed.), (1956) *Studies in the Quantity Theory of Money*, Chicago, Ill.: Chicago University Press.

Friedman, M. and Schwartz, A. (1963) *A Monetary History of the United States*, Princeton, N.J.: Princeton University Press.

Friedman, M. and Schwartz, A. (1982) *Monetary Trends in the United Kingdom and the United States*, Chicago, Ill.: Chicago University Press.

Fry, M. (1978) 'The Permanent Income Hypothesis in Underdeveloped Economies: Additional Evidence', *Journal of Development Economics*, 5(4): 399–402.

Fry, M. (1981), 'Inflation and Economic Growth in Pacific Basin Developing Economies', *Federal Reserve Bank of San Francisco Economic Review*, Fall: 8–18.

Fry, M. (1983), 'Inflation and Monetary Policy in Hong Kong, Indonesia, Korea, Malaysia, Philippines, Singapore, Taiwan and Thailand, 1960–1982', in *Conference on Inflation in East Asian Countries*, Taipei: Chung-Hua Institution for Economic Research.

Fry, M. (1984) 'Saving, Financial Intermediation and Economic Growth in Asia', *Asian Development Review*, 2(1): 82–102.

Fry, M. (1985) 'Financial Structure, Monetary Policy, and Economic Growth in Hong Kong, Singapore, Taiwan and South Korea, 1960–1983', in Corbo, V., Krueger, A. and Ossa, F. (eds), *Export-oriented Development Strategies: The Success of Five Newly Industrializing Countries*, Boulder, Col.: Westview Press.

Fry, M. (1988) *Money, Interest, and Banking in Economic Development*, Baltimore, Md.: Johns Hopkins University Press.

Fry, M. (1990) 'Nine Financial Sector Issues in Eleven Asian Developing Countries', International Finance Group Working Paper (IFGWP-90–09), University of Birmingham.

Fry, M. (1991) 'Domestic Resource Mobilization in Developing Asia: Four Policy Issues', *Asian Development Review*, 19(1): 14–39

Fry, M. (1993) 'Financial Repression and Economic Growth', International Finance Group Working Paper (IFGWP–93–07), University of Birmingham.

Fuller, W. (1976) *Introduction to Statistical Time Series*, New York: John Wiley.

Galbis, N. (1979) 'Money, Investment and Growth in Latin America, 1961–1973', *Economic Development and Cultural Change*, 27: 423–443.

Gelb, A.H. (1989) 'Financial Policies, Growth and Efficiency', PRE Working Paper 202, Washington, D.C.: World Bank.

Gelb, A. and Honohan, P. (1991) *Restructuring Economies in Distress: Policy Reform and the World Bank*, New York: Oxford University Press.

Genberg, H. (1991) 'On the Sequencing of Reforms in Eastern Europe', *Working Paper WP/91/13*, Washington D.C.: International Monetary Fund.

Georgescu-Roegen, N. (1970) 'Structural Inflation-lock and Balanced Growth', *Economies et sociétés*, March, 557–605.

Gersovitz, M. (1988) 'Saving and Development', in Chenery, H. and Srinivasan, T. (eds), *Handbook of Development Economics*, vol. 1, Amsterdam: Elsevier.

Ghafur, A. and Chowdhury, O. (1988) *Financing Public Sector Development Expenditure in Selected Countries: Bangladesh*, Manila: Asian Development.

Ghani, E. (1992) 'How Financial Markets Affect Long-run Growth – a Cross-Country Study', Policy Research Working Paper no. 843, Washington, D.C.: World Bank.

Ghate, P. (1992) 'Interaction Between the Formal and Informal Financial Sectors: the Asian Experience', *World Development*, 20: 859–872.

Gibson, W. (1972) 'Demand and Supply Functions for Money in the United States: Theory and Measurement', *Econometrica*, 40: 361–370.

Gillis, M., Perkins, D., Roemer, M. and Snodgrass, D. (1992) *Economics of Development*, New York: W.W. Norton.

Giovannini, A. (1985) 'Savings and Real Interest Rate in LDCs', *Journal of Development Economics*, 18(2): 195–218.

Giovannini, A. and de Melo, M. (1993) 'Government Revenue from Financial Repression', *American Economic Review*, 83(4): 953–963.

Glezakos, C. (1978) 'Inflation and Growth: a Reconsideration of the Evidence from the LDCs', *Journal of Developing Areas*, 12: 171–182.

Godley, W. and Cripps, F. (1983) *Macroeconomics*, London: Fontana.

Goh, K.S. (1982) Press Interview, *The Sunday (Straits) Times*, August.

Goldfeld, S. (1973) 'The Demand for Money Revisited', *Brookings Papers on Economic Activity*, 3: 577–638.

Goldfeld, S. (1976) 'The Case of the Missing Money', *Brookings Papers on Economic Activity* 6: 683–730.

Goldfeld, S. and Sichel, S. (1987) 'Money Demand: the Effects of Inflation and Alternative Adjustment Mechanisms', *Review of Economics and Statistics*, 69: 511–515.

Gordon, R.J. (1981) 'Output Fluctuations and Gradual Price Adjustment', *Journal of Economic Literature*, 19(July): 493–530.

Gordon, R. (1984) 'The Short-run Demand for Money: a Reconsideration', *Journal of Money, Credit, and Banking*, 16(4, part 1): 403–434.

Gordon, R.J. (1988) 'Back to the Future: European Unemployment Today Viewed from America in 1939', *Brookings Papers on Economic Activity*, 19(1): 271–304.

Gordon, R.J. (1993) *Macroeconomics*, New York: HarperCollins.

Greene, J. and Villanueva, D. (1991) 'Private Investment in Developing Countries', *IMF Staff Papers*, 38(1): 33–580.

Gruber, H. and Ryan, T. (1979) 'A Monetary Model of Kenya's Balance of Payments', University of Nairobi, mimeo.

Haberler, G. (1941) *Prosperity and Depression*, Geneva: League of Nations.

Hafer, R. (1989) 'Does Dollar Depreciation Cause Inflation?', Federal Reserve Bank of St Louis *Economic Review*, July/August.

Haliassos, M. and Tobin, J. (1990) 'The Macroeconomics of Government Finance' in Friedman, B.M. and Hahn, F.H. (eds), *Handbook of Monetary Economics*, vol. 2, Amsterdam: North-Holland.

Hansen, B. (1969) 'Employment and Wages in Rural Egypt', *American Economic Review*, 59(3): 298–313.

Hanson, J.A. (1980) 'The Short-run Relation between Growth and Inflation in Latin America: Quasi-rational or Consistent Expectations Approach', *American Economic Review*, 70: 972–989.

Hanson, J. and de Melo, J. (1985) 'External Shocks, Financial Reforms, and Stabilisation Attempts in Uruguay During 1974–83', *World Development*, 13(8): 917–939.

Harberger, A. (1963) 'The Dynamics of Inflation in Chile', in Christ, C. *et al.* (eds), *Measurement in Economics: Studies in Mathematical Economics and Econometrics in Memory of Yehudi Grunfeld*, Stanford, Calif.: Stanford University Press.

Harberger, A. (1964) 'Some Notes on Inflation', in Baer, W. and Kertenetzky, I. (eds), *Inflation and Growth in Latin America*, Homewood, Ill.: Irwin.

Harberger, A. (1982) 'The Chilean Economy in the 1970s: Crisis, Stabilization, Liberalization, Reform', in Brunner, K. and Meltzer, A.H. (eds), *Economic Policy in a World of Change*, Amsterdam: North-Holland.

Harris, B. (1983) 'Money and Commodities: Their Interaction in a Rural Indian Setting', *EDI Series in Economic Development*, Washington, D.C.: World Bank.

Harris, L. (1985) *Monetary Theory*, New York: McGraw-Hill.

Harrod, R. (1939) 'An Essay in Economic Theory', *Economic Journal*, 49: 14–33.

Hayek, F.A. (1931) *Prices and Production*, London: Routledge.

Healy, J. and Page, S. (1993) 'The Use of Monetary Policy', in Page (ed.) (1993).

Hetzel, R. (1990) 'Central Banks' Independence in Historical Perspective: a Review Essay', *Journal of Monetary Economics*, 25(1): 165–176.

Hinds, M. (1988) 'Economic Effects of Financial Crises', PPR Working Paper WPS 104, Washington, D.C.: World Bank.

Ho, Y.K. (1983) 'An Analysis of Inflation in Hong Kong', in *Conference on Inflation in East Asian Countries*, Chung-Hua Institution for Economic Research, Taipei.

Hohohan, P. (1992) 'Financial Repression', in Eatwell, J. *et al.* (eds), *The New Palgrave Dictionary of Money and Finance*, London: Macmillan.

Hoover, K. (1988) *The New Classical Macroeconomics: a Skeptical Inquiry*, Oxford: Blackwell.

Hossain, A. (1988) 'Theories of Inflation and Balance of Payments in Developing Countries: a Survey', *Indian Economic Journal*, 36(1): 55–75.

Hossain, A. (1989) *Inflation, Economic Growth and the Balance of Payments: A Macroeconometric Study 1974–85*, PhD thesis, La Trobe University, Australia.

Hossain, A. (1993), 'Financial Reforms, Stability of the Money Demand Function, and Monetary Policy in Bangladesh: an Econometric Investigation', *Indian Economic Review*, 28(1): 85–100

Hossain, A. (1994), 'The Search of a Stable Money Demand Function for Pakistan', paper presented to the 10th Annual Conference of the Pakistan Society of Development Economists, Islamabad, 2–5 April.

Hossain, A. and Chowdhury, A. (1994) 'Monetary Policy in Bangladesh' in Zafarullah, H., Taslim, M. and Chowdhury, A. (eds), *Policy Issues in Bangladesh*, New Delhi: South Asia Publishing.

211

Howitt, P. (1989) 'Money Illusion', in Eatwell, J. *et al.* (eds), *Money*, London: Macmillan.

Hume, D. (1752) 'Of Money', 'Of Interest', and 'Of the Balance of Trade', reprinted in Hume, D. (1970) *Writings on Economics*, (ed.), Rotwein, E., Madison, Wis.: University of Wisconsin Press.

International Financial Statistics Yearbook (various years), Washington, D.C.: International Monetary Fund.

International Monetary Fund (IMF) (1982) *World Economic Outlook: A Survey by the Staff of the International Monetary Fund*, Occasional Paper no. 9, Washington, D.C.: World Bank.

Islam, I. (1995), 'Governance, International Competitiveness and Economic Development: Some Analytical Considerations', in Kapur, B., Quah, E. and Hoon, N. (eds), *Festschrift in Honour of Professor Lim Chong-Yah*, Singapore: Prentice-Hall.

Johnson, H.G. (1969) *Essays in Monetary Economics*, London: Allen & Unwin.

Johnson, H.G. (1972) 'The Monetary Approach to Balance of Payments', *Journal of Financial and Quantitative Analysis*, 4: 1555–1572.

Johnson, H.G. (1978) *Selected Essays in Monetary Economics*, London: Allen & Unwin.

Johnson, O. (1974) 'Credit Controls as Instruments of Development Policy in the Light of Economic Theory', *Journal of Money, Credit, and Banking*, 6: 85–99.

Johnson, O. (1984) 'On Growth and Inflation in Developing Countries', *IMF Staff Papers*, 31: 636–660.

Jonson, P. and Rankin, R. (1986), 'On Some Recent Developments in Monetary Economics', *Economic Record*, 62: 257–267

Jung, W. (1986) 'Financial Development and Economic Growth: International Evidence', *Economic Development and Cultural Change*, 34(2): 333–346.

Kahil, R. (1973) *Inflation and Economic Development in Brazil, 1946–63*, Oxford: Clarendon Press.

Kaldor, N. (1955–6) 'Alternative Theories of Distribution', *Review of Economic Studies*, 23: 83–100.

Kalecki, M. (1976) *Essays on Development Economics*, Brighton, Sussex; Harvester Press.

Kandil, M. (1991) 'Structural Differences between Developing and Developed Countries: Some Evidence and Implications', *Economic Notes*, 20(2): 254–278.

Kapur, B. (1976), 'Alternative Stabilization Policies for Less Developed Economies', *Journal of Political Economy*, 84(4, pt. 1): 777–795

Kapur, B. (1981) 'Exchange Rate Flexibility and Monetary Policy', in Monetary Authority of Singapore, *Papers on Monetary Economics*, Singapore: Singapore University Press.

Kapur, B. (1992) 'Formal and Informal Financial Markets, and the Neo-structuralist Critique of the Financial Liberalization Strategy in Less Developed Countries', *World Development*, 38(1): 63–77.

Kaufman, H. (1992) *Money and Banking*, Lexington, Mass.: Heath.

Keller, P. (1980) 'Implications of Credit Policies for Output and the Balance of Payments', *IMF Staff Papers*, 27: 451–477.

Keynes, J.M. (1930) *Treatise on Money*, London: Macmillan.

Keynes, J.M. (1931) *Essays in Persuasion*, London: Macmillan.

Keynes, J.M. (1936) *The General Theory of Employment, Interest, and Money*, London: Macmillan.

Khan, M. (1980) 'Monetary Shocks and the Dynamics of Inflation', *IMF Staff Papers*, 27(2): 250–284.

Khan, M.S. (1987a) 'Macroeconomic Adjustment in Developing Countries: a Policy Perspective', *World Bank Research Observer*, 2(1): 23–42.

Khan, M.S. (1987b) 'Stabilization and Economic Growth in Developing Countries', *Pakistan Development Review*, 16(3): 341–361.

Khan, M. and Knight, M. (1982) 'Unanticipated Monetary Growth and Inflationary Finance', *Money, Credit, and Banking*, 14(3): 347–364.

Khan, M.S. and Reinhart, C.M. (1990) 'Private Investment and Economic Growth in Developing Countries', *World Development*, 18: 19–27.

Khan, M. *et al.* (1990) 'Adjustment with Growth', *Journal of Development Economics*, 32: 155–179.

Khatkhate, D.R. (1972) 'Analytic Basis of the Working of Monetary Policy in Less Developed Countries', *IMF Staff Papers*, 19(3): 533–558.

Kiguel, M. (1989) 'Budget Deficits, Stability and the Monetary Dynamics of Hyperinflation', *Journal of Money, Credit, and Banking*, 21(2): 61–80.

Killick, T. (1984) *The Quest for Economic Stabilization*, London: Heinemann.

Killick, T. (1990) *A Reaction Too Far: Economic Theory and the Role of the State in Developing Countries*, London: Overseas Development Institute.

Killick, T. and Mwega, F. (1993) 'Kenya, 1967–88', in Page (ed.) (1993).

King, J. (1979 *Stabilization Policy in an African Setting: Kenya, 1963–73*, London: Heinemann Educational Books.

King, R. and Levine, R. (1992) 'Financial Indicators and Growth in Cross Section of Countries', *Policy Research Working Papers no. 819*, Washington, D.C.: World Bank.

King, R.G. and Levine, R. (1993) 'Financial Intermediation and Economic Development', in Mayer, C. and Vives, X. (eds), *Capital Markets and Financial Intermediation*, Cambridge: Cambridge University Press.

Kirkpatrick, C. and Nixson, F. (1989) 'Inflation and Stabilisation Policy in LDCs', in Gemmel, N. (ed.), *Survey in Development Economics*, Oxford: Blackwell.

Kopits, G. and Robinson, D. (1989) 'Fiscal Policy and External Performance: the Turkish Experience', Working Paper WP/89/20, Washington, D.C.: International Monetary Fund.

Kreinin, M.E. and Officer, L.H. (1978) 'The Monetary Approach to the Balance of Payments: a Survey', *Princeton Studies in International Finance*, no. 43., Princeton, N.J.: Princeton University Press.

Krueger, A.O. (1984) 'Problems of Liberalization', in Harberger, A.C. (ed.), *World Economic Growth*, San Francisco,: Institute for Contemporary Studies.

Krueger, A.O. (1993) *The Political Economy of Policy Reform in Developing Countries*, Cambridge, Mass.: MIT Press.

Krugman, P. (1979) 'A Model of Balance-of-payments Crises', *Journal of Money, Credit and Banking*, 11: 311–335.

Krugman, P. and Taylor, L. (1978) 'Contractionary Effects of Devaluation', *Journal of International Economics*, 8(3): 445–456.

Laidler, D. (1966) 'Some Evidence on the Demand for Money', *Journal of Political Economy*, 74: 55–68.

Laidler, D. (1971) 'The Influence of Money on Economic Activity – a Survey of Some Current Problems', in Clayton, G. *et al.* (eds), *Monetary Theory and Monetary Policy in the 1970s*, London: Oxford University Press.

Laidler, D. (1982) *Monetarist Perspectives*, Oxford: Phillip Allan.

Laidler, D. (1985) *The Demand for Money: Theories and Evidence*, New York: Harper & Row.

Laidler, D. (1986) 'What Do We Really Know About Monetary Policy?', *Australian Economic Papers*, (June): 1–16.

Laidler, D. (1990) *Taking Money Seriously*, New York: Philip Allan.

Lal, D. (1984) 'Trends in Real Wages in Rural India 1880–1980', *World Bank Research Paper*, Washington, D.C.: World Bank.

Lane, C., Cole, D. and Slade, B. (1993), 'Indonesia, 1974–90', in Page, S. (ed.), *Monetary Policy in Developing Countries*, London: Routledge.

Lee, C.H. (1992) 'The Government Financial System, and Large Private Enterprises in the Economic Development of South Korea', *World Development*, 20(2): 187–197.

Leeahtam, P., Patrawimolpon, P. and Spapongse, M. (1991) 'Monetary Policy in Asian Economic Development', *Asian Development Review*, 9: 59–89.

Leijonhufvud, A. (1968) *On Keynesian Economics and the Economics of Keynes*, New York: Oxford University Press.

Leontief, W. (1936) 'The Fundamental Assumption of Mr Keynes' Monetary Theory of Unemployment', *Quarterly Journal of Economics*, 51: 192–197.

Leung, S. (1989) 'Financial Liberalisation in Australia and New Zealand', Discussion Paper no. 208, Centre for Economic Policy Research, Australian National University, Canberra.

Levhari, D. and Patinkin, D. (1968) 'The Role of Money in a Simple Growth Model', *American Economic Review*, 58: 713–753.

Levy, B. and Spiller, P.T. (1994) 'Regulation, Institutions, and Commitment in Telecommunications: a Comparative Analysis of Five Country Studies', in Proceedings of the World Bank Annual Conference on Development Economics 1993: 225–266.

Lewis, A. (1947) 'Closing Remarks', in Baer, W. and Kertenetzky, I. (eds), *Inflation and Growth in Latin America*, Homewood, Ill.: Irwin.

Lim, J. (1987), 'The New Structuralist Critique of the Monetarist Theory of Inflation: the Case of the Philippines', *Journal of Development Economics*, 25: 45–61.

Little, I.M.D. (1982) *Economic Development: Theory, Policy and International Relations*, New York: Basic Books.

Liviatan, N. (ed.) (1993) *Proceedings of a Conference on Currency Substitution and Currency Boards*, World Bank Discussion Paper 207, Washington, D.C.: World Bank.

Long, M. (1993) 'Financial Reforms: A Global Perspective', in Faruqi, S. (ed.), *Financial Sector Reforms in Asian and Latin American Countries: Lessons of Comparative Experience*, Washington, D.C.: Economic Development Institute of the World Bank.

Long, M. and Vittas, D. (1991) 'Financial Regulation: Changing the Rules of the Game', Policy Research Working Papers WPS803, Washington, D.C.: World Bank.

Lucas, R. E. (1972) 'Expectations and the Neutrality of Money', *Journal of Economic Theory*, 4: 103–124

Lucas, R.E. (1988) 'On the Mechanics of Economic Development', *Journal of Monetary Economics*, 22: 3–42.

Lucas, R. and Sargent, T. (eds), (1981) *Rational Expectations and Econometric Practice*, London: George Allen & Unwin.

Mammen, T. (1970) 'A Test of Friedman's Theory of Demand for Money with Indian Data', *Indian Economic Review*, 17(4–5): 494–499.

Manasan, R. (1988) *Financing Public Sector Development Expenditure in Selected Countries: Philippines*, Manila: Asian Development Bank.

Mangla, I. (1979) 'An Annual Money Demand Function for Pakistan: Some Further Results', *Pakistan Development Review*, 18(1): 21–33.

Marquez, J. (1987) 'Money Demand in Open Economies: a Currency Substitution Model for Venezuela', *Journal of International Money and Finance*, 6: 167–178.

Marty, A.L. (1967) 'Growth and the Welfare Cost of Inflationary Finance', *Journal of Political Economy*, 75: 71–76

Marty, A.L. (1968) 'The Optimal Rate of Growth of Money', *Journal of Political Economy*, 76: 860–873.

Marty, A.L. (1973) 'Growth, Satiety, and the Tax Revenue from Money Creation', *Journal of Political Economy*, 81: 1136–1152

Mathieson, R. (1986) 'International Capital Flows, Capital Controls, and Financial Reforms', in Cheng, H.S. (ed.), *Financial Policy Reform in Pacific Basin Countries*, Lexington, Mass.: Lexington Books.

Matin, K.M. (1986) *Bangladesh and the IMF: An Exploratory Study*, Dhaka: Bangladesh Institute of Development Studies.

McKinnon, R.I. (1964) 'Foreign Exchange Constraints in Economic Development and Efficient Aid Allocation', *Economic Journal*, 74: 388–409.

McKinnon, R.I. (1973) *Money and Capital in Economic Development*, Washington, D.C.: Brookings Institution.

McKinnon, R.I. (1974) 'Money, Growth, and the Propensity to Save', in Horwich, G. and Samuelson, P.A. (eds), *Trade, Stability, and Macroeconomics: Essays in Honor of Lloyd Metzler*, New York: Academic Press.

McKinnon, R.I. (1976) 'International Transfers and Non-traded Commodities: the Adjustment Problem', in Leipziger, D.M. (ed.), *The International Monetary System and the Developing Countries*, Washington, D.C.: Agency for International Development.

McKinnon, R.I. (1981) 'Financial Repression and the Liberalization Problem within Less Developed Countries', in Grassman, E. and Lundberg, E. (eds), *The Past and Prospects for the World Economic Order*, London: Macmillan.

McKinnon, R.I. (1982) 'The Order of Economic Liberalization: Lessons from Chile and Argentina', *Carnegie-Rochester Conference Series on Public Policy*, 17: 159–186.

McKinnon, R.I. (1986) 'Issues and Perspectives: an Overview of Banking Regulations and Monetary Control', in Tan, A. and Kapur, B. (eds), *Pacific Growth and Financial Interdependence*, Sydney: Allen & Unwin.

McKinnon, R.I. (1989a) 'Financial Liberalization and Economic Development: A Reassessment of Interest Rate Policies in Asia and Latin America', *Oxford Review of Economic Policy*, 5(4): 29–54

McKinnon, R.I. (1989b) 'Financial Liberalization in Retrospect: Interest Rate Policies in LDCs', in Ranis, G. and Schultz, T.P. (eds), *The State of Development Economics*, New York: Blackwell.

McKinnon, R.I. (1991) *The Order of Economic Liberalization: Financial Control in the Transition to a Market Economy*, Baltimore, Md.: Johns Hopkins University Press.

Meltzer, A.H. (1963) 'The Demand for Money: the Evidence from the Time Series', *Journal of Political Economy*, 71(3): 219–246.

Meltzer, A.H. (1981) 'Keynes's General Theory: a Different Perspective', *Journal of Economic Literature*, 19(1): 34–64.

Meltzer, A.H. (1988) *Keynes's Monetary Theory*, Cambridge: Cambridge University Press.

Metzler, L.A. (1951) 'Wealth, Saving, and the Rate of Interest', *Journal of Political Economy*, 59: 93–116.

Michaelly, M. (1982) 'The Sequencing of a Liberalization Policy: a Preliminary Statement of Issues', unpublished paper, cited in Edwards and Edwards (1987).

Mikesell, R. (1969) 'Inflation in Latin America', in Nisbet, C. (ed.), *Latin America: Problems in Economic Development*, New York: Free Press.

Milbourne, R. (1983) 'Price Expectations and the Demand for Money: Resolution of a Paradox', *Review of Economics and Statistics*, 65: 633–638.

Mishkin, F. (1992) *The Economics of Money, Banking, and Financial Markets*, New York: HarperCollins.

Modigliani, F. (1944) 'Liquidity Preference and the Theory of Interest and Money', *Econometrica*, 12: 45–88.

Modigliani, F. (1971) 'Monetary Policy and Consumption', in *Consumer Spending and Monetary Policy: The Linkages*, Boston, Mass.: Federal Reserve Bank of Boston, 9–84.

Modigliani, F. (1977) 'The Monetarist Controversy, or Should We Forsake Stabilization Policies?', *American Economic Review*, 67: 1–19.

Montes, M. (1987), *Stabilization and Adjustment Policies and Programmes, Country Study: The Philippines*, Helsinki: World Institute for Development Economics Research of the United Nations.

Monteil, P. (1986) 'An Optimizing Model of Household Behaviour under Credit Rationing', *IMF Staff Papers*, 33(3): 583–615.

Montiel, P.J. (1991), 'The Transmission Mechanism for Monetary Policy in Developing Countries', *IMF Staff Papers*, 38(1): 83–108

Mundell, R. (1963) 'Inflation and Real Interest', *Journal of Political Economy*, 71: 280–283.

Mundell, R. (1965) 'Growth, Stability and Inflationary Finance', *Journal of Political Economy*, 73: 97–109.

Mundell, R. (1968) *International Economics*, New York: Macmillan.

Mundell, R. (1971) *Monetary Theory*, San Francisco, Cal.: Goodyear Publishing.

Mussa, M. (1978) 'The Exchange Rate, the Balance of Payments, and Monetary and Fiscal Policy under a Regime of Controlled Floating', in Frenkel, J. and Johnson, H. (eds), *The Economics of Exchange Rates*, London: Addison-Wesley.

Muth, J.F. (1961) 'Rational Expectations and the Theory of Price Movement', *Econometrica*, 29(2), 315–335.

Nascimento, J. (1990) 'The Crisis in the Financial Sector and the Authorities' Reaction: the Case of the Philippines', Working Paper WP/90/26, Washington, D.C.: International Monetary Fund.

Nelson, R.R. (1964) 'Aggregate Production Functions', *American Economic Review*, 54(5): 575–606.

Olivera, J.H.G. (1964), 'On Structural Inflation and Latin-American Structuralism', *Oxford Economic Papers*, 16(3) (new series): 321–332.

Oncham, T. (1985) 'Informal Credit and the Development of Non-farm Enterprises in Thailand', research paper prepared for USAID.

Orphanides, O. and Solow, R.M. (1990) 'Money, Inflation and Growth', in Friedman, B.M. and Hahn, F.H. (eds), *Handbook of Monetary Economics*, vol. 1, Amsterdam: North-Holland.

Ortiz, G. (1983) 'Currency Substitution in Mexico: the Dollarization Problem', *Journal of Money, Credit, and Banking*, 15: 174–185.

Page, S. (1993) 'The Relationship Between Formal and Informal Finance', in Page (ed.) (1993).

Page, S. (ed.) (1993) *Monetary Policy in Developing Countries*, London and New York: Routledge.

Page, S. and Healey, J. (1993) 'The Financial Sector', in Page (ed.), paper presented to SEACEN Seminar in Jakarta, Indonesia.

Pangestu, M. (1991) 'Macroeconomic Management in the ASEAN Countries', in Ariff, M. (ed.), *The Pacific Economy: Growth and External Stability*, Sydney: Allen & Unwin.

Papademos, L. and Modigliani, F. (1990) 'The Supply of Money and the Control of Nominal Income', in Friedman, B. and Hahn, F. (eds), *Handbook of Monetary*

Economics, Amsterdam, New York and Oxford: North-Holland.

Papanek, G. (1981) 'Comment on "Stabilization Policies in Pakistan: the 1970–77 Experience" by Guisinger', in Cline, W. and Weintraub, S. (eds), *Developing Countries*, Washington, D.C.: Brookings Institution.

Paris, S. (1961), 'Some Mathematical Notes on the Quantity Theory of Money in an Open Economy', *IMF Staff Papers*, 8: 210–126

Park, Y.C. (1973) 'The Role of Money in Stabilization Policy in Developing Countries', *IMF Staff Papers*, 20: 379–418.

Park, Y.C. (1983) 'Inflation and Stabilization Policies in Korea, 1960–1980, in *Conference on Inflation in East Asian Countries*, Chung-Hua Institution for Economic Research, Taipei.

Park, Y.C. (1990) 'Growth, Liberalization and Internationalization of Korea's Financial Sector, 1970–89', Conference on Financial Development in Japan, Korea and Taiwan, 27–28 August, Teipei: Academia Sinica.

Park, Y.C. (1991) 'Financial Repression and Liberalization' in Krause, L. and Kihwan, K. (eds), *Liberalization in the Process of Economic Development*, Berkeley, Cal.: University of California Press.

Park, Y.C. (1994) 'Comment on *The Role of the State in Financial Markets*, in *Proceedings of the World Bank Annual Conference on Development Economics* 1993: 57–58.

Pastor, M. (1987) 'The Effects of IMF Programs in the Third World: Debate and Evidence from Latin America', *World Development*, 15(2): 249–262.

Patinkin, D. (1949) 'The Indeterminacy in Absolute Prices in Classical Economic Theory', *Econometrica*, 17(1): 1–27.

Patinkin, D. (1972) 'On the Short Run Non-neutrality of Money in the Quantity Theory', *Banca Nazionale del Lavoro Quarterly Review*, no. 100 (March): 3–22.

Patinkin, D. (1989) 'Neutrality of Money', in Eatwell, J. *et al.* (eds), *Money*, London: Macmillan.

Patinkin, D. (1992) 'Neutrality of Money', in Eatwell, J. *et al.* (eds), *The Palgrave Dictionary of Money and Finance*, vol. 3, London: Macmillan.

Patinkin, D. and Steiger, O. (1989) 'In Search of the Veil of Money and the Neutrality of Money: a Note on the Origin of Terms', *Scandinavian Journal of Economics*, 91(1): 131–146.

Patrick, H. (1966) 'Financial Development and Economic Growth in Underdeveloped Countries', *Economic Development and Cultural Change*, 14(2): 174–189.

Paul, S., Kearney, C. and Chowdhury, K. (1992) 'The Relationship between Inflation and Economic Growth: a Multicountry Empirical Analysis', Working Paper, Department of Economics and Finance, University of Western Sydney, Macarthur.

Payer, C. (1974) *The Debt Trap: The IMF and the Third World*, New York: Monthly Review Press.

Persson, T. and Svensson, L. (1989) 'Checks and Balances on the Government Budget', *Quarterly Journal of Economics*, 104: 325–345.

Persson, T. and Tabellini, G. (1990) *Macroeconomic Policy, Credibility and Politics*, Chur, Switzerland: Harwood.

Phelps, E. (1973) 'Inflation in the Theory of Public Finance', *Swedish Journal of Economics*, 75: 67–82.

Polak, J. (1957) 'Monetary Analysis of Income Formation and Payments Problems' *IMF Staff Papers*, 6: 1–50.

Polak, J. and Argy, V. (1971) 'Credit Policy and the Balance of Payments', *IMF Staff Papers*, 18: 1–24.

Porter, R. (1961) 'The Dangers of Monetary Policy in Agrarian Economies', *Pakistan Development Review*, 1: 59–72.

Prachowny, M. (1975) *Small Open Economies*, London: Lexington Books.

Ramirez-Rojas, C.L. (1985) 'Currency Substitution in Argentina, Mexico and Uruguay', *IMF Staff Papers*, 32: 627–667.

Rao, V.K.R.V. (1952) 'Investment, Income and the Multiplier in an Underdeveloped Economy', *Indian Economic Review*, 1(1): 55–67.

Reichmann, T.M. and Stillson, R.T. (1978) 'Experience with Programs of Balance of Payments Adjustment: Stand-by Arrangements in the Higher Tranches, 1963–72', *IMF Staff Papers*, 25: 292–310.

Rivera-Batiz, F. and Rivera-Batiz, L. (1985) *International Finance and Open Economy Macroeconomics*, New York: Macmillan.

Robinson, J. (1962) 'A Model of Accumulation', in *Essays in the Theory of Economic Growth*, London: Macmillan.

Roe, A. (1993) 'Seminar Proceedings: a Summary Report', in Faruqi, S. (ed.), *Financial Sector Reforms in Asian and Latin American Countries: Lessons of Comparative Experience*, Washington D.C.: Economic Development Institute of the World Bank.

Romer, P.M. (1986) 'Increasing Returns and Long-run Growth', *Journal of Political Economy*, 94: 1002–1037.

Romer, P.M. (1989) 'Capital Accumulation in the Theory of Long-run Growth', in Barro, R. (ed.), *Modern Business Cycle Theory*, Cambridge, Mass.: Harvard University Press.

Romer, P.M. (1990) 'Endogenous Technological Change', *Journal of Political Economy*, 98: S71–103.

Rosenzweig, M. (1988) 'Labor Markets in Low-income Countries', in Chenery, H. and Srinivasan, T. (eds), *Handbook of Development Economics*, vol. 1 Amsterdam: Elsevier.

Roubini, N. (1991) 'Economic and Political Determinants of Budget Deficits in Developing Countries', *Journal of International Money and Finance*, 10 (March Supplement): S49–72.

Roubini, N. and Sala-i–Martin, X. (1992) 'Financial Repression and Economic Growth', *Journal of Development Economics*, 39: 1–30.

Rozenzweig, M. (1980) 'Neoclassical Theory and the Optimizing Peasant: an Econometric Analysis of Market Family Labour Supply in a Developing Country', *Quarterly Journal of Economics*, 94: 31–55.

Sabirin, S. (1993) 'Capital Account Liberalization: the Indonesian Experience', in Faruqi, S. (ed.), *Financial Sector Reforms in Asian and Latin American Countries*, Washington, D.C.: World Bank.

Sachs, J. (ed.), (1989) *Developing Country Debt and the World Economy*, Chicago, Ill.: Chicago University Press.

Sachs, J. and Larrain, F. (1993) *Macroeconomics in the Global Economy*, New York: Harvester Wheatsheaf.

Sargent, T. and Wallace, N. (1975) 'Rational Expectations, the Optimal Monetary Instrument, and the Optimal Money Supply Rule', *Journal of Political Economy*, 83(2): 241–254.

Schelling, T. (1982) 'Establishing Credibility: Strategic Considerations', *American Economic Review*, 72(2): 77–80.

Scitovsky, T. (1985) 'Economic Development in Taiwan and South Korea, 1965–81', *Food Research Institute Studies*, 19(3): 215–264.

Seck, D. and Nil, Y.H. (1993) 'Financial Liberalization in Africa', *World Development*, 21(11): 1867–1881.

Seers, D. (1962) 'A Theory of Inflation and Growth in Underdeveloped Economies Based on the Experience of Latin America', *Oxford Economic Papers*, 14: 173–195.

Seers, D. (1964) 'Inflation and Growth: the Heart of the Controversy', in Baer, W. and Kertenetzky, I. (eds), *Inflation and Growth in Latin America*, Homewood, Ill.: Irwin.

Sen, A.K. (1988) 'The Concept of Development' in Chenery, H. and Srinivasan, T.N. (eds), *Handbook of Development Economics* vol. 1, Amsterdam: North-Holland.

Shaw, E. (1973) *Financial Deepening in Economic Development*, New York: Oxford University Press.

Sidrauski, M. (1967) 'Inflation and Economic Growth', *Journal of Political Economy*, 75: 796–810.

Solow, R.M. (1956) 'A Contribution to the Theory of Economic Growth', *Quarterly Journal of Economics*, 70: 65–94.

Solow, R.M. (1957) 'Technical Change and the Aggregate Production Function', *Review of Economics and Statistics*, 39: 312–320.

Sowa, N.K. (1993) 'Ghana, 1957–88', in Page (ed.), (1993).

Squire, L. (1981) *Employment Policy in Developing Countries: A Survey of Issues and Evidence*, New York: Oxford University Press.

Stein, J.L. (1970) 'Monetary Growth Theory in Perspective', *American Economic Review*, 60: 85–106.

Stiglitz, J.E. (1985) 'Credit Markets and the Control of Capital', *Journal of Money, Credit and Banking*, 17(1): 133–152.

Stiglitz, J.E. (1988) 'Economic Organization, Information, and Development', in Chenery, H. and Srinivasan, T.N. (eds), *Handbook of Development Economics*, vol. 1, Amsterdam: North-Holland.

Stiglitz, J.E. (1989) 'Financial Markets and Development', *Oxford Review of Economic Policy*, 5(4): 55–68.

Stiglitz, J.E. (1990) *Economic Role of the State*, London: Allen & Unwin.

Stiglitz, J.E. (1994) 'The Role of the State in Financial Markets', Proceedings of the World Bank Annual Conference on Development Economics 1993: Supplement to *World Bank Economic Review and World Bank Research Observer*, 1:19–62.

Stiglitz, J. and Weiss, A. (1981) 'Credit Rationing in Markets with Imperfect Information', *American Economic Review*, 71(3): 393–410.

Streeten, P. (1981) *Development Perspectives*, London: Macmillan.

Sundaram, K. and Pandit, V. (1984) 'Informal Credit Markets, Black Money and Monetary Policy: Some Analytical and Empirical Issues', *Economic and Political Weekly*, 18(16).

Sundararajan, V. and Balino, T. (1990) 'Issues in Recent Banking Crises in Developing Countries', Working Paper WP/90/19, Washington, D.C.: International Monetary Fund.

Sundararajan, V. and Molho, L. (1988) 'Financial Reform and Monetary Control in Indonesia', Working Paper WP/88/4, Washington, D.C.: International Monetary Fund.

Sundararajan, V. and Thakur, S. (1980) 'Public Investment, Crowding Out, and Growth: A Dynamic Model Applied to India and Korea', *IMF Staff Papers*, 27: 814–855.

Sunkel, O. (1960) 'Inflation in Chile: an Unorthodox Approach', *International Economic Papers*, 10: 107–131.

Swan, T.W. (1956) 'Economic Growth and Capital Accumulation', *Economic Record*, 32: 334–361.

Swinburne, M. and Castello-Branco, M. (1991) 'Central Bank Independence and Central Bank Functions', in Downes, P. and Vaez-Zadeh, R. (eds), *The Evolving Role of Central Banks*, Washington, D.C.: International Monetary Fund.

Swoboda, A. (1976) 'Monetary Approaches to Balance of Payments Theory', in Classen, E. and Salin, P. (eds.), *Recent Issues in International Monetary Economics*, Amsterdam: North-Holland, 3–23.

Tabellini, G. and Alesina, A. (1990) 'Voting on the Budget Deficit', *American Economic Review*, 80: 37–49.

Tanzi, V. (1982) 'Fiscal Disequilibrium in Developing Countries', *World Development*, 10: 1069–1082.

Tanzi, V. (1985) 'Fiscal Deficits and Interest Rates in the United States', *IMF Staff Papers*, 32(4): 551–576.

Tanzi, V. (1989) 'Lags in Tax Collection and the Case for Inflationary Finance: Theory with Simulations', in Blejer, M. and Chu, K. (eds), *Fiscal Policy, Stabilization, and Growth in Developing Countries*, Washington, D.C.: International Monetary Fund.

Tanzi, V. and Blejer, M. (1982) 'Inflation, Interest Rate Policy, and Currency Substitution in Developing Economies: a Discussion of Some Major Issues', *World Development*, 10: 781–790.

Taylor, J. (1982) 'Establishing Credibility: a Rational Expectations Viewpoint', *American Economic Review*, 72(2): 81–85.

Taylor, L. (1979) *Macro-models for Developing Countries*, New York: McGraw-Hill.

Taylor, L. (1983) *Structuralist Macroeconomics*, New York: Basic Books.

Taylor, L. (1988) *Varieties of Stabilization Experience: Towards Sensible Macroeconomics in the Third World*, Oxford: Clarendon Press.

Thirlwall, A. (1974) *Inflation, Saving and Growth in Developing Economies*, London: Macmillan.

Thirlwall, A.P. (1989) *Growth and Development with Special Reference to Developing Countries*, London: Macmillan.

Thirlwall, A. and Barton, C. (1971) 'Inflation and Growth: the International Evidence', *Banca Nazionale del Lavoro Quarterly Review*, 98: 263–275.

Tobin, J. (1956) 'The Inter-elasticity of Transactions Demand for Cash', *Review of Economics and Statistics*, 38(3): 241–247.

Tobin, J. (1958) 'Liquidity Preference as Behaviour Towards Risk', *Review of Economic Studies*, 25: 65–86.

Tobin, J. (1961) 'Money, Capital and other Stores of Value', *American Economic Review*, 51(2): 26–37.

Tobin, J. (1965) 'Money and Economic Growth', *Econometrica*, 33: 671–684.

Todaro, M. (1989) *Economic Development in the Third World*, New York: Longman.

Treadgold, M. (1990), 'Macroeconomic Management in Asian-Pacific Developing Countries', *Asian-Pacific Economic Literature*, 4(1): 3–40.

Trivedi, M. (1980), 'Inflationary Expectations and Demand for Money in India', *Indian Economic Journal*, 28(1): 62–76.

Trivedi, M. (1983), 'Inflationary Expectations and Demand for Per Capita Real Balances: Evidence from Indian Economy', *Artha Vijnana*, 25(1): 21–36.

Tseng, W. and Corker, R. (1991) 'Financial Liberalization, Money Demand, and Monetary Policy in Asian Countries', *Occasional Paper 84*, Washington, D.C.: International Monetary Fund.

Tun Wai, U. (1959) 'The Relation between Inflation and Economic Development: a Statistical Inductive Study', *IMF Staff Papers*, 7: 302–317.

Tun Wai, U. and Wong, C. (1982) 'Determinants of Private Investment in Developing Countries', *Journal of Development Studies*, 19: 19–36.

Velasco, A. (1988) 'Liberalization, Crisis, Intervention: the Chilean Financial System, 1975–1985', Working Paper WP/88/66, Washington, D.C.: International Monetary Fund.

Villaneuva, D. and A. Mirakhor (1990) 'Interest Rate Policies, Stabilization, and Bank Supervision in Developing Countries: Strategies for Financial Reforms', Working Paper WP/90/8, Washington D.C.: International Monetary Fund.

Vogel, R. (1974) 'The Dynamics of Inflation in Latin America', *American Economic Review*, 64: 102–114.

Vongpradhip, D. (1985) 'Urban Unorganized Money Market in Thailand', paper presented to SEACEN Seminar in Jakarta, Indonesia.

Wachtel, P. (1989) *Macroeconomics: From Theory to Practice*, New York: McGraw Hill.

Wachter, S. (1976) *Latin American Inflation*, Lexington, Mass.: Lexington Books.

Wade, R. (1988) 'The Role of Government in Overcoming Market Failure: Taiwan, Republic of Korea and Japan', in Hughes, H. (ed.), *Achieving Industrialization in Asia*, Cambridge: Cambridge University Press.

Wade, R. (1990) *Governing the Market: Economic Theory and the Role of Government in East Asian Industrialization*, Princeton, N.J.: Princeton University Press.

Wallich, H.C. (1969) 'Money and Growth: a Cross Country Cross-section Analysis', *Journal of Money, Credit and Banking*, 1(2): 281–302.

Walters, A. (1965) 'Professor Friedman on the Demand for Money', *Journal of Political Economy*, 73: 545–551.

Wijnbergen, S. van (1982) 'Stagflationary Effects of Monetary Stabilization Policies', *Journal of Development Economics*, 10(2): 133–169.

Wijnbergen, S. van (1985) 'Macroeconomic Effects of Changes in Bank Interest Rates: Simulation Results from South Korea', *Journal of Development Economics*, 18: 541–554.

Willett, T. (ed.), (1988) *Political Business Cycles: The Political Economy of Money, Inflation and Unemployment*, Durham, N.C.: Duke University Press.

Woo, W.T. and Nasution, A. (1989) 'Indonesia's Economic Policies and their Relation to External Debt Management', in Sachs, J.D. and Collins, S.N. (eds), *Developing Country Debt and Economic Performance*, Chicago, Ill.: Chicago University Press.

World Bank (1989) *World Bank Report*, New York: Oxford University Press.

World Bank (1993) *The East Asian Miracle: Economic Growth and Public Policy*, New York: Oxford University Press.

Zahler, R. (1993) 'Financial Sector Reforms and Liberalization: Welcome Address', in Faruqi, S. (ed.), *Financial Sector Reforms in Asian and Latin American Countries: Lessons from Comparative Experience*, Washington, D.C.: World Bank.

Zysman, J. (1983) *Government, Markets and Growth: Financial Systems and the Politics of Industrial Change*, Ithaca, N.Y.: Cornell University Press.

NAME INDEX

SUBJECT INDEX